Rethinking the Western Tradition

*The volumes in this series
seek to address the present debate
over the Western tradition
by reprinting key works of
that tradition along with essays
that evaluate each text from
different perspectives.*

Groundwork for the Metaphysics of Morals

IMMANUEL KANT

Edited and translated by Allen W. Wood
with essays by
J. B. Schneewind
Marcia Baron
Shelly Kagan
Allen W. Wood

Yale University Press

New Haven and London

Published with assistance from the Ernst Cassirer Publications Fund.

Printed in the United States of America by
Vail-Ballou Press, Binghamton, New York.

Library of Congress Cataloging-in-Publication Data

Kant, Immanuel, 1724–1804.
[Grundlegung zur Metaphysik der Sitten. English]
Groundwork for the metaphysics of morals / Immanuel Kant ;
edited and translated by Allen W. Wood ; with essays by J. B. Schneewind . . . [et al.].
p. cm. — (Rethinking the Western tradition)
Includes bibliographical references and index.
ISBN 0-300-09486-8 (cloth) — ISBN 0-300-09487-6 (paper)
1. Ethics — Early works to 1800. I. Wood, Allen W. II. Schneewind, J. B. (Jerome B.) III.
Title. IV. Series.
B2766.E6 W6613 2002
170 — dc21   2002002605

A catalogue record for this book is available from the British Library.
The paper in this book meets the guidelines
for permanence and durability of the Committee on
Production Guidelines for Book Longevity of the
Council on Library Resources.

10 9 8 7 6 5 4 3

Contributors

J. B. Schneewind is professor of philosophy (emeritus) at Johns Hopkins
University.

Marcia Baron is professor of Philosophy at Indiana University.

Shelly Kagan is Henry R. Luce Professor of Social Thought and Ethics at Yale
University.

Allen W. Wood is Ward W. and Priscilla B. Woods Professor at Stanford
University.

Contents

Editor's Preface

Kant's little book of 1785 is one of the most significant texts in the history of ethics. It has been a standard of reference — sometimes a model to be developed and expanded on, sometimes a target of criticism — for moral philosophers from the German idealist and German Romantic traditions, for Victorians of the utilitarian school such as Mill and Sidgwick, for later British idealists such as Green and Bradley, for the neo-Kantians, for twentieth-century philosophers in both the continental and the anglophone traditions, and for moral philosophers of all persuasions right down to the present day. From the standpoint of the depth and originality of the ideas it contains, it undoubtedly deserves this influence. But in the development of Kant's own moral thinking, it occupies a place that ought to make us question the wisdom of treating it, the way moral philosophers customarily do, as the definitive statement of Kant's views on ethics.

Kant first gave notice of his intention to produce a system of moral philosophy under the title "metaphysics of morals" about 1768. It took him eighteen years to deliver even the first installment of the promised system, which he gave a title indicative of the tentativeness and incompleteness of what he thought he had so far accomplished: he was only *laying the ground for* a "metaphysics of morals" by seeking out and establishing its first principle.

Kant apparently began composing the *Groundwork* late in 1783. Letters written by Kant's brilliant but eccentric friend J. G. Hamann report that he began writing about moral philosophy in order to provide an 'anticritique' of Christian Garve's 1783 book on Cicero's treatise *On Duties*. But according to Hamann, during the spring of 1784 this critical discussion of Garve on Cicero was transformed into something quite different, a "Prodromus der Moral" (Ak 4:626–28). The title "Grundlegung zur Metaphysik der Sitten" is first mentioned in a letter from Hamann in September 1784.

Hamann's correspondence reveals him to be an avid Kant-watcher, sometimes a helpfully critical one. But there is reason to be skeptical about his account of the genesis of the *Groundwork*. Hamann's account has inspired scholars as reputable as Klaus Reich and H. J. Paton to seek in the *Groundwork* for allusions to Cicero, and even to think that they have found them. But there are no explicit references either to Cicero or to Garve's book about him. Kant may have been drawn to the subject of ethics in part by reading and reflecting on Garve's book or Cicero's classical treatise, but it seems unlikely that the *Groundwork,* as we now have it, could have grown out of a critical discussion of Garve on Cicero. The "Prodromus der Moral" would seem to be a project independent of any 'anticritique' of Garve that Kant could have been undertaking.

Kant was working on other topics in 1784 whose affinity with the ethical theory presented in the *Groundwork* is also worth noting. For instance, he was reviewing Herder's *Ideas for the Philosophy of History of Humanity* and writing two other short essays, *Idea for a Universal History from a Cosmopolitan Standpoint* and *Answer to the Question: What Is Enlightenment?* that reflect on human history, the social sources of the evil in human nature, the role of autonomous reason in directing our lives, and the rational prospects for the moral progress of the human species. But perhaps no special explanation is needed for the fact that Kant finally got around to addressing a subject he had been promising to write on for the past sixteen years.

Whatever the actual history of its genesis, the *Groundwork* went into press with Johann Hartknoch of Riga late in 1784. Throughout the winter, and into the spring of 1785, Kant's followers waited impatiently for its appearance (Ak 4:628). Apparently the first copies were available on April 7. A second edition, altered in a number of passages throughout (but never very greatly in any of them), appeared in 1786. This second edition went through six more reprintings during Kant's lifetime.

Kant seems always to have treated the *Groundwork* as a successful laying of the ground for the ethical theory presented in his later writings. But clearly he soon came to regard it as not providing a complete or wholly clear presentation even of the foundations of his system, for only three years later he wrote a *Critique of Practical Reason* (1788) with the aim of clarifying those foundations, correcting misunderstandings, and answering criticisms of his moral philosophy that had come from readers of the *Groundwork*. It is a matter of controversy how far what is said in the second *Critique* involves revisions of what Kant said in the *Groundwork*, but many scholars think that Kant meant to supplant the argument of the Third Section, where the *Groundwork* establishes freedom of the will and relates freedom to the moral law. In the following decade Kant wrote a number of essays and treatises on topics involving the application of his moral philosophy to politics, history, international relations, education, and religion. But it was only after he had retired from university teaching, and as he began to realize that his mental powers were beginning to fail him, that he finally assembled from the notes and drafts of many years a work he called the *Metaphysics of Morals*, which was published as one of his very last works.

Kant's essays and treatises of the 1790s, and especially the *Metaphysics of Morals* (1798), give us explicit accounts of many matters on which readers of the *Groundwork* customarily try to deduce the "Kantian view" (by triangulation, as it were) from what he says in this little foundational treatise. Many doctrines standardly attributed to Kant on the basis of these triangulations — on topics such as the nature of moral motivation, the relation between reason and feeling in human action, the structure of everyday moral reasoning, and the nature of the will's freedom — do not harmonize very well with what Kant actually says in the *Metaphysics of Morals, Religion within the Boundaries of Mere Reason,* or other later works. This discrepancy strongly suggests that the *Groundwork* does not give us Kant's final word on everything, and implies that where the *Groundwork* itself is not entirely explicit, it ought perhaps to be interpreted (often very differently from the customary ways of interpreting it) in light of his other, later, more explicit writings. But so influential has the *Groundwork* been, in comparison with his other ethical writings, that Kant will perhaps always be burdened with what the long tradition of moral philosophers have read of (and sometimes read into) what he said in his first foundational text on moral philosophy.

The *Groundwork* is unquestionably the starting point not only for any study of Kant's moral theory, but for any attempt to understand, develop, or criticize any of the wide variety of "Kantian" ideas that have exercised such a powerful influence on people's thinking about morality, politics, and religion in the centuries since this little book was first published. The translator and editor of this volume, as well as the writers of the four essays that follow the text, hope they have presented Kant's *Groundwork* in a way that will further its ongoing appropriation by everyone who thinks about the fundamental issues raised in it.

A Note on the Translation

Kant's *Grundlegung zur Metaphysik der Sitten* has had many English translations. The most estimable are those by Thomas K. Abbott (1883), H. J. Paton (1948), Lewis White Beck (1949, revised several times, most notably in 1959 and 1990), and Mary J. Gregor (1996). Yet I have found even these fine translations unsatisfying at certain points because, in order to provide a smoother English reading, they are too often content to remain at a distance from what Kant actually said, and because they sometimes commit themselves too much to one possible interpretation where the original text is tantalizingly ambiguous. Also, over the years I have come to be aware that some of their words and phrases, even some that now echo in the ears of us who have for many years been reading the *Groundwork* in translation, are not the very best choices to translate precisely what Kant was saying.

In the present translation my aim has been to place the English reader, as far as possible, in the same interpretive position as the German reader of the original. Doing so has dictated taking pains to achieve accuracy and literalness in the translation, as far as this can be made consistent with intelligibility. It has also led to the attempt to preserve, as far as possible, a consistency in terminology, not only with technical terms but even with nontechnical ones. Where variations in meaning or context require the same term to be translated in different ways, a numbered footnote informs the reader of what is going on. (The unnumbered footnotes are Kant's own.) Kant's paragraphing and even sentence structure have been respected, because Kant's sentences often constitute units of argument, and modifying them for the sake of more graceful English prose often makes the argument harder to comprehend. Further, since my aim has been to put the English reader in the same interpretive position as the German reader of the original, I have not attempted to make the translation clearer or more elegant than Kant's German is; in fact, where Kant's writing is obscure or awkward, I have tried to reproduce the same murkiness and cumbersomeness in English that the German reader would encounter.

For these reasons, some will perhaps find this translation less smooth and readable in places than the existing ones. Yet greater literalness and transparency in a translation can often be as clarifying as confusing, as much an invitation to ponder the meaning of the text as an obstacle to understanding it. In such cases, the increased difficulty is, I believe, more than compensated for by greater consistency, accuracy, and precision. I am translating for those who want to know, insofar as they can know it from an English translation, exactly what Kant said, so that they can have an accurate basis for their own thinking, exegetical and critical, about what Kant said. That sort of person will not be looking for easy reading.

The priorities in translating a text must obviously depend on the nature and purpose of the text itself. Poetry should probably be translated only by poets; philosophy certainly needs to be translated by philosophers. What matters in a philosophical text is almost exclusively *what it means*. What a philosophical text means is constituted by the range of possible alternative constructions that a reader's philosophical imagination can justifiably put on the words in which the text expresses its questions, doctrines, and arguments. A translation succeeds, therefore, to the extent that it provides a reliable basis for this work of imagination, neither constraining the reader to adopt the translator's own preferred imaginings nor suggesting possible meanings that the original text cannot bear. Faithfulness to the precise wording of the text is one way of achieving this; another is the use of a consistent terminology, even if the reader must adjust slightly to an English idiolect needed to convey the thoughts Kant expressed in German.

To a philosophical mind, the meaning of the text, taken in this sense, matters incomparably more than the smoothness of the prose; difficult prose is even an advantage if it provokes the kind of questioning, or even the bewilderment, that leads to fruitful philosophical reflections that are also really about what Kant was saying. To such a mind, in fact, there is something intellectually offensive about a translation that merely gestures in the direction of what Kant said, leaving it to the common sense of readers (that is, to the philosophical prejudices that a great historical text should help them to unlearn) not merely to resolve the ambiguities, but even to determine where they are. Likewise, there is even something aesthetically repugnant about a translation whose smoothness of style glosses over philosophical difficulties for the sake of achieving a facility of comprehension or a rhetorical elegance that were not in the original text.

Abbott's translations of Kant's foundational writings on ethics were remarkable for their time because Abbott attempted accuracy when other translators of philosophical works were often content with highly interpretive paraphrases, or sought to interpose their own idiosyncratic readings of

a text between it and the English reader. Paton, Beck and Gregor are superior to the degree that they represent increasing attentiveness to what the
text says. Such a trend seems healthy or even inevitable. The more carefully
a text is studied, the more closely and subtly it will be read, and the more
sensitive its readers will become to the need for translations that reproduce
as far as possible precisely the same interpretive situation as that confronted
by a reader of the original. Once a translation is available that achieves this
to a higher degree, philosophical readers will adjust to the inconveniences
they must incur in order to obtain the advantage. Readers who want to think
hard about what the text says will not be content with something less
accurate just because it is easier to read.

Another direct incitement to do a new translation of the *Groundwork* at
this time was the availability of the new edition of the German text, published by Bernd Kraft and Dieter Schönecker in Felix Meiner Verlag's
Philosophische Bibliothek series. This text of the *Grundlegung* was used as
the basis for the present translation. One of the special virtues of the new
Meiner Verlag edition is its attention to variations between the two earliest
versions of the text, the first published in 1785, the second a year later. The
edition usually follows the 1786 version, but notes inform the reader of the
differences. The present translation does likewise wherever textual differences make a difference in translation (which they usually do). In a few
places I have also followed the editors of the new text in making textual
emendations where the sense seems to require it. But I have done this only
reluctantly (and less often than the editors of the original text did); wherever emendations are made, of course, a numbered footnote informs the
reader; in some cases, a note suggests a possible emendation, and what it
would have meant in the translation, but without actually adopting it.

This translation has benefited greatly from careful comments by, and
long discussions with, Dieter Schönecker. His care, precision, and linguis-
tic expertise and his intimate knowledge of the text of the *Grundlegung*
saved me from many errors and led to many improvements in the translation. Schönecker and Kraft also made available to me a draft of their edi-
torial notes; I tried to reciprocate this favor by providing them with some
informational notes they did not yet have. Also helpful were textual correc-
tions and thoughtful stylistic suggestions made by Derek Parfit. In identifying Kant's references to classical philosophy and literature, I also benefited
from the expertise, erudition, and generosity of Tad Brennan, John Cooper,
and Elizabeth Tylawsky.

Abbreviations

Like this translation of the *Groundwork*, most writings of Kant available in English provide marginal volume: page numbers from the definitive German edition (Ak). In the footnotes to this text of the *Groundwork*, the writings of Kant are cited by title in English and by Ak volume:page number. In the essays, they are cited by abbreviations listed here.

Ak   *Immanuel Kants Schriften.* Ausgabe der königlich preussischen Akademie der Wissenschaften (Berlin: W. de Gruyter, 1902–)

Ca   *Cambridge Edition of the Writings of Immanuel Kant* (New York: Cambridge University Press, 1992–)

G   *Grundlegung zur Metaphysik der Sitten* (1785), Ak 4
   Groundwork for the Metaphysics of Morals

KrV   *Kritik der reinen Vernunft* (1781, 1787), cited by A/B pagination
   Critique of Pure Reason, Ca

KpV   *Kritik der praktischen Vernunft* (1788), Ak 5
   Critique of Practical Reason, Ca *Practical Philosophy*

MA   *Mutmasslicher Anfang der Menschengeschichte* (1786), Ak 8
   Conjectural Beginning of Human History, Ca *Anthropology, History and Education*

MS   *Metaphysik der Sitten* (1797–1798), Ak 6
   Metaphysics of Morals, Ca *Practical Philosophy*

R   *Religion innerhalb der Grenzen der bloßen Vernunft* (1793–1794), Ak 6
   Religion within the Boundaries of Mere Reason, Ca *Religion and Rational Theology*

VA   *Anthropologie in pragmatischer Hinsicht* (1798), Ak 7
   Anthropology from a Pragmatic Standpoint, Ca *Anthropology, History and Education*
   Vorlesungen über Anthropologie, Ak 25

VE   *Vorlesungen über Ethik,* Ak 27
   Lectures on Ethics, Ca *Lectures on Ethics*

VL   *Vorlesungen über Logik*, Ak 9, 24
        Lectures on Logic, Ca *Lectures on Logic*
WA   *Beantwortung der Frage: Was ist Aufklärung?* (1784), Ak 8
        An Answer to the Question: What Is Enlightenment? Ca *Practical
        Philosophy*

Formulations of the Moral Law

Kant formulates the moral law in three principal ways. The first and third of
these have variants which are intended to bring the law closer to intuition
and make it easier to apply. These five principal formulations of the moral
law are abbreviated as follows.

First formula:
FUL   *The Formula of Universal Law*: "Act only in accordance with that
        maxim through which you can at the same time will that it become
        a universal law" (G 4:421; cf. G 4:402)
with its variant
FLN   *The Formula of the Law of Nature*: "So act as if the maxim of your
        action were to become through your will a **universal law of na-
        ture**" (G 4:421; cf. G 4:436)

Second formula:
FH   *The Formula of Humanity as End in Itself*: "*Act so that you use
        humanity, as much in your own person as in the person of every
        other, always at the same time as end and never merely as means*"
        (G 4:429; cf. G 4:436)

Third formula:
FA   *Formula of Autonomy:* "the idea of the will of every rational being
        as a will giving universal law" (G 4:431; cf. G 4:432) or "Not to
        choose otherwise than so that the maxims of one's choice are at
        the same time comprehended with it in the same volition as uni-
        versal law" (G 4:440; cf. G 4:432, 434, 438)
with its variant,
FRE   *The Formula of the Realm of Ends:* "Act in accordance with
        maxims of a universally legislative member for a merely possible
        realm of ends" (G 4:439; cf. G 4:433, 437, 438)

Groundwork
for
the Metaphysics of Morals

Preface

Ancient Greek philosophy was divided into three sciences: **physics, ethics,** and **logic**.[1] This division is perfectly suitable to the nature of the thing and one cannot improve upon it, except only by adding its principle, in order in this way partly to secure its completeness and partly to be able to determine correctly the necessary subdivisions.

All rational cognition is either *material*, and considers some object, or *formal*, and concerns itself merely with the form of the understanding and of reason itself and the universal rules of thinking in general, without distinction among objects.[2] Formal philosophy is called **logic**, but material philosophy, which has to do with determinate objects and the laws to which they are subjected, is once again twofold. For these laws are either laws of **nature** or of **freedom**. The science of the first is called **physics**, and that of the other is **ethics**; the former is also named 'doctrine of nature', the latter 'doctrine of morals'.

Logic can have no empirical part, i.e., a part such that the universal and necessary laws of thinking rest on grounds that are taken from experience; for otherwise it would not be logic, i.e., a canon for the understanding or reason which is valid for all thinking and must be demonstrated. By contrast, natural and moral philosophy can each have their empirical part, because the former must determine its laws of nature as an object of experience, the latter must determine the laws for the will of the human being insofar as he is affected by nature — the first as laws in accordance with which everything happens, the second as those in accordance with which everything ought to happen, but also reckoning with the conditions under which it often does not happen.

One can call all philosophy, insofar as it is based on grounds of experi-

---

1. According to Diogenes Laertius, *Lives and Opinions of the Eminent Philosophers* 7.39, this division was first devised by Zeno of Citium (335–265 B.C.) and was characteristic of the Stoics. See, e.g., Seneca, *Epistles* 89.9; Cicero, *On Ends* 4.4.

2. Cf. *Critique of Pure Reason*, A50–55/B74–79.

ence, *empirical*, but that which puts forth its doctrines solely from principles *a priori*, *pure* philosophy. The latter, when it is merely formal, is called *logic;* but if it is limited to determinate objects of the understanding, then[3] it is called *metaphysics.*

In such a wise there arises the idea of a twofold metaphysics, the idea of a *metaphysics of nature* and of a *metaphysics of morals*. Physics will thus have its empirical but also a rational part; and ethics likewise; although here the empirical part in particular could be called *practical anthropology*, but the rational part could properly be called *morals*.[4]

All trades, handicrafts, and arts have gained through the division of labor, since, namely, one person does not do everything, but rather each limits himself to a certain labor which distinguishes itself markedly from others by its manner of treatment, in order to be able to perform it in the greatest perfection and with more facility. Where labors are not so distinguished and divided, where each is a jack-of-all-trades, there the trades still remain in the greatest barbarism. But it might be a not unworthy object of consideration to ask whether pure philosophy in all its parts does not require each its particular man, and whether it would not stand better with the learned trade as a whole if those who, catering to the taste of the public, are accustomed to sell the empirical along with the rational, mixed in all sorts of proportions[5] unknown even to themselves — calling themselves 'independent thinkers',[6] and those who prepare the merely rational part 'quibblers'[7] — if they were warned not to carry on simultaneously two enterprises that are very different in their mode of treatment, each of which perhaps requires a particular talent, and the combination of which in a single person produces only bunglers: thus I here ask only whether the nature of the science does not require the empirical part always to be carefully separated from the rational, placing ahead of a genuine (empirical) physics a metaphysics of nature, and ahead of practical anthropology a metaphysics of morals, which must be carefully cleansed of everything

3. 1785: "understanding, is called"

4. Kant later includes "principles of application" drawn from "the particular nature of human beings" *within* "metaphysics of morals" itself, leaving "practical anthropology" to deal "only with the subjective conditions in human nature that hinder people or help them in fulfilling the laws of a metaphysics of morals" (*Metaphysics of Morals*, Ak 6:217).

5. *Verhältnisse*

6. *Selbstdenker*

7. *Grübler*

empirical, in order to know how much pure reason could achieve in both [Ak 4: 389] cases; and from these sources pure reason itself creates its teachings *a priori*, whether the latter enterprise be carried on by all teachers of morals (whose name is legion) or only by some who feel they have a calling for it.

Since my aim here is properly directed to moral philosophy, I limit the proposed question only to this: whether one is not of the opinion that it is of the utmost necessity to work out once a pure moral philosophy which is fully cleansed of everything that might be in any way empirical and belong to anthropology; for that there must be such is self-evident from the common idea of duty and of moral laws. Everyone must admit that a law, if it is to be valid morally, i.e., as the ground of an obligation, has to carry absolute necessity with it; that the command 'You ought not to lie' is valid not merely for human beings, as though other rational beings did not have to heed it; and likewise all the other genuinely moral laws; hence that the ground of obligation here is to be sought not in the nature of the human being or the circumstances of the world in which he is placed, but *a priori* solely in concepts of pure reason, and that every other precept grounded on principles of mere experience, and even a precept that is universal in a certain aspect, insofar as it is supported in the smallest part on empirical grounds, perhaps only as to its motive, can be called a practical rule, but never a moral law.

Thus not only are moral laws together with their principles essentially distinguished among all practical cognition from everything else in which there is anything empirical, but all moral philosophy rests entirely on its pure part, and when applied to the human being it borrows not the least bit from knowledge about him (anthropology), but it gives him as a rational being laws *a priori*, which to be sure require a power of judgment sharpened through experience, partly to distinguish in which cases they have their application, and partly to obtain access for them to the will of the human being and emphasis for their fulfillment, since he,[8] as affected with so many inclinations, is susceptible to the idea of a pure practical reason, but is not so easily capable of making it effective *in concreto* in his course of life.

Thus a metaphysics of morals is indispensably necessary not merely from a motive of speculation, in order to investigate the source of the [Ak 4:390] practical principles lying *a priori* in our reason, but also because morals themselves remain subject to all sorts of corruption as long as that guiding

8. Kant's text reads *diese*, which would be translated "the latter" and refer to "fulfillment"; editors suggest amending it to *dieser*, which would refer to 'the human being'.

thread and supreme norm of their correct judgment is lacking. For as to what is to be morally good, it is not enough that it *conform* to the moral law, but it must also happen *for the sake of this law*; otherwise, that conformity is only contingent and precarious, because the unmoral ground will now and then produce lawful actions, but more often actions contrary to the law. But now the moral law in its purity and genuineness (which is precisely what most matters in the practical) is to be sought nowhere else than in a pure philosophy; hence this (metaphysics) must go first, and without it there can be no moral philosophy at all; that which mixes those pure principles among empirical ones does not even deserve the name of a 'philosophy' (for this distinguishes itself from common rational cognition precisely by the fact that what the latter conceives only as mixed in, it expounds in a separate science), still less of a 'moral philosophy', because precisely through this mixture it violates the purity of morals and proceeds contrary to its own end.

One should not think that what is here demanded we already have in the propadeutic of the famous *Wolff* in his moral philosophy, namely in what he calls *universal practical philosophy*,[9] and thus that here an entirely new field is not to be entered on. Precisely because it is supposed to be a "universal practical philosophy," it has not drawn into consideration any will of a particular kind, such as one determined without any empirical motives fully from principles *a priori*, which one could call a 'pure will', but only volition in general, with all actions and conditions that pertain to it in this universal signification; and thereby it is distinguished from a metaphysics of morals just as general logic is from transcendental philosophy, of which the first expounds the actions and rules of thinking *in general*, but the latter merely the particular actions and rules of **pure** thinking, i.e., those through which objects can be cognized fully *a priori*. For the metaphysics of morals is to investigate the idea and principles of a possible *pure* will, and not the actions and conditions of human volition in general, which are for the most part drawn from psychology. It constitutes no objection to my assertion that moral laws and duty are also discussed in universal practical philosophy (though contrary to all warrant). For in this too the authors of that science remain faithful to their idea of it; they do not distinguish the

9. Christian Wolff (1679–1754), *Philosophia Practica Universalis* (1738–1739). Kant uses the same title himself, however, as a subtitle to the section of the introduction to the *Metaphysics of Morals* titled "Preliminary Concepts of the Metaphysics of Morals," in which he discusses concepts such as freedom, duty, personhood, maxims, and laws (Ak 6:221–28).

motives that are represented as such fully *a priori* merely through reason, and are properly moral, from the empirical ones that understanding raises to universal concepts through the comparison of experiences; but rather they consider them, without respecting the distinction of their sources, only in accordance with their greater or smaller sum (since they are all regarded as homogeneous), and through that they make for themselves their concept of *obligation*, which is to be sure not less than moral, but is so constituted as can be demanded only in a philosophy that does not judge about the *origin* of all practical concepts, whether they occur *a priori* or merely *a posteriori*.

Now intending someday to provide a metaphysics of morals, I issue this groundwork in advance.[10] There is, to be sure, really no other foundation for it than the critique of a *pure practical reason*,[11] just as for metaphysics there is the already provided critique of pure speculative reason. Yet in part the former is not of such utmost necessity as the latter, because in what is moral human reason, even in the most common understanding, can easily be brought to great correctness and completeness, whereas in its theoretical but pure use it is entirely dialectical; in part I require for a critique of a pure practical reason that if it is to be completed, its unity with the[12] speculative in a common principle must at the same time be exhibited, because it can in the end be only one and the same reason that is distinguished merely in its application. But I could not bring it to such a completeness here without bringing in considerations of an entirely different kind and confusing the reader. It is for the sake of this that instead of the term *Critique of pure practical reason* I have used instead *Groundwork for the metaphysics of morals*.

But, thirdly, because a metaphysics of morals, despite its intimidating title, is yet susceptible to a high degree of popularity and suitability to the common understanding, I find it useful to separate from it this preliminary work of laying the ground, in order that in the future I need not attach [Ak 4:392] subtleties, which are unavoidable in it, to more easily grasped doctrines.

The present groundwork is, however, nothing more than the search for

10. Kant's *Metaphysics of Morals*, Ak 6:205–493, was published in 1797–1798.

11. Kant published the *Critique of Practical Reason*, Ak 5:1–163, in 1788. But he appears not to have intended to write a separate work with that title in 1785–1786. He apparently planned to include a "practical" section in the second edition of the *Critique of Pure Reason* (1787), but published the *Critique of Practical Reason* separately when it grew too long for that.

12. In 1785 the definite article *der* is repeated; that version would be translated: "its unity with the critique of speculative reason in a common principle."

and establishment *of the supreme principle of morality*, which already constitutes an enterprise whole in its aim and to be separated from every other moral investigation. To be sure, my assertions about this important and principal question, whose discussion has hitherto been far from satisfactory, would receive much light through the application of the same principle to the entire system, and of confirmation through the adequacy it manifests every-where; yet I had to dispense with this advantage, which would also be basically more a matter of my self-love than of the common utility, because the facility of use and the apparent adequacy of a principle provide no wholly secure proof of its correctness, but rather awaken a certain partiality not to investigate and consider it for itself without any regard for the consequences.

The method I have taken in this work, I believe, is the one best suited if one wants to take the way analytically from common cognition to the determination of its supreme principle and then, in turn, synthetically from the testing of this principle and its sources back to common cognition, in which its use is encountered. Hence the division turns out thus:

First Section: Transition from common rational moral cognition to philosophical moral cognition.

Second Section: Transition from popular moral philosophy to the metaphysics of morals.

Third Section: Final step from the metaphysics of morals to the critique of pure practical reason.

First Section

Transition

FROM COMMON RATIONAL MORAL COGNITION

TO PHILOSOPHICAL MORAL COGNITION

There is nothing it is possible to think of anywhere in the world, or indeed anything at all outside it, that can be held to be good without limitation, excepting only a **good will**. Understanding, wit, the power of judgment,[1] and like *talents* of the mind,[2] whatever they might be called, or courage, resoluteness, persistence in an intention, as qualities of *temperament*, are without doubt in some respects good and to be wished for; but they can also become extremely evil and harmful, if the will that is to make use of these gifts of nature, and whose peculiar constitution is therefore called *character*,[3] is not good. It is the same with *gifts of fortune*. Power, wealth, honor,[4] even health and that entire well-being and contentment with one's condition, under the name of *happiness*, make for courage and thereby often also for arrogance,[5] where there is not a good will to correct their influence on the mind,[6] and thereby on the entire principle of action, and make them universally purposive; not to mention that a rational impartial spectator can never take satisfaction even in the sight of the uninterrupted welfare of a being, if it is adorned with no trait of a pure and good will; and so the good will appears to constitute the indispensable condition even of the worthiness to be happy.

Some qualities are even conducive to this good will itself and can make its work much easier, but still have despite this no inner unconditioned worth, yet always presuppose a good will, which limits the esteem[7] that one

---

1. See *Anthropology in a Pragmatic Respect*, Ak 7:196–201.

2. *Geist*

3. For Kant's distinction between "temperament" and "character," see *Anthropology in a Pragmatic Respect*, Ak 7:286–95; see also Ak 4:398–99 below.

4. Power, wealth, and honor are for Kant the three objects of the principal social passions. See *Anthropology in a Pragmatic Respect*, Ak 7:271–274.

5. *Mut und hierdurch öfters auch Übermut*

6. *Gemüt*

7. 1786: *Hochschätzung*; 1785: *Schätzung* ("estimation")

otherwise rightly has for them, and does not permit them to be held absolutely good. Moderation in affects and passions,[8] self-control, and sober reflection not only are good for many aims, but seem even to constitute a part of the *inner* worth of a person; yet they lack much in order to be declared good without limitation (however unconditionally they were praised by the ancients).[9] For without the principles of a good will they can become extremely evil, and the cold-bloodedness of a villain makes him not only far more dangerous but also immediately more abominable in our eyes than he would have been held without it.

The good will is good not through what it effects or accomplishes, not through its efficacy for attaining any intended end, but only through its willing, i.e., good in itself, and considered for itself, without comparison, it is to be estimated far higher than anything that could be brought about by it in favor of any inclination, or indeed, if you prefer, of the sum of all inclinations. Even if through the peculiar disfavor of fate, or through the meager endowment of a stepmotherly nature, this will were entirely lacking in the resources to carry out its aim, if with its greatest effort nothing of it were accomplished, and only the good will were left over (to be sure, not a mere wish, but as the summoning up of all the means insofar as they are in our control): then it would shine like a jewel for itself, as something that has its full worth in itself. Utility or fruitlessness can neither add to nor subtract anything from this worth. It would be only the setting, as it were, to make it easier to handle in common traffic, or to draw the attention of those who are still not sufficiently connoisseurs, but not to recommend it to connoisseurs and determine its worth.

There is, however, something so strange in this idea of the absolute worth of the mere will, without making any allowance for utility in its estimation, that despite all the agreement with it even of common reason, there must nevertheless arise a suspicion that perhaps it is covertly grounded merely on a high-flown fantasy, and that nature might have been falsely understood in the aim it had in assigning reason to govern our will. Hence we will put this idea to the test from this point of view.

[Ak 4:395]

In the natural predispositions of an organized being, i.e., a being arranged purposively for life, we assume as a principle that no instrument is to

8. In Kant's empirical theory of the faculty of desire, affects and passions are the two principal obstacles to rational self-control. See *Metaphysics of Morals*, Ak 6:407–9; *Anthropology in a Pragmatic Respect*, Ak 7:251–67.

9. Courage and self-control were, for the ancients, two of the primary moral virtues, along with wisdom, justice, and sometimes piety. See Plato, *Meno* 78d–e, *Republic* 427e; Aristotle, *Nicomachean Ethics* 3.6–12; Cicero, *On Duties* 1.15.

be encountered in it for any end except that which is the most suitable to and appropriate for it.[10] Now if, in a being that has reason and a will, its *preservation*, its *welfare* — in a word, its *happiness* — were the real end of nature, then nature would have hit on a very bad arrangement in appointing reason in this creature to accomplish the aim. For all the actions it has to execute toward this aim, and the entire rule of its conduct, would be prescribed to it much more precisely through instinct, and that end could be obtained far more safely through it than could ever happen through reason; and if, over and above this, reason were imparted to the favored creature, it would have served it only to make it consider the happy predisposition of its nature, to admire it, to rejoice in it, and to make it grateful to the beneficent cause of it, but not to subject its faculty of desire to that weak and deceptive guidance, and meddle in the aim of nature; in a word, nature would have prevented reason from breaking out into *practical use* and from having the presumption, with its weak insight, to think out for itself the project of happiness and the means of attaining it; nature would have taken over the choice not only of the ends but also of the means, and with wise provision would have entrusted both solely to instinct.[11]

In fact we also find that the more a cultivated reason gives itself over to the aim of enjoying life and happiness, the further the human being falls short of true contentment; from this arises in many, and indeed in those most practiced in the cultivated use of reason, if only they are sincere enough to admit it, a certain degree of *misology*, i.e., hatred of reason;[12] for after reckoning all the advantages they draw, I do not say from the invention of all the arts of common luxury,[13] but even from the sciences (which also

10. Kant's reasons for accepting this proposition as an *a priori* maxim of reflective judgment are presented in the *Critique of the Power of Judgment* (1790), § 66, Ak 5:376–77.

11. Kant rejects the proposition that human happiness is an end of nature in his writings on history and in his review of the chief work of his former student J. G. Herder (1762–1802). See *Idea toward a Universal History with a Cosmopolitan Aim* (1784), Ak 8:19–20; Reviews of Herder's *Ideas for the Philosophy of History of Humanity* (1785–1786), Ak 8:64–65; *Conjectural Beginning of Human History* (1786), Ak 8:114–18. See also *Critique of the Power of Judgment*, Ak 5:429–31. Though not an end of nature, human happiness is an end of reason, and of morality; see *Critique of Practical Reason*, Ak 5:61–62, 110–13; *Metaphysics of Morals*, Ak 6:387–88.

12. See Plato, *Phaedo* 89d–91b.

13. "Luxury (luxus) is excessive convenience in the social life of a community (so that its convenience works against its welfare)"; *Anthropology in a Pragmatic Respect*, Ak 7:249.

seem to them in the end to be[14] a luxury of the understanding), they nevertheless find that they have in fact only brought more[15] hardship down on their shoulders than they have gained in happiness, and on this account in the end they sooner envy than despise human beings of the more common stamp, who are closer to the guidance of mere natural instinct and do not permit their reason much influence over their deeds and omissions. And we must admit this much, that the judgment of those who very much moderate the boastful high praise of the advantages that reason is supposed to supply us in regard to happiness and contentment with life, or who even reduce it below zero, is by no means morose or ungrateful toward the kindness of the world's government; but rather these judgments are covertly grounded on the idea of another aim for their existence, possessing much greater dignity, for which, and not for their happiness, reason has been given its wholly authentic vocation, and to which, therefore, as a supreme condition, the private aims of the human being must for the most part defer.

For since reason is not sufficiently effective in guiding the will safely in regard to its objects and the satisfaction of all our needs (which it in part itself multiplies), and an implanted natural instinct would have guided us much more certainly to this end, yet since reason nevertheless has been imparted to us as a practical faculty, i.e., as one that ought to have influence on the *will*, its true vocation must therefore be not to produce volition *as a means* to some other aim, but rather to produce a *will good in itself*, for which reason was absolutely necessary, since everywhere else nature goes to work purposively in distributing its predispositions. This will may therefore not be the single and entire good, but it must be the highest good, and the condition for all the rest, even for every demand for happiness, in which case it can be united with the wisdom of nature, when one perceives that the culture of reason, which is required for the former, limits in many ways the attainment of the second aim, which is always conditioned, namely of happiness, at least in this life, and can even diminish it to less than nothing without nature's proceeding unpurposively in this; for reason, which recognizes its highest practical vocation in the grounding of a good will, is capable in attaining this aim only of a contentment after its own kind, namely from the fulfillment of an[16] end that again only reason determines,

14. 1785 reads *scheint* instead of *zu sein scheinen*, which would have the effect in translation of eliminating the words "to be" from this sentence.

15. 1785: "more of"

16. 1785: "of the end"

even if this should also be bound up with some infringement of the ends of inclination.

[Ak 4:397]

But now in order to develop the concept of a good will, to be esteemed in itself and without any further aim, just as it dwells already[17] in the naturally healthy understanding, which does not need to be taught but rather only to be enlightened, this concept always standing over the estimation of the entire worth of our actions and constituting the condition for everything else: we will put before ourselves the concept of **duty**, which contains that of a good will, though under certain subjective limitations and hindrances, which, however, far from concealing it and making it unrecognizable, rather elevate it by contrast and let it shine forth all the more brightly.

I pass over all actions that are already recognized as contrary to duty, even though they might be useful for this or that aim; for with them the question cannot arise at all whether they might be done *from duty*, since they even conflict with it. I also set aside the actions which are actually in conformity with duty, for which, however, human beings have immediately *no inclination*, but nevertheless perform them because they are driven to it through another inclination. For there it is easy to distinguish whether the action in conformity with duty is done *from duty* or from a self-seeking aim. It is much harder to notice this difference where the action is in conformity with duty and the subject yet has besides this an *immediate* inclination to it. E.g., it is indeed in conformity with duty that the merchant should not overcharge his inexperienced customers, and where there is much commercial traffic, the prudent merchant also does not do this, but rather holds a firm general price for everyone, so that a child buys just as cheaply from him as anyone else. Thus one is *honestly* served; yet that is by no means sufficient for us to believe that the merchant has proceeded thus from duty and from principles of honesty; his advantage required it; but here it is not to be assumed that besides this, he was also supposed to have an immediate inclination toward the customers, so that out of love, as it were, he gave no one an advantage over another in his prices. Thus the action was done neither from duty nor from immediate inclination, but merely from a self-serving aim.

By contrast, to preserve one's life is a duty, and besides this everyone has an immediate inclination to it. But the often anxious care that the greatest part of humankind takes for its sake still has no inner worth, and its maxim has no moral content. They protect their life, to be sure, *in conformity with duty*, but not *from duty*. If, by contrast, adversities and hopeless grief have

[Ak 4:398]

17. This word added in 1786

entirely taken away the taste for life, if the unhappy one, strong of soul, more indignant than pusillanimous or dejected over his fate, wishes for death and yet preserves his life without loving it, not from inclination or fear, but from duty: then his maxim has a moral content.

To be beneficent where one can is a duty, and besides this there are some souls so sympathetically attuned[18] that, even without any other motive of vanity or utility to self, take an inner gratification in spreading joy around them, and can take delight in the contentment of others insofar as it is their own work. But I assert that in such a case the action, however it may conform to duty and however amiable it is, nevertheless has no true moral worth, but is on the same footing as other inclinations, e.g., the inclination to honor, which, when it fortunately encounters something that in fact serves the common good and is in conformity with duty, and is thus worthy of honor, deserves praise and encouragement, but not esteem; for the maxim lacks moral content, namely of doing such actions not from inclination but *from duty*. Thus suppose the mind of that same friend of humanity were clouded over with his own grief, extinguishing all his sympathetic participation[19] in the fate of others; he still has the resources to be beneficent to those suffering distress, but the distress of others does not touch him because he is[20] sufficiently busy with his own; and now, where no inclination any longer stimulates him to it, he tears himself out of this deadly insensibility and does the action without any inclination, solely from duty; only then does it for the first time have its authentic moral worth. Even more: if nature had put little sympathy at all in the heart of this or that person, if he (an honest man, to be sure) were by temperament cold and indifferent toward the sufferings of others, perhaps because he himself is provided with particular gifts of patience and strength to endure his own, and also presupposes or even demands the same of others; if nature has not really formed[21] such a man into a friend of humanity (although he would not in truth be its worst product), nevertheless would he not find a source within himself to give himself a far higher worth than that which a good-natured temperament might have? By all means! Just here begins the worth of character, which is moral and the highest without any comparison, namely that he is beneficent not from inclination but from duty.

To secure one's own happiness is a duty (at least indirectly), for the lack

[Ak 4:399]

18. *teilnehmend gestimmte Seelen*
19. *Teilnehmung*
20. 1785: *wäre*
21. *gebildet*

of contentment with one's condition, in a crowd of many sorrows and amid unsatisfied needs, can easily become a great *temptation to the violation of duties*. But even without looking at duty, all human beings always have of themselves the most powerful and inward inclination to happiness, because precisely in this idea all inclinations are united in a sum. Yet the precept of happiness is for the most part so constituted that it greatly infringes on some inclinations and yet the human being cannot make any determinate and secure concept of the sum of satisfaction of them all, under the name of 'happiness'; hence it is not to be wondered at that a single inclination, which is determinate in regard to what it promises and the time in which its satisfaction can be obtained, can outweigh a wavering idea; and the human being, e.g., a person with gout, could choose to enjoy what tastes good and to suffer what he must, because in accordance with his reckoning, here at least he has not sacrificed the enjoyment of the present moment through expectations, perhaps groundless, of a happiness that is supposed to lie in health. But also in this case, if the general inclination to happiness does not determine his will, if for him, at least, health does not count as so necessary in his reckoning, then here, as in all other cases, there still remains a law, namely to promote his happiness not from inclination but from duty, and then his conduct has for the first time its authentic moral worth.

It is in this way, without doubt, that those passages in scripture are to be understood in which it is commanded to love our neighbor and even our enemy. For love as inclination cannot be commanded; but beneficence solely from duty, even when no inclination at all drives us to it, or even when natural and invincible disinclination resists, is *practical* and not *pathological* love, which lies in the will and not in the propensity of feeling, in the principles of action and not in melting sympathy;[22] but the former alone can be commanded.

The second proposition[23] is: an action from duty has its moral worth *not in the aim* that is supposed to be attained by it, but rather in the maxim in accordance with which it is resolved upon; thus[24] that worth depends not on the actuality of the object of the action, but merely on the *principle of the volition*, in accordance with which the action is done, without regard to any object of the faculty of desire. It is clear from the preceding that the aims we may have in actions, and their effects, as ends and incentives of the will, can

[Ak 4:400]

22. *schmelzender Teilnehmung*

23. Kant does not say explicitly what the "first proposition" was, but presumably it is that an action has moral worth only if it is done from duty.

24. This word added in 1786

impart to the actions no unconditioned and moral worth. In what, then, can this worth lie, if it is not supposed to exist in the will, in the relation of the actions to the effect hoped for? It can lie nowhere else *than in the principle of the will*, without regard to the ends that can be effected through such action; for the will is at a crossroads, as it were, between its principle *a priori*, which is formal, and its incentive *a posteriori*, which is material, and since it must somehow be determined by something, it must be determined through the formal principle in general of the volition if it does an action from duty, since every material principle has been withdrawn from it.

The third proposition, as a consequence of the first two, I would express thus: *Duty is the necessity of an action from respect for the law.* For the object, as an effect of my proposed action, I can of course have an *inclination*, but *never respect*, just because it[25] is merely an effect and not the activity of a will.[26] Just as little can I have respect for inclination in general, whether my own or another's; I can at most approve it in the first case, in the second I can sometimes even love it, i.e., regard it as favorable to my own advantage. Only that which is connected with my will merely as a ground, never as an effect, only what does not serve my inclination but outweighs it, or at least wholly excludes it from the reckoning in a choice, hence only the mere law for itself, can be an object of respect and hence a command. Now an action from duty is supposed entirely to abstract from[27] the influence of inclination, and with it every object of the will, so nothing is left over for the will that can determine it except the *law* as what is objective and subjectively *pure respect* for this practical law, hence the maxim* of complying with such a law, even when it infringes all my inclinations.

The moral worth of the action thus lies not in the effect to be expected from it; thus also not in any principle of action which needs to get its motive from this expected effect. For all these effects (agreeableness of one's condition, indeed even the furthering of the happiness of others) could be brought about through other causes, and for them the will of a rational being

---

*A *maxim* is the subjective principle of the volition; the objective principle (i.e., that which would serve all rational beings also subjectively as a practical principle if reason had full control over the faculty of desire) is the practical *law*.

25. Kant's pronoun here is in the feminine, which could refer to "effect" but not to "object," which seems to be the intended referent. Editors therefore often emend the pronoun to the neuter.

26. 1785: "an effect of my will"

27. *absondern*

is therefore not needed; but in it alone the highest and unconditioned good can nevertheless be encountered. Nothing other than the *representation of the law* in itself, *which obviously occurs only in the rational being* insofar as it, and not the hoped-for effect, is the determining ground of the will, therefore[28] constitutes that so pre-eminent good which we call 'moral', which is already present in the person himself who acts in accordance with it, but must not first of all be expected from the effect.** [Ak 4:402]

But what kind of law can it be, whose representation, without even

**One could accuse me of merely taking refuge behind the word *respect* [Ak4:401] in an obscure feeling instead of giving a distinct reply to the question through a concept of reason. Yet even if respect is a feeling, it is not one *received* through influence but a feeling *self-effected* through a concept of reason and hence specifically distinguished from all feelings of the first kind, which may be reduced to inclination or fear. What I immediately recognize as a law for me, I recognize with respect, which signifies merely the consciousness of the *subjection* of my will to a law without any mediation of other influences on my sense. The immediate determination of the will through the law and the consciousness of it is called *respect*, so that the latter is to be regarded as the *effect* of the law on the subject and not as its *cause*. Authentically, respect is the representation of a worth that infringes on my self-love. Thus it is something that is considered as an object neither of inclination nor of fear, even though it has something analogical to both at the same time. The *object* of respect is thus solely the law, and specifically that law that we *lay upon ourselves* and yet also as in itself necessary. As a law we are subject to it without asking permission of self-love; as laid upon us by ourselves, it is a consequence of our will, and has from the first point of view an analogy with fear, and from the second with inclination. All respect for a person is properly only respect for the law (of uprightness, etc.) of which the person gives us the example. Because we regard the expansion of our talents also as a duty, we represent to ourselves a person with talents also as an *example of a law*, as it were (to become similar to the person in this) and that constitutes our respect. All so-called moral *interest* consists solely in *respect* for the law. [The parenthetical material in the penultimate sentence was added in 1786. Cf. *Critique of Practical Reason*, Ak 5:71–89. In the *Metaphysics of Morals*, Kant lists *four* feelings that are produced directly by reason and can serve as moral motivation. These are "moral feeling," "conscience," "love of human beings," and "respect" (*Metaphysics of Morals*, Ak 6:399–403).]

28. 1785: "thus"

taking account of the effect expected from it, must determine the will, so that it can be called good absolutely and without limitation? Since I have robbed the will of every impulse that could have arisen from the obedience to any law, there is nothing left over except the universal lawfulness of the action in general which alone is to serve the will as its principle, i.e., I ought never to conduct myself except so *that I could also will that my maxim become a universal law.* Here it is mere lawfulness in general (without grounding it on any law determining certain actions) that serves the will as its principle, and also must so serve it, if duty is not to be everywhere an empty delusion and a chimerical concept; common human reason,[29] indeed, agrees perfectly with this in its practical judgment, and has the principle just cited always before its eyes.

Let the question be, e.g.: When I am in a tight spot, may I not make a promise with the intention of not keeping it? Here I easily make a distinction in the signification the question can have, whether it is prudent, or whether it is in conformity with duty, to make a false promise. The first can without doubt often occur. I do see very well that it is not sufficient to get myself out of a present embarrassment by means of this subterfuge, but rather it must be reflected upon whether from this lie there could later arise much greater inconvenience than that from which I am now freeing myself, and, since the consequences of my supposed *cunning* are not so easy to foresee, and a trust once lost to me might become much more disadvantageous than any ill I think I am avoiding, whether it might not be more *prudent* to conduct myself in accordance with a universal maxim and make it into a habit not to promise anything except with the intention of keeping it. Yet it soon occurs to me here that such a maxim has as its ground only the worrisome consequences. Now to be truthful from duty is something entirely different from being truthful out of worry over disadvantageous consequences; in the first case, the concept of the action in itself already contains a law for me, whereas in the second I must look around elsewhere to see which effects might be bound up with it for me. For if I deviate from the principle of duty, then this is quite certainly evil; but if I desert my maxim of prudence, then that can sometimes be very advantageous to me, even though it is safer to remain with it. Meanwhile, to inform myself in the shortest and least deceptive way in regard to my answer to this problem, whether a lying promise is in conformity with duty, I ask myself: Would I be content with it if my maxim (of getting myself out of embarrassment through an untruthful promise) should be valid as a universal law (for

[Ak 4:403]

29. 1785: "but common human reason"

myself as well as for others), and would I be able to say to myself that anyone may make an untruthful promise when he finds himself in embarrassment which he cannot get out of in any other way? Then I soon become aware that I can will the lie but not at all a universal law to lie; for in accordance with such a law there would properly be no promises, because it would be pointless to avow my will in regard to my future actions to those who would not believe this avowal, or, if they rashly did so, who would pay me back in the same coin; hence my maxim, as soon as it were made into a universal law, would destroy itself.

Thus I need no well-informed shrewdness to know what I have to do in order to make my volition morally good. Inexperienced in regard to the course of the world, incapable of being prepared for all the occurrences that might eventuate in it, I ask myself only: Can you will also that your maxim should become a universal law? If not, then it is reprehensible, and this not for the sake of any disadvantage impending for you or someone else, but because it cannot fit as a principle into a possible universal legislation; but for this legislation reason extorts immediate respect from me, from which, to be sure, I still do not have *insight* into that on which it is grounded (which the philosopher may investigate), but I at least understand this much, that it is an estimation of a worth which far outweighs everything whose worth is commended by inclination, and that the necessity of my actions from *pure* respect for the practical law is what constitutes duty, before which every other motive must give way because it is the condition of a will that is good *in itself*, whose worth surpasses everything.

Thus in the moral cognition of common human reason we have attained to its principle, which it obviously does not think abstractly in such a universal form, but actually has always before its eyes and uses as its standard of judgment. It would be easy here to show how, with this compass [Ak 4:404] in its hand, it knows its way around very well in all the cases that come before it, how to distinguish what is good, what is evil, what conforms to duty or is contrary to duty, if, without teaching it the least new thing, one only makes it aware of its own principle, as Socrates did;[30] and thus that it needs no science and philosophy to know what one has to do in order to be honest and good, or indeed, even wise and virtuous. It might even have been conjectured in advance that the acquaintance with what every human being is obliged to do, hence to know, would also be the affair of everyone,

---

30. This would appear to be Kant's interpretation of Socrates' "human wisdom" (Plato, *Apology* 20c–24b). Compare *Metaphysics of Morals*, Ak 6:411.

even of the most common human being. Here[31] one cannot regard without admiration the way the practical faculty of judgment is so far ahead of the theoretical in the common human understanding. In the latter, if common reason ventures to depart from the laws of experience and perceptions of sense, then it falls into sheer inconceivabilities and self-contradictions, or at least into a chaos of uncertainty, obscurity, and inconstancy. But in the practical, the power of judgment first begins to show itself to advantage when the common understanding excludes from practical laws all sensuous incentives. It then even becomes subtle, caviling with its conscience, or with other claims in reference to what is to be called right, or even in wanting sincerely to determine the worth of actions for its own instruc-tion,[32] and, what is most striking, it can in the latter case do so with just as good a hope of getting things right as any philosopher might promise to do; indeed, it is almost more secure in this even than the latter, because the philosopher has[33] no other principle than the common understanding, but the philosopher's judgment is easily confused by a multiplicity of consider-ations that are alien and do not belong to the matter and can make it deviate from the straight direction. Would it not accordingly be more advisable in moral things to stay with the judgment of common reason, and bring in philosophy at most only in order to exhibit the system of morals all the more completely and comprehensibly, and its rules in a way that is more conve-nient for their use (still more for disputation), but not in order to remove the common human understanding in a practical respect out of its happy sim-plicity, and through philosophy to set it on a new route of investigation and instruction?

[Ak 4:405]   There is something splendid about innocence, but it is in turn very bad that it cannot be protected very well and is easily seduced. On this account even wisdom — which consists more in deeds and omissions than in knowl-edge — also needs science, not in order to learn from it but in order to provide entry and durability for its precepts. The human being feels in himself a powerful counterweight against all commands of duty, which reason represents to him as so worthy of esteem, in his needs and inclina-tions, whose satisfaction he summarizes under the name of 'happiness'. Now reason commands its precepts unremittingly, without promising any-thing to inclinations, thus snubbing and disrespecting, as it were, those impetuous claims, which at the same time seem so reasonable (and will not

31. 1785: "Nevertheless"
32. 1785: *Belohnung* ("reward"); 1786: *Belehrung* ("instruction")
33. 1785: "can have"

be done away with by any command). From this, however, arises a *natural dialectic*, that is, a propensity to ratiocinate against those strict laws of duty and to bring into doubt their validity, or at least their purity and strictness, and,[34] where possible, to make them better suited to our wishes and inclinations, i.e., at ground to corrupt them and deprive them of their entire dignity, which not even common practical reason can in the end call good.

Thus *common human reason* is impelled, not through any need of speculation (which never assaults it as long as it is satisfied with being mere healthy reason), but rather from practical grounds themselves, to go outside its sphere and to take a step into the field of *practical philosophy*, in order to receive information and distinct directions about the source of its principle and its correct determination in opposition to the maxims based on need and inclination, so that it may escape from its embarrassment concerning the claims of both sides and not run the risk of being deprived, through the ambiguity into which it easily falls, of all genuine ethical principles. Thus even in common practical reason, when it is cultivated, there ensues unnoticed a *dialectic*, which necessitates it to seek help in philosophy, just as befalls it in its theoretical use; and therefore the first will find no more tranquillity than the other anywhere except in a complete critique of our reason.

---

34. 1785: "at least"

Second Section

TRANSITION FROM POPULAR MORAL PHILOSOPHY

TO

THE METAPHYSICS OF MORALS

If we have thus far drawn our concept of duty from the common use of our practical reason, it is by no means to be inferred from this that we have treated it as a concept of experience. Rather, if we attend to the experience of the deeds and omissions of human beings, we encounter frequent and, as we ourselves concede, just complaints that one could cite no safe examples of the disposition to act from pure duty; that, even if some of what is done may *accord* with what *duty* commands, nevertheless it always[1] remains doubtful whether[2] it is really done *from duty* and thus has a moral worth. Hence[3] in all ages there have been philosophers who have absolutely denied the actuality of this disposition in human actions, and have ascribed everything to a more or less refined self-love, yet without bringing the correctness of the concept of morality into doubt; rather, they have mentioned[4] with inward regret the fragility and impurity of human nature,[5] which is, to be sure, noble enough to make an idea so worthy of respect into its precept, but at the same time is too weak to follow it, and uses reason, which ought to serve it for legislation, only in order to take care of the interest of inclinations, whether singly or at most in their greatest compatibility with

one another.

In fact it is absolutely impossible to settle with complete certainty through experience whether there is even a single case in which the maxim

1. 1785: "thus"

2. 1785: "that"

3. 1785 omits this word and treats the following sentence as a clause subordinate to the previous sentence.

4. 1786 adds this verb construction *Erwähnung* taten

5. In *Religion within the Boundaries of Mere Reason*, Kant lists "fragility" (the inability to hold to good maxims, once they are adopted) and "impurity" (the need for nonmoral incentives to do one's duty) as the two lesser degrees of the radical evil in human nature, along with the highest degree, "depravity" (the propensity to place incentives of inclination ahead of those of duty) (Ak 6:29–30).

of an otherwise dutiful action has rested solely on moral grounds and on the representation of one's duty. For it is sometimes the case that with the most acute self-examination we encounter nothing that could have been powerful enough apart from the moral ground of duty to move us to this or that good action and to so great a sacrifice; but from this it cannot be safely inferred that it was not actually some covert impulse of self-love, under the mere false pretense of that idea, that was the real determining cause of the will; so we would gladly flatter ourselves with a false presumption of a nobler motive, while in fact even through the most strenuous testing, we can never fully get behind the covert incentives, because when we are talking about moral worth, it does not depend on the actions, which one sees, but on the inner principles, which one does not see.[6]

One cannot better serve the wishes of those who ridicule all morality, as a mere figment of the mind overreaching itself though self-conceit, than to concede to them that the concepts of duty must be drawn solely from experience (as one is gladly persuaded, for the sake of convenience, in the case of all other concepts); for in this way one prepares for them a certain triumph. From love of humanity I will concede that most of our actions are in conformity with duty; but if one looks more closely at "the imagination of the thoughts of their hearts,"[7] then everywhere one runs into the dear self, which is always thrusting itself forward;[8] it is upon this that the aim is based, and not on the strict command of duty, which would often demand self-renunciation. One does not need to be an enemy of virtue, but only a cold-blooded observer, who does not take the liveliest wish for the good straightway as its reality, in order (especially with advancing years, and a power of judgment grown shrewder through experience and more acute for observation) to become doubtful at certain moments whether any true virtue is ever really to be encountered in the world. And here nothing can protect us from falling away entirely from our ideas of duty and preserve in our soul a well-grounded respect toward its law, except the clear conviction that even if there have never been actions that have arisen from such pure

6. Cf. 2 Corinthians 4:18: "While we look not at the things which are seen, but at the things which are not seen: for the things that are seen are temporal; but the things which are not seen are eternal."

7. *ihr Dichten und Trachten;* this is an allusion to the phrase *Tichten und Trachten* in the Lutheran translation of Genesis 6:5, which reads (in the King James version): "And God saw that the wickedness of man was great in the earth, and that every imagination of the thoughts of his heart was only evil continually."

8. See *Anthropology in a Pragmatic Respect,* § 2, Ak 7:128–30.

sources, yet nevertheless we are not talking here about whether this or that happens, but rather reason commands, for itself and independently of all appearances, what ought to happen; hence actions, of which perhaps the world has up to now given no example and about which one might, grounding everything on experience, very much doubt even their feasibility, are nevertheless commanded unremittingly by reason; and that, e.g., pure honesty in friendship can no less be demanded of every human being, even if up to now there may not have been a single honest friend,[9] because this duty, as duty in general, lies prior to all experience in the idea of a reason determining the will through *a priori* grounds.

If one adds that unless one wants to dispute whether the concept of morality has any truth and relation to any possible object, one could not deny that its law is of such an extensive significance that it would have to be valid not merely for human beings but for all *rational beings in general*, and not merely under contingent conditions and with exceptions, but with *absolute necessity*, then it is clear that no experience could give occasion for inferring even the possibility of such apodictic laws.[10] For with what right could we bring into unlimited respect, as a universal precept for every rational nature, that which is perhaps valid only under the contingent conditions of humanity, and how should laws for the determination of *our* will be taken as laws for the determination of the will of a rational being in general, and only as such also for our will, if they were merely empirical and did not take their origin fully *a priori* from pure but practical reason?

Nor could one give worse advice to morality than by trying to get it from examples. For every example of morality that is to be represented to me as such must itself be previously judged in accordance with principles of

---

9. "Friendship thought of as attainable in its purity or completeness (between Orestes and Pylades, Thesesus and Pirithous) is the hobbyhorse of writers of romances. On the other hand, Aristotle says: 'My dear friends, there are no friends!' " (*Metaphysics of Morals*, Ak 6:470). The statement attributed to Aristotle is based on Diogenes Laertius, *Lives and Opinions of Eminent Philosophers* 5.1.21.

10. The original meaning of 'apodictic' is 'self-evident' (from the Greek 'από + δείκνυμι). But Kant more typically uses it in the sense of 'necessary' (this is its apparent meaning in the Table of Judgments, *Critique of Pure Reason* A70/B95); yet an epistemic element of certainty is often intended as well. For example: "Geometrical propositions are all apodictic, i.e., combined with consciousness of their necessity" (*Critique of Pure Reason* B 41; cf. A160/B199); "[Mathematical cognition] carries with it thoroughly apodictic certainty (i.e., absolute necessity), hence rests on no grounds of experience" (*Prolegomena to Any Future Metaphysics*, § 6, Ak 4:280).

morality as to whether it is worthy to serve as an original[11] example, i.e., as a model; but it can by no means by itself[12] supply the concept of morality. Even the holy one of the Gospel must first be compared with our ideal of moral perfection before one can recognize him as holy; he says this about himself too: Why do you call me (whom you see) good? No one is good (the archetype of the good) except the one God (whom you do not see).[13] But where do we get the concept of God as the highest good? Solely from the [Ak 4:409] *idea* that reason projects *a priori* of moral perfection and connects inseparably with the concept of a free will. In morality there is no imitation, and examples serve only for encouragement, i.e., they place beyond doubt the feasibility of what the law commands, they make intuitive what the practical rule expresses universally; but they can never justify setting aside their true original,[14] which lies in reason, and in directing ourselves in accordance with examples.

If, then, there is no genuine supreme principle of morality which does not have to rest on pure reason independent of all experience, then I believe it is not necessary even to ask whether it is good to expound these concepts in general (*in abstracto*), as they, together with the principles belonging to them, are fixed *a priori*, provided that this cognition is distinguished from common cognition and is to be called 'philosophical'. But in our age this might well be necessary. For if one were to collect votes on which is to be preferred, a pure rational cognition abstracted from everything empirical, hence a metaphysics of morals, or popular practical philosophy, then one would soon guess on which side the preponderance[15] will fall.[16]

11. 1785. "genuine"

12. *zu oberst*

13. " 'Why do you call me good?' Jesus answered. 'No one is good except God alone' " (Luke 18:19; cf. Matthew 19:17, Mark 10:18). As in note 6 above, compare also 2 Corinthians 4:18.

14. *Original*

15. 1785: "the truth"

16. Kant's references to "popular philosophy" are primarily allusions to a movement of German Enlightenment philosophers, centered chiefly in Berlin, whose best-known representatives were Christian Garve (1742–1798), Moses Mendelssohn (1729–1786), Christoph Meiners (1747–1810), and Christoph Friedrich Nicolai (1733–1811). Other critical references to this movement can be found throughout Kant's writings (*Critique of Pure Reason* A x, A855/B883; *Prolegomena*, Ak 4:261–62, 371–83; *What Does It Mean To Orient Oneself in Thinking?* Ak 8:133–46; *On the Common Saying "That May Be Correct in Theory, but Does Not Work in Practice"* Ak 8:278–89; *Metaphysics of Morals,*

This condescension to popular concepts[17] is to be sure very laudable when the elevation to principles of pure reason has already been achieved to full satisfaction, and that would mean first *grounding* the doctrine of morals on metaphysics, but procuring *entry* for it by means of popularity, once it stands firm. But it is quite absurd to want to humor popularity in the first investigation, upon which depends the correctness of principles. Not only can this procedure never lay claim to the extremely rare merit of a true *philosophical popularity*, since there is no art in being commonly understandable if one relinquishes all well-grounded insight; this produces only a disgusting mish-mash of patched-together observations and half-reasoned principles, in which superficial minds revel, because there is always something serviceable for everyday chitchat, but which insightful people disregard, feeling confused and dissatisfied without being able to help themselves; yet philosophers, who can very well see through the illusion,[18] find

[Ak 4:410] little hearing when for certain occasions they decry this supposed popularity, in order, through acquiring determinate insight, finally to gain the right to be popular .

One need only look at the essays on morality adapted to this favored taste; then one will sometimes encounter the particular vocation of human nature (but occasionally also the idea of a rational nature in general), sometimes perfection, sometimes happiness, here moral feeling, there fear of God, some of this and some of that, all in a wondrous mixture, without its occurring to anyone to ask whether the principles of morality are to be sought anywhere in the knowledge of human nature (which we can obtain only through experience); and if not, if these principles are to be encountered in pure concepts of reason, fully *a priori*, free from everything empirical, and nowhere else even in the smallest part, then one may seize the

---

Ak 6:206; *On Turning Out Books*, Ak 8: 433–37; *Logic*, Ak 9:19–20, 148). Despite this, Kant was on terms of friendship and mutual admiration with at least two members of the movement, namely Mendelssohn and Garve. Some scholars have maintained the thesis that Garve's translation, with notes, of Cicero's *On Duties* greatly influenced the *Groundwork* itself, including its account of the good will and its three formulations of the moral law. See Klaus Reich, "Kant and Greek Ethics," *Mind* 47 (1939), and A. R. C. Duncan, *Practical Reason and Morality* (London: Nelson, 1957), chap. 11. For a convincing refutation of this thesis, see Reiner Wimmer, *Universalisierung in der Ethik* (Frankfurt: Suhrkamp, 1980), pp. 183–84; and Dieter Schönecker, *Kant*: Grundlegung *III. Die Deduktion des kategorischen Imperativs* (Freiburg: Alber Verlag, 1999), pp. 61–67.

17. *Volksbegriffen*
18. *Blendwerk*

initiative by entirely separating this investigation as pure practical philosophy, or (if one may use such a disreputable term) as metaphysics* of morals,
bringing it for itself alone to its entire completeness, and deferring the
expectations of the public, which demands popularity, until the completion
of this undertaking.

But such a fully isolated metaphysics of morals, mixed with no anthropology, with no theology, with no physics or hyperphysics, still less with
occult qualities (which one might call 'hypophysical'), is not only an indispensable substrate of all theoretical cognition of duties which is securely
determined, but it is at the same time also a desideratum of the highest
importance for the actual fulfillment of its precepts. For the pure representation of duty and the moral law in general, mixed with no alien addition from
empirical stimuli, has, by way of reason alone (which thereby for the first
time becomes aware that it can for itself be practical), an influence on the
human heart so much more powerful than all other incentives** that might   [Ak 4:411]

*One can, if one wants, distinguish the 'pure' philosophy of morals
(metaphysics) from the 'applied' (namely to human nature) (just as 'pure'
mathematics and 'pure' logic are distinguished from 'applied'). By this
terminology one is directly reminded that moral principles are not grounded
on the peculiarities of human nature, but must be subsistent *a priori* for
themselves; but from them human practical rules must be derivable, as for
every rational nature.

**I have a letter from the late excellent *Sulzer*, in which he asks me what
the cause might be that the doctrines of virtue, however convincing they
may be to reason, yet accomplish so little. My answer, through being prepared so as to be complete, came too late. Yet it is nothing except that the
teachers have not brought their concepts to purity, and because they were
trying to do too much by scaring up motivations to be morally good from
everywhere, in trying to strengthen their medicine they ruin it. For the most
common observation shows that when one represents an upright action as it
is carried out with a steadfast soul even under the greatest temptations of
distress or of enticement, separate from every intention for any advantage
in this or in another world, it leaves far behind and eclipses every similar
action which is affected even in the slightest with an alien incentive; it
elevates the soul and inspires the wish to be able also to act that way. Even
moderately young children feel this impression, and one should never represent duty to them otherwise than this. [Johann Georg Sulzer (1720–
1779), director of the philosophical division of the Prussian Academy of
Sciences (1777–1779). The letter in question is usually thought to be the

be summoned from the empirical field, that reason, in the consciousness of its dignity, despises the latter, and can gradually become their master; in place of this, a mixed doctrine of morals, composed from incentives of feelings and inclinations and simultaneously from concepts of reason, must make the mind waver between motivations that cannot be brought under any principle, and can lead us only very contingently to the good, but often also to the evil.

From what we have adduced it is clear that all moral concepts have their seat and origin fully *a priori* in reason, and this as much in the most common human reason as in that reason which is in highest measure speculative; that these concepts cannot be abstracted from any empirical, and therefore mere contingent, cognition; that their dignity lies precisely in this purity of their origin, so that[19] they serve us as supreme practical principles; that whatever one adds to them of the empirical, one withdraws that much from their genuine influence and from the unlimited worth of actions; that it is not only of the greatest necessity for theoretical aims, when it is merely a matter of speculation, but it is also of the greatest practical importance, to demand that their concepts and laws should be taken from pure reason, to expound them pure and unmixed, indeed, to determine the range of this entire practical or pure rational cognition, i.e., the entire faculty of pure practical reason; but not as speculative philosophy permits, or indeed at [Ak 4:412]   times finds necessary, making the principles dependent on the particular nature of human reason, but rather, since moral laws are to be valid for every rational being in general, to derive them from the universal concept of a rational being in general; and in such a way all morality, which needs

---

one dated December 8, 1770 (see Ak 13:51), which, however, does not directly raise the question Kant says it does. What Sulzer does say is this: "I really wished to hear from you whether we may soon hope to see your work on the metaphysics of morals. This work is of the highest importance, given the present unsteady state of moral philosophy. I have tried to do something of this sort myself in attempting to resolve the question, 'What actually is the physical or psychological difference between a soul that we call virtuous and one which is vicious?' I have sought to discover the true dispositions of virtue and vice in the first manifestations of representations and sensations, and I now regard my undertaking of this investigation as less futile, since it has led me to concepts that are simple and easy to grasp, and which one can effortlessly apply to the teaching and raising of children. But this work, too, is impossible for me to complete at present" (Ak 10:112).]
    19. This word added in 1786

anthropology for its *application* to human beings, must first be expounded completely, independently of anthropology, as pure philosophy, i.e., as metaphysics (which it is possible to do in this species of entirely separate cognitions); but we must also be conscious that without being in possession of this, it would be futile, I will not say to determine precisely for speculative judgment what is moral about duty in everything that conforms to duty, but that it would even be impossible in a common and practical use, chiefly in moral instruction, to ground morality on its genuine principles and thereby to effect pure moral dispositions and implant them in people's minds for the highest good of the world.[20]

But now in order to progress by natural steps in this work not merely from the common moral judgment (which is here worthy of great respect) to the philosophical, as has already been done, but also from a popular philosophy, which goes no further than it can get through groping by means of examples, up to metaphysics (which is not any longer held back by anything empirical and, since it must cover the entire sum total of rational cognition of this kind, goes as far as ideas, where even examples desert us), we must follow and distinctly exhibit the practical faculty of reason from its universal rules of determination up to where the concept of duty arises from it.

Every thing in nature works in accordance with laws. Only a rational being has the faculty to act *in accordance with the representation* of laws, i.e., in accordance with principles, or a *will*. Since for the derivation of actions from laws *reason* is required, the will is nothing other than practical reason. If reason determines the will without exception, then the actions of such a being, which are recognized as objectively necessary, are also subjectively necessary, i.e., the will is a faculty of choosing *only that* which reason, independently of inclination, recognizes as practically necessary, i.e., as good. But if reason for itself alone does not sufficiently determine the will, if the will is still subject to subjective conditions (to certain incentives) which do not always agree with the objective conditions, in a word, if the   [Ak 4:413] will is not *in itself* fully in accord with reason (as it actually is with human beings), then the actions which are objectively recognized as necessary are subjectively contingent, and the determination of such a will, in accord with objective laws, is *necessitation*, i.e., the relation of objective laws to a will which is not thoroughly good is represented as the determination of the will of a rational being through grounds of reason to which, however, this will in accordance with its nature is not necessarily obedient.

20. *Vom höchsten Weltbesten*

The representation of an objective principle, insofar as it is necessitating for a will, is called a 'command' (of reason), and the formula of the command is called an **imperative**.

All imperatives are expressed through an *ought* and thereby indicate the relation of an objective law of reason to a will which in its subjective constitution is not necessarily determined by that law (a necessitation). They say that it would be good to do or refrain from something, but they say it to a will that does not always do something just because it is represented to it as good to do. Practical *good*, however, is that which determines the will by means of representations of reason, hence not from subjective causes, but objectively, i.e., from grounds that are valid for every rational being as such. It is distinguished from the *agreeable*, as that which has influence on the will only by means of sensation from merely subjective causes, those which are valid only for the senses of this or that one, and not as a principle of reason, which is valid for everyone.*

[Ak 4:414]

A perfectly good will would thus stand just as much under objective laws (of the good), but it would not be possible to represent it as *necessitated* by them to lawful actions, because of itself, in accordance with its subjective constitution, it can be determined only through the representation of the good. Hence for the *divine* will, and in general for a *holy* will, no imperatives are valid; the *ought* is out of place[21] here, because the *volition* is of itself already necessarily in harmony with the law. Hence imperatives are

[Ak4:413]

*The dependence of the faculty of desire on sensations is called 'inclination', and this always therefore proves a *need*. But the dependence of a contingently determinable will on principles of reason is called an *interest*. This occurs, therefore, only with a dependent will, which does not always of itself accord with reason; with the divine will one cannot think of any interest. But the human will, too, can *take an interest* without therefore *acting from interest*. The former signifies the *practical* interest in the action, the second the *pathological* interest in the object of the action. The first indicates only the dependence of the will on principles of reason in itself, the second on those principles of reason on behalf of inclination, where, namely, reason furnishes only the practical rule as to how the need of inclination is to be supplied. In the first case the action interests me, in the second the object of the action (insofar as it is agreeable to me). In the First Section we have seen that with an action from duty it is not the interest in an object that has to be looked to, but merely the action itself and its principle in reason (the law).

[Ak4:414]

21. *am unrechten Orte*

only formulas expressing the relation of objective laws of volition in general to the subjective imperfection of the will of this or that rational being, e.g., to the human being.

Now all *imperatives* command either *hypothetically* or *categorically*. The former represent the practical necessity of a possible action as a means to attain something else which one wills (or which it is possible that one might will). The categorical imperative would be that one which represented an action as objectively necessary for itself, without any reference to another end.

Because every practical law represents a possible action as good, and therefore as necessary for a subject practically determinable by reason, all imperatives are formulas of the determination of action, which is necessary in accordance with the principle of a will which is good in some way.[22] Now if the action were good merely as a means to *something else*, then the imperative is *hypothetical*; if it is represented as good *in itself*, hence necessary, as the principle of the will, in a will that in itself accords with reason, then it is *categorical*.

The imperative thus says which action possible through me would be good, and represents the practical rule in relation to a will[23] that does not directly do an action because it is good, in part because the subject does not always know that it is good, in part because if it did know this, its maxims could still be contrary to the objective principles of a practical reason.

The hypothetical imperative thus says only that the action is good for some *possible* or *actual* aim. In the first case it is a **problematically**,[24] in the second an **assertorically** practical principle. The categorical imperative, which declares the action for itself as objectively necessary without reference to any aim, i.e., also without any other end, is valid as an **apodictically** practical principle.   [Ak 4:415]

One can think of that which is possible only through the powers of some rational being also as a possible aim of any will, and hence the principles of the action, insofar as it is represented as necessary in order to achieve any aim to be effected through it, are infinitely many. All sciences have some

22. 1785: "for some aim"

23. 1785: "the will"

24. In his (unpublished) First Introduction to the *Critique of the Power of Judgment* (Ak 20:200 note), Kant retracts the term 'problematical' for this kind of imperative, replacing it with the term 'technical', which he also uses already in the *Groundwork* (Ak 4:416).

practical part, consisting of the problems whether[25] any end is possible for us and of imperatives about how it can be attained. These can therefore in general be called imperatives of **skill**. Whether the end is rational and good is not the question here, but only what one has to do in order to achieve them. The precepts for the physician, how to make his patient healthy in a well-grounded way, and for the poisoner, how to kill him with certainty,[26] are to this extent of equal worth, since each serves to effect its aim perfectly. Because in early youth one does not know what ends he will run up against in life, parents seek chiefly to have their children learn *many things*, and they concern themselves about *skill* in the use of means toward all kinds of *discretionary* ends, about none of which they can determine whether it will perhaps actually become an aim of his pupil in the future, but about any of which, however, it is *possible* that he might someday have it, and this concern is so great that they commonly neglect to educate and correct their judgment over the worth of the things that they may perhaps make their ends.

There is *one* end, however, that one can presuppose as actual for all rational beings (insofar as imperatives apply to them, namely as dependent beings) and thus one aim that they not merely *can* have, but of which one can safely presuppose that without exception[27] they *do have* it in accordance with a natural necessity, and that is the aim at *happiness*. The hypothetical imperative that represents the practical necessity of the action as a means to furthering happiness is **assertoric.** One may expound it as necessary not merely to an uncertain, merely possible aim, but to an aim that one

[Ak 4:416] can presuppose safely and *a priori*[28] with every human being, because it belongs to his essence.[29] Now one can call skill in the choice of means to his own greatest well-being *prudence** in the narrowest sense. Thus the imper-

*The word 'prudence' is taken in a twofold sense; in the first it can bear the name of 'worldly prudence' and in the second that of 'private prudence.' The first is the skill of a human being to have influence on others, in order to use them for his aims. The second is the insight to unite all these aims to his own enduring advantage. The latter is really that to which the worth of the first is reduced, and about someone who is prudent in the first way but not in the second way one can better say that he is clever and sly, but on the whole imprudent.

25. *Aufgaben, daß*, a construction somewhat opaque in meaning and almost as awkward in German as "problems that" would be in English.

26. *sicher*, which could also be translated "safely"

27. *insgesamt*

28. "and *a priori*" added in 1786

29. 1785: "to his nature"

ative that refers to the choice of means to one's own happiness, i.e., the precept of prudence, is always *hypothetical*; the action is commanded not absolutely but only as a means to another aim.

Finally, there is one imperative that, without being grounded on any other aim to be achieved through a certain course of conduct as its condition, commands this conduct immediately. This imperative is **categorical**. It has to do not with the matter of the action and what is to result from it, but with the form and the principle from which it results; and what is essentially good about it consists in the disposition, whatever the result may be. This imperative may be called that **of morality**.

The volition in accordance with these three kinds of principles is also clearly distinguished by a *difference*[30] in the necessitation of the will. Now in order to make this noticeable too, I believe that the most suitable terminology to use in ordering them is to say that they are either *rules* of skill, or *counsels* of prudence or *commands (laws)* of morality. For only *law* carries with it the concept of an *unconditional* and objective, hence universally valid *necessity*, and commands are laws that must be obeyed, i.e., followed even against inclination. The *giving of counsel* contains necessity, to be sure, but can be valid merely under a subjective, pleasing[31] condition, whether this or that human being counts this or that toward his happiness; the categorical imperative, by contrast, is not limited by any condition, and as absolutely, though practically necessary, can be called quite authentically a command. One could also call the first imperative *technical* (belonging to art), the second *pragmatic** (to welfare), the third *moral* (belonging to free conduct in general, i.e., to morals). [Ak 4:417]

Now the question arises: How are all these imperatives possible? This

---

*It seems to me that the authentic signification of the word 'pragmatic' could be determined most precisely in this way. For those *sanctions* are called 'pragmatic' which really flow not from the rights of states, as necessary laws, but from *provision* for the general welfare. A *history* is written 'pragmatically' when it makes us *prudent*, i.e., teaches how the world could take care of its advantage better than, or at any rate at least as well as, the world of antiquity has done.

30. *Ungleichheit*, which might also be translated "inequality." Kant may be suggesting, that is, not only that the three imperatives are different in kind, but also that the three kinds of necessitation have unequal rational weight: moral necessitation is unconditional, hence prior to the other two, overriding them in cases of conflict; pragmatic necessitation by imperatives of prudence, in turn, overrides technical necessitation by imperatives of skill that merely tell us how to achieve some optional end we have contingently chosen.

31. *gefälliger*; editors often correct this to *zufälliger*, "contingent."

question does not demand the knowledge how to think the execution of the action that the imperative commands, but rather merely how to think the necessitation of the will that the imperative expresses in the problem. How an imperative of skill is to be possible probably needs no particular discussion. Whoever wills the end, also wills (insofar as reason has decisive influence on his actions) the means that are indispensably necessary to it that are in his control. As far as volition is concerned, this proposition is analytic; for in the volition of an object, as my effect, is already thought my causality as an acting cause, i.e., the use of means; and the imperative extracts the concept of actions necessary for this end out of the concept of a volition of this end (to be sure, synthetic propositions belong to determining the means themselves to a proposed aim, but they have nothing to do with the ground, with making the act[32] of the will actual, but rather with how to make the object actual). That in order to divide a line into two equal parts in accordance with a secure principle I must draw two arcs from its endpoints — this mathematics obviously teaches only through synthetic propositions; but that if I know that the specified effect can occur only through such an action, then if I completely will the effect, I would also will the action that is required for it — that is an analytic proposition; for to represent something as an effect possible through me in a certain way and to represent myself, in regard to it, acting in this same way — those are entirely the same.

Imperatives of prudence would be equally analytic, and entirely coincide with those of skill, if only it were so easy to provide a determinate concept of happiness. For here, as there, it would be said: whoever wills the end, also wills (necessarily in accord with reason) the sole means to it in his control. Yet it is a misfortune that the concept of happiness is such an indeterminate concept that although every human being wishes to attain it, he can never say, determinately and in a way that is harmonious with himself, what he really wishes and wills. The cause of this is that all the elements that belong to the concept of happiness are altogether empirical, i.e., have to be gotten from experience, while for the idea of happiness an absolute whole, a maximum of welfare, is required, in my present and in every future condition. Now it is impossible for the most insightful, and at the same time most resourceful, yet finite being to make a determinate concept of what he really wills here. If he wills wealth, how much worry, envy, and harassment[33] will he not bring down on his shoulders?[34] If he

[Ak 4:418]

---

32. *Aktus*

33. *Nachstellung*

34. Kant ends this sentence, which seems halfway between an assertion and a rhetorical question, with a period instead of a question mark.

wills much cognition and insight, perhaps that could only give him a more acute eye, to show him all the more terribly those ills that are now hidden from him and yet cannot be avoided, or to burden his desires, which already give him quite enough to do, with still more needs. If he wills a long life, who will guarantee him that it would not be a long misery? If he wills at least health, how often have bodily discomforts not deterred him from excesses into which unlimited health would have allowed him to fall, etc.? In short, he is not capable of determining with complete certainty, in accordance with any principle, what will make him truly happy, because omniscience would be required for that. Thus one cannot act in accordance with determinate principles in order to be happy, but only in accordance with empirical counsels, e.g., of diet, frugality, politeness, restraint, etc., of which experience teaches that they most promote welfare on the average. It follows from this that the imperatives of prudence, to speak precisely, cannot command at all, i.e., cannot exhibit actions objectively as practically *necessary*; that they are sooner to be taken as advisings *(consilia)* than as commands *(praecepta)* of reason; that the problem of determining, certainly[35] and universally, what action will promote the happiness of a rational being, is fully insoluble, hence no imperative in regard to it is possible, which would command us, in the strict sense, to do what would make us happy, because happiness is an ideal not of reason but of imagination, resting merely on empirical grounds, of which it would be futile to expect   [Ak 4:419] that they should determine an action through which to attain the totality of a series of consequences which are in fact infinite. This imperative of prudence, meanwhile, would be an analytically practical proposition if one assumes that the means to happiness could be specified with certainty;[36] for it is distinguished from the imperative of skill only in this, that with the latter the end is merely possible, but with the former it is given: since, however, both merely command the means to that which it is presupposed that one wills as an end, then the imperative that commands the volition of the means for him who wills the end is in both cases analytic. Thus there is also no difficulty in regard to the possibility of such an imperative.

By contrast, how the imperative of *morality* is possible is without doubt the sole question in need of a solution, since it is not at all hypothetical, and thus the necessity, represented as objective, cannot be based on any presupposition, as with the hypothetical imperatives. Yet in this connection it must not be left out of account that whether there is any such imperative anywhere cannot be settled *by any example*, hence not empirically; but the

35. *sicher*
36. *sicher*

worry is rather that all those that seem categorical might be, in some hidden wise, hypothetical. E.g., if it is said: "You ought not to make a deceiving promise," and one assumes that the necessity of this omission is not mere advice for the avoidance of some ill or other, so that it might really mean: "You should not make a lying promise, so that if it were revealed then you would lose your credit"; if an action of this kind[37] must be considered as evil for itself, then the imperative forbidding it would be categorical; then one still cannot with certainty give an example in which the will is determined merely by the law, without any other incentive, although it might[38] appear so; for it is always possible that fear of disgrace, or perhaps also an obscure worry about other dangers, might secretly have had an influence on the will. Who[39] can prove through experience the nonexistence of a cause, since experience teaches us nothing beyond the fact that we do not perceive one? But in such a case the so-called moral imperative, which appears as such to be categorical and unconditioned, would in fact be only a pragmatic precept, which alerts us to our own advantage and merely teaches us to pay attention to it.

[Ak 4:420]   Thus we will have to investigate the possibility of a *categorical* imperative entirely *a priori*, since here we cannot have the advantage that its reality is given in experience, so that its possibility would be necessary not for its establishment but only for its explanation.[40] Meanwhile, we can provisionally[41] have insight into this much: that the categorical imperative alone can be stated as a practical **law**, while the others collectively are, to be sure, *principles* of the will, but cannot be called 'laws'; for what it is necessary to do for the attainment of a discretionary aim can be considered in itself to be contingent, and we can always be rid of the precept if we give up the aim; whereas the unconditioned command leaves the will no free discretion in regard to the opposite, hence it alone carries with it that necessity which we demand for a law.

Secondly, with this categorical imperative, or law of morality, the ground of difficulty (of having insight into its possibility) is very great

37. 1785: "but rather if one asserts that an action of this kind"

38. 1785: "even if it might appear so"

39. 1785: "For who"

40. *Erklärung*, which could also be translated "definition." Kant holds that for a well-formed (real) definition of a thing, we require a demonstration of its (real) possibility. See *Critique of Pure Reason* A727–30/B755–59.

41. 1785: "But we can provisionally"

indeed. It is a synthetically practical proposition* *a priori*, and since there is so much difficulty in gaining insight into the possibility of propositions of this kind in theoretical cognition, it is easy to gather that there will be no less in the practical.

Regarding this problem we will first try to see whether perhaps the mere concept of a categorical imperative does not also provide us with its formula, containing the proposition which alone can be a categorical imperative; for how such an absolute command is possible, even if we know how it is stated, will still demand particular and difficult effort, which, however, we will postpone until the last section.

If I think of a *hypothetical* imperative in general, then I do not know beforehand what it will contain until the condition is given to me. But if I think of a *categorical* imperative, then I know directly what it contains. For since besides the law, the imperative contains only the necessity of the maxim,** that it should accord with this law, but the law contains no   [Ak 4:421] condition to which it is limited, there remains nothing left over with which the maxim of the action is to be in accord, and this accordance alone is what the imperative really represents necessarily.

The categorical imperative is thus only a single one, and specifically this: *Act only in accordance with that maxim through which you can at the same time will that it become a universal law.*

Now if from this one imperative all imperatives of duty can be derived as from their principle, then although we leave unsettled whether in general

---

*I connect the deed *a priori* with the will, without a presupposed condi-   [Ak4:420] tion from any inclination, hence necessarily (though only objectively, i.e., under the idea of reason, which would have full control over all subjective motivations). This is therefore a practical proposition that does not derive the volition of an action analytically from any other volition already presupposed (for we have no such perfect will), but is immediately connected with the concept of the will of a rational being, as something not contained in it.

**A *maxim* is the subjective principle for action, and must be distinguished from the *objective principle*, namely the practical law. The former   [Ak4:421] contains the practical rule that reason determines in accord with the conditions of the subject (often its ignorance or also its inclinations), and is thus the principle in accordance with which the subject *acts*; but the law is the objective principle, valid for every rational being, and the principle in accordance with which it *ought to act*, i.e., an imperative.

what one calls 'duty' is an empty concept, we can at least indicate what we are thinking in the concept of duty and what this concept means.[42]

Because the universality of the law in accordance with which effects happen constitutes that which is really called *nature* in the most general sense (in accordance with its form), i.e., the existence of things insofar as it is determined in accordance with universal laws, thus the universal imperative of duty can also be stated as follows: *So act as if the maxim of your action were to become through your will a **universal law of nature***.

Now we will enumerate[43] some duties, in accordance with their usual division into duties toward ourselves and toward other human beings, and into perfect and imperfect duties:*

[Ak 4:422]   (1) One person, through a series of evils that have accumulated to the point of hopelessness, feels weary of life but is still so far in possession of his reason that he can ask himself whether it might be contrary to the duty to himself to take his own life. Now he tries out whether the maxim of his action could become a universal law of nature. But his maxim is: 'From self-love, I make it my principle to shorten my life when by longer term it threatens more ill than it promises agreeableness'. The question is whether this principle of self-love could become a universal law of nature. But then one soon sees that a nature whose law it was to destroy life through the same feeling[44] whose vocation it is to impel the furtherance of life would contra-

[Ak4:421]   *Here one must note well that I reserve the division of duties entirely for a future *metaphysics of morals*; the division here therefore stands only as a discretionary one (to order my examples). For the rest, I understand by a perfect duty that which permits no exception to the advantage of inclination, and I do have *perfect duties* that are not merely external but also internal, which runs contrary to the use of words common in the schools; but I do not mean to defend that here, because for my aim it is all the same whether or not one concedes it to me. [Cf. *Metaphysics of Morals*, Ak 6:240, 391–98, 413, and the detailed taxonomy of duties of virtue, Ak 6:417–68. The "use of words common in the schools," according to which perfect duties are externally enforceable actions, is based on Samuel Pufendorf (1632–1694), *De Jure Naturale* (1672), 1.1.19–20. But Pufendorf's distinction was anticipated by Hugo Grotius (1583–1645) and had been taken up also by, among others, Christian Thomasius (1655–1728) and J. G. Sulzer.]

42. *sagen wolle*

43. *herzählen*, which could also be translated "reckon" or "calculate"

44. *Empfindung*

dict itself, and thus could not subsist as nature; hence that maxim could not possibly obtain as a universal law of nature, and consequently it entirely contradicts the supreme principle of all duty.

(2) Another sees himself pressured by distress into borrowing money. He knows very well that he will not be able to pay, but he also sees that nothing will be lent him if he does not firmly promise to pay at a determinate time. He wants to make such a promise; yet he has conscience enough to ask himself: "Is it not impermissible and contrary to duty to get out of distress in such a way?" Supposing he nevertheless resolved on it, his maxim would be stated as follows: 'If I believe myself to be in pecuniary distress, then I will borrow money and promise to pay it back, although I know this will never happen'. Now this principle of self-love, or of what is expedient for oneself, might perhaps be united with my entire future welfare, yet the question now is: "Is it right?" I thus transform this claim[45] of self-love into a universal law and set up the question thus: "How would it stand if my maxim became a universal law?" Yet I see right away that it could never be valid as a universal law of nature and still agree with itself, but rather it would necessarily contradict itself. For the universality of a law that everyone who believes himself to be in distress could promise whatever occurred to him with the intention of not keeping it would make impossible the promise and the end one might have in making it, since no one would believe that anything has been promised him, but rather would laugh about every such utterance as vain pretense.

(3) A third finds in himself a talent, which could, by means of some   [Ak 4:423] cultivation, make him into a human being who is useful for all sorts of aims. But he sees himself as in comfortable circumstances and sooner prefers to indulge[46] in gratification than to trouble himself with the expansion and improvement of his fortunate natural predispositions. Yet he still asks whether, apart from the agreement of his maxim of neglecting his gifts of nature with his propensity to amusement, it also agrees with what one calls 'duty'. Then he sees that, although a nature could still subsist in accordance with such a universal law, though then the human being (like the South Sea Islanders) would think only of letting his talents rust and applying his life merely to idleness, amusement, procreation, in a word, to enjoyment; yet it is impossible for him to **will** that this should become a universal law of nature, or that it should be implanted in us as such by natural instinct. For as a rational being he necessarily wills that all the faculties in him should be

45. *Zumutung*
46. 1785: "and he prefers it that he indulge"

developed, because they are serviceable and given[47] to him for all kinds of possible aims.

(4)[48] Yet a *fourth* — for whom it is going well, while he sees that others have to struggle with great hardships (with which he could well help them) — thinks: "What has it to do with me? Let each be as happy as heaven wills, or as he can make himself, I will not take anything from him or even envy him; only I do not want to contribute to his welfare or to his assistance in distress!" Now to be sure, if such a way of thinking were to become a universal law of nature, then the human race could well subsist, and without doubt still better than when everyone chatters about sympathetic participation[49] and benevolence, and even on occasion exerts himself to practice them, but, on the contrary also deceives wherever he can,[50] sells out, or otherwise infringes on the right of human beings. But although it is possible that a universal law of nature could well subsist in accordance with that maxim, yet it is impossible to **will** that such a principle should be valid without exception[51] as a natural law. For a will that resolved on this would conflict with itself, since the case could sometimes arise in which he needs the love and sympathetic participation of others, and where, through such a natural law arising from his own will, he would rob himself of all the hope of assistance that he wishes for himself.

Now these are some of the many actual duties, or at least of what we take [Ak 4:424]   to be duties, whose partitioning[52] from the single principle just adduced

47. "and given" added in 1786

48. Kant's text, although it emphasizes the word "fourth," omits the (4) required by the parallel with his three other examples.

49. *Teilnehmung*

50. 1785: "wherever one can"

51. *allenthalben*

52. *Abteilung*; some editors correct this to *Ableitung*, "derivation." In favor of the emendation is that if Kant meant 'classification,' one would expect him to use *Einteilung* ("division," as he did above, Ak 4:421); *Abteilung* refers more properly to one of the parts or subcategories marked out by a division or classification than it does to the act of dividing or classifying or to the entire system of classification; where it does refer to an act of dividing, *abteilen* means the partitioning off of one space from another, and not the creation of a system of classification. The construction *Abteilung aus dem einigen Prinzip* is also awkward, in the same way that this English translation of it is; and no such construction is found anywhere else in Kant's writings. Further, Kant did speak earlier of being able to "derive" (*ableiten*) all imperatives of duty from a single categorical imperative (Ak 4:421). But despite all these reasons, the emendation to *Ableitung* ("derivation")

clearly meets the eye. One must *be able to will* that a maxim of our action should become a universal law: this is the canon of the moral judgment of this action in general. Some actions are so constituted that their maxim cannot even be *thought* without contradiction as a universal law of nature, much less could one *will* that it *ought* to become one. With others, that internal impossibility is not to be encountered, but it is impossible to *will*

---

remains doubtful. Against it is the following: Kant goes on in the present paragraph to discuss the relation of his principle only to the *classification* of duties, not to their *derivation*. Further, it is not at all clear that when Kant spoke of deriving duties from a single categorical imperative, he meant to restrict the formula of that imperative to the two formulations that have been presented so far. He may well have meant that a derivation of duties would require the entire system of formulas, first introduced later at Ak 4:436. His practice in the *Metaphysics of Morals* strongly suggests the latter position. There Kant does propose to derive an entire system of ethical duties; but only the duty of beneficence (which pertains only to the fourth example here) is related to anything in the present formula of the moral law (Ak 6:453). This is possible only because the maxim of pursuing one's own happiness (and the consequent volition of others' voluntary assistance, as required to achieve this end) can be ascribed to all rational beings, so that the principle of morality can require them to adopt it in a universalizable form. Apart from this unique case, universalizability enables us only to disqualify certain specific maxims, and cannot yield anything like a positive duty (e.g., to refrain from suicide, keep promises, or develop talents). All fifteen of the other ethical duties explicitly enumerated there (including three of the four that are exemplified here) are derived by appeal to the second formula, that of humanity as end in itself (first stated in the *Groundwork* at Ak 4:429). Kant says that suicide is a "debasing of humanity in one's person" (Ak 6:422–423); the duty to develop one's natural perfection is "bound up with the end of humanity in our own person" (Ak 6:391–92; cf. 6:444–46). In the *Metaphysics of Morals*, Kant treats promising under the heading of externally enforceable right rather than of ethics (as his use here of the term 'right' might also imply). There Kant even denies that it is either possible or necessary to demonstrate that promises ought to be kept (Ak 6:273). The principle of right is distinct from the supreme principle of morality (Ak 6:230); but the fundamental right (the innate human right to freedom) is said "to belong to every human being by virtue of his humanity" (Ak 6:237). But he does discuss the ethical duty not to lie under the heading of strict duties to oneself, where it is said to be a violation of "the humanity in his own person" because it uses his capacity to communicate as a mere means (Ak 6:429). Kant's definitive presentation of the duties enumerated here thus has far less affinity with the present discussion of them (based on the formula of the law of nature) than it does with his discussion of them below in connection with the second formula, that of humanity as end in itself (Ak 4:429–30).

that their maxims should be elevated to the universality of a natural law, because such a will would contradict itself.[One easily sees that the first conflict with strict or narrow (unremitting) duty, the second only with wide (meritorious) duty, and thus all duties regarding the kind of obligation (not the object of their action) have been completely set forth[53] through these examples in their dependence on the one principle.]

Now if we attend to ourselves in every transgression of a duty, then we find that we do not actually will that our maxim should become a universal law, for that is impossible for us, but rather will that its opposite should remain a law generally; yet we take the liberty of making an *exception* for ourselves, or (even only for this once) for the advantage of our inclination. Consequently, if we weighed everything from one and the same point of view, namely that of reason, then we would encounter a contradiction in our own will, namely that objectively a certain principle should be necessary as a universal law and yet subjectively that it should not be universally valid, but rather that it should admit of exceptions. But since we consider our action at one time from a point of view that accords entirely with reason, and then, however, also the same action from the point of view of a will affected by inclination, there is actually no contradiction here, but only a resistance of inclination against the precept of reason *(antagonismus)*, through which the universality of the principle *(universalitas)* is transformed into a mere general validity *(generalitas)*, so that the practical principle of reason is supposed to meet the maxim halfway. Now although this cannot be justified in our own impartially rendered judgment, it proves that we actually recognize the validity of the categorical imperative and (with every respect for it) allow ourselves only a few exceptions, which are, as it seems to us, insignificant and forced upon us.

[Ak 4:425]

Thus we have established at least this much: that if duty is a concept that is to contain significance and actual legislation for our actions, then this duty could be expressed only in categorical imperatives, but by no means in hypothetical ones; likewise, which is already quite a bit, we have exhibited distinctly and for every use the content of the categorical imperative which would have to contain the principle of all duty (if there is such a thing at all). But we are still not ready to prove *a priori* that there actually is such an imperative, that there is a practical law which commands for itself absolutely and without any incentives, and that it is a duty to follow this law.

With the aim of attaining that, it is of the utmost importance to let this serve as a warning that one must not let it enter his mind to try to derive the

---

53. 1785: "are completely set forth"

reality of this principle from the *particular quality of human nature*. For duty ought to be the practically unconditioned necessity of action; thus it must be valid for all rational beings (for only to them can an imperative apply at all), and must *only for this reason* be a law for every human will. That which, by contrast, is derived only from what is proper to the particular natural predisposition of humanity, or from certain feelings and propensities, or indeed, if possible, from a particular direction of human reason, and would not have to be valid necessarily for the will of every rational being — that can, to be sure, be a maxim for us, but cannot yield any law; it can yield a subjective principle, in accordance with which we may have a propensity and inclination, but not an objective one, in accordance with which we would be *assigned* to act, even if it were to go directly contrary to all our propensities, inclinations, and natural adaptations; it even proves all the more the sublimity and inner dignity of the command in a duty, the less subjective causes are for it and the more they are against it, without on this account the least weakening the necessitation through the law or taking anything away from its validity.

Now here we see philosophy placed in fact at a perilous standpoint, which is to be made firm, regardless of anything either in heaven or on earth from which it may depend or by which it may be supported. Here it should prove its purity[54] as self-sustainer of its own laws, not as a herald of those that an implanted sense or who knows what tutelary nature whispers to it, which, taken collectively, although they may be better than nothing at all, yet they can never yield the principles that reason dictates and that must have their source fully *a priori* and therewith at the same time their commanding authority: expecting nothing of the inclination of the human being, but everything from the supremacy of the law and the respect owed to it; or else, if that fails, condemning the human being to self-contempt and inner abhorrence.

Thus everything that is empirical is, as a contribution toward the principle of morality, not only entirely unfit for it, but even highly disadvantageous to the purity[55] of morals themselves, in which precisely consists the sublime[56] worth of a will absolutely good in itself and elevated above all price,[57] that the principle of the actions is free of all influences of contingent grounds that only experience can provide. One cannot be given too many or

[Ak 4:426]

too frequent warnings against this negligent or even base way of thinking, which seeks out the principle among empirical motivations and laws, since human reason in its weariness gladly reposes on this pillow and, in the dream of sweet illusions[58] (which lets it embrace a cloud instead of Juno),[59] supplants the place of morality with a bastard patched together from limbs of quite diverse ancestry, which looks similar to whatever anyone wants to see, but not to virtue, for him who has once beheld it in its true shape.*

The question is therefore this: Is it a necessary law *for all rational beings* to judge their actions always in accordance with those maxims of which they themselves can will that they should serve as universal laws? If it is, then it must be bound up (fully *a priori*) with the concept of the will of a rational being in general. But in order to discover this connection, one must, however much one may resist it, take one step beyond, namely to metaphysics, though into a domain of metaphysics that is distinguished from [Ak 4:427] that of speculative philosophy, namely into the metaphysics of morals. In a practical philosophy, where what are to be established are not grounds for what *happens*, but laws for what *ought to happen*, even if it never does happen, i.e., objectively practical laws, there we do not find it necessary to institute an investigation into the grounds why something pleases or displeases, how the gratification of mere sensation is to be distinguished from taste, and whether the latter is distinct from a universal satisfaction of

[Ak4:426]   *To behold virtue in its authentic shape is nothing other than to exhibit morality denuded of all admixture of the sensible and all ungenuine adornment of reward or self-love. How completely it eclipses everything else that appears charming to inclinations, everyone can easily be aware of by means of the least attempt of his reason, if it is not entirely corrupted for abstraction.

58. *Vorspiegelungen*

59. In Greek mythology, Ixion (a legendary king of Thessaly) schemed to win the love of Hera, queen of the gods (Latin name: Juno). Her husband, Zeus, discovered his intention and formed a cloud, Nephelē, that resembled Hera. By the cloud Ixion conceived Centaurus (for which the scholiast gives the false etymology "what penetrates the air"). Centaurus was the ancestor of the centaurs, a race of beings half human and half equine (perhaps Kant's "bastard patched together from limbs of quite diverse ancestry" is a reference to them). Zeus punished Ixion for his presumptuousness by having him bound on a wheel in Hades that turns forever. The myth is told by Pindar, *Pythian Ode* 2.21–50. Since Kant's knowledge of Latin poetry was better, he is more likely to have known the Ixion story from Ovid (*Metamorphoses* 4.461, 9.124, 10.42, 12.503–5) or Virgil (*Georgics* 3.38, 4.484; *Aeneid* 6.601), although these later versions emphasize Ixion's underworld punishment rather than the story of Juno and the cloud.

reason; on what the feelings of pleasure and displeasure rest, and how from them arise desires and inclinations, and from these, again, through the cooperation of reason, maxims arise; for all that belongs to an empirical doctrine of the soul, which constitutes the second part of the doctrine of nature, if one considers it as *philosophy of nature* insofar as it is grounded on *empirical laws*. Here, however, we are talking about objectively practical laws, hence about the relation of a will to itself insofar as it determines itself merely through reason, such that everything that has reference to the empirical falls away of itself; because if *reason for itself alone* determines conduct (the possibility of which we will investigate right now), it must necessarily do this *a priori*.

The will is thought as a faculty of determining itself to action *in accord with the representation of certain laws*. And such a faculty can be there to be encountered only in rational beings. Now that which serves the will as the objective ground of its self-determination is the *end*, and this, if it is given through mere reason, must be equally valid for all rational beings. By contrast, what contains merely the ground of the possibility of the action whose effect is the end is called the *means*. The subjective ground of desire is the *incentive*, the objective ground of volition is the *motive*; hence the distinction between subjective ends, which rest on incentives, and objective ones, which depend on motives that are valid for every rational being. Practical principles are *formal* when they abstract from all subjective ends; but they are *material* when they are grounded on these, hence on certain incentives. The ends that a rational being proposes as *effects* of its action at its discretion (material ends) are all only relative; for only their relation to a particular kind of faculty of desire of the subject gives them their worth, which therefore can provide no necessary principles valid universally for all [Ak 4:428] rational beings and hence valid for every volition, i.e., practical laws. Hence all these relative ends are only the ground of hypothetical imperatives.

But suppose there were something *whose existence in itself* had an absolute worth, something that, as *end in itself*, could be a ground of determinate laws; then in it and only in it alone would lie the ground of a possible categorical imperative, i.e., of a practical law.

Now I say that the human being, and in general every rational being, *exists* as end in itself, *not merely as means* to the discretionary use of this or that will, but in all its actions, those directed toward itself as well as those directed toward other rational beings, it must always *at the same time* be considered as an *end*. All objects of inclinations have only a conditioned worth; for if the inclinations and the needs grounded on them did not exist, then their object would be without worth. The inclinations themselves, however, as sources of needs, are so little of absolute worth, to be wished for in themselves, that rather to be entirely free of them must be the universal wish of every rational being.⁶⁰ Thus the worth of all objects *to be acquired* through our action is always conditioned. The beings whose existence rests not on our will but on nature nevertheless have, if they are beings without reason, only a relative worth as means, and are called *things*; rational beings, by contrast, are called *persons*, because their nature already marks them out as ends in themselves, i.e., as something that may not be used merely as means, hence to that extent limits all arbitrary choice⁶¹ (and is an object of respect). These are not merely subjective ends whose existence as effect of our action has a worth *for us*; but rather *objective ends*, i.e., things whose existence in itself is an end, and specifically an end such that no other end can be set in place of it, to which it should do service *merely* as means, because without this nothing at all of *absolute worth* would be encountered anywhere; but if all worth were conditioned, hence contingent, then for reason no supreme practical principle could anywhere be encountered.

If, then, there is supposed to be a supreme practical principle, and in regard to the human will a categorical imperative, then it must be such from the representation of that which, being necessarily an end for everyone, [Ak 4:429]   because it is an *end in itself*, constitutes an *objective* principle of the will, hence can serve as a universal practical law. The ground of this principle is: *Rational nature exists as end in itself.* The human being necessarily represents his own existence in this way;⁶² thus to that extent it is a *subjective* principle of human actions. But every other rational being also represents his existence in this way as consequent on the same rational ground as is valid for me;* thus it is at the same time an *objective* principle, from which, as a supreme practical ground, all laws of the will must be able to be derived. The practical imperative will thus be the following: *Act so that you*

---

*This proposition I here set forth as a postulate. In the last section one will find the grounds for it.

60. "*Considered in themselves*, natural inclinations are *good*, i.e., not reprehensible, and to want to extirpate them would be not only futile, but harmful and blameworthy as well; we must rather only curb them, so that they will not wear each other out but will instead be harmonized into a whole called 'happiness' " (*Religion within the Boundaries of Mere Reason*, Ak 6:58).

61. *Willkür*

62. See *Conjectural Beginning of Human History*, Ak 8:114; *Anthropology in a Pragmatic Respect*, Ak 7:127, 130.

use humanity,[63] *as much in your own person as in the person of every other, always at the same time as end and never merely as means.* We will see whether this can be accomplished.

In order to remain with the previous examples,

First, in accordance with the concept of the necessary duty toward one-self, the one who has suicide in mind will ask himself whether his action could subsist together with the idea of humanity *as an end in itself*. If he destroys himself in order to flee from a burdensome condition, then he makes use of a person merely as *a means*, for the preservation of a bearable condition up to the end of life. The human being, however, is not a thing, hence not something that can be used *merely* as a means, but must in all his actions always be considered as an end in itself. Thus I cannot dispose of the human being in my own person, so as to maim, corrupt, or kill him.[64] (The nearer determination of this principle, so as to avoid all misunder-standing, e.g., the amputation of limbs in order to preserve myself, or the risk at which I put my life in order to preserve my life, etc., I must here pass over; they belong to morals proper.)[65]

Second, as to the necessary or owed duty toward others, the one who has it in mind to make a lying promise to another will see[66] right away that he wills to make use of another human being *merely as means*, without the end also being contained in this other. For the one I want to use for my aims through such a promise cannot possibly be in harmony with my way of

---

63. *Menschlichkeit*; this term refers to one of our three fundamental predispositions: (1) animality (through which we have instincts for survival, procreation, and sociability); (2) humanity, through which we have the rational capacities to set ends, use means to them, and organize them into a whole (happiness); and (3) personality, through which we have the capacity to give ourselves moral laws and are accountable for following them (see *Religion within the Boundaries of Mere Reason*, Ak 6:26–28; *Anthropology in a Pragmatic Respect*, Ak 7:322–25). 'Humanity' thus means the same as 'rational nature', and Kant's use of it involves no retraction of the claim that moral commands must be valid for all rational beings, not only for members of the human species.

64. In the *Metaphysics of Morals*, Kant discusses the duty not to maim oneself in connection with the duty forbidding suicide (Ak 6:422–23). *Verderben* ("corrupt") there-fore probably carries with it the broad sense of ruining or destroying (sc. one's body or parts of it) rather than the narrower sense of *moral* corruption. Duties to oneself as a moral being, which Kant classifies as duties against lying, avarice, false humility (or servility), and duties as moral judge of oneself, are dealt with separately, 6:428–42.

65. *zur eigentlichen Moral*

66. *einsehen*

conducting myself toward him and thus contain in himself the end of this action.[67] Even more distinctly does this conflict with the principle of other human beings meet the eye if one approaches it through examples of attacks on the freedom and property of others. For then it is clearly evident that the one who transgresses the rights of human beings is disposed to make use of the person of others merely as a means, without taking into consideration that as rational beings, these persons ought always to be esteemed at the same time as ends, i.e., only as beings who have to be able to contain in themselves the end of precisely the same action.*

Third, in regard to the contingent (meritorious) duty toward oneself, it is not enough that the action does not conflict with humanity in our person as end in itself; it must also *harmonize with it*. Now in humanity there are predispositions to greater perfection, which belong to ends of nature in regard to the humanity in our subject; to neglect these would at most be able to subsist with the *preservation* of humanity as end in itself, but not with the *furthering* of this end.

Fourth, as to the meritorious duty toward others, the natural end that all human beings have is their own happiness. Now humanity would be able to subsist if no one contributed to the happiness of others yet did not intentionally remove anything from it; only this is only a negative and not a positive agreement with *humanity as end in itself*, if everyone does not aspire, as much as he can, to further the ends of others. For regarding the subject which is an end in itself: if that representation is to have its *total* effect on me, then its ends must as far as possible also be *my* ends.

This principle of humanity and of every rational nature in general *as end*

*Let one not think that the trivial *quod tibi non vis fieri, etc.* [What you do not want to be done to yourself do not do to another] could serve here as a standard or principle. For it is only derived from that principle, though with various limitations; it cannot be a universal law, for it does not contain the ground of duties toward oneself, nor that of the duties of love toward others (for many would gladly acquiesce that others should not be beneficent to him, if only he might be relieved from showing beneficence to them), or finally of owed duties to one another, for the criminal would argue on this ground against the judge who punishes him, etc. [Here Kant is distinguishing his principle from the so-called Golden Rule of the Gospels: "Therefore, all things whatsoever ye would that men should do to you, do ye even so to them" (Matthew 7:12; cf. Luke 6:31).]

67. It is essential to Kant's conception of a promise that it involves a "united will" of the promisor and the promisee (*Metaphysics of Morals*, Ak 6: 272).

in itself (which is the supreme limiting condition of the freedom of the
actions of every human being) is not gotten from experience, first, on
account of its universality, since it applies to all rational beings in general,
and no experience is sufficient to determine anything about that; second,
because in it humanity is represented not as an end of human beings[68]
(subjectively), i.e., as an object that one actually from oneself makes into an
end, but as an objective end which, whatever ends we may have, is to
constitute as a law the supreme limiting condition of all subjective ends,
hence must arise from pure reason. The ground of all practical legislation,
namely, lies *objectively in the rule* and the form of universality, which
makes it capable of being a law (at least a law of nature) (in accordance with
the first principle), but *subjectively* it lies in the *end*; but the subject of all
ends is every rational being as end in itself (in accordance with the second
principle): from this now follows the third practical principle of the will, as
the supreme condition of its harmony with universal practical reason, the
idea *of the will of every rational being as a will giving universal law.*

All maxims are repudiated in accordance with this principle which cannot subsist together with the will's own universal legislation. The will is
thus not solely subject to the law, but is subject in such a way that[69] it must
be regarded also *as legislating to itself,*[70] and precisely for this reason as
subject to the law (of which it can consider itself as the author).[71]

Imperatives represented in the above way, namely of the lawfulness of
actions generally similar to an *order of nature*, or of the universal *preference of the end* of rational beings themselves, just by being represented as
categorical, excluded from their commanding authority all admixture of
any interest as an incentive; but they were only *assumed* as categorical,
because one had to assume such a thing if one wanted to explain the concept

68. 1785: "of the human being"

69. 1785: "not subject to the law except in such a way that"

70. 1785: "as a self-legislating [being]"

71. On the distinction between the "legislator" of a law (who promulgates and
attaches sanctions to it) and the "author" of a law (whose will actually imposes the
obligation), see *Metaphysics of Morals*, Ak 6:227. Although Kant frequently speaks here
of the rational being as "legislator" of the moral law, his position (more precisely expressed, in this terminology) is that only the rational being who is obligated can be the
author of the law; Kant allows that we can speak of God (or the "supreme head of the
realm of ends") as the *legislator* of the moral law (see below, 4:433–34; *Moral Philosophy Collins*, Ak 27:282–83; and *Religion within the Boundaries of Mere Reason*, Ak
6:99–100.

of duty. But that there are practical propositions which command categorically cannot be proven for itself here, just as little as this can still happen[72] anywhere in this section; yet one thing could have happened, namely that the withdrawal of all interest in the case of volition from duty, in the imperative itself, through any determination that it could contain, is indicated as the specific sign distinguishing the categorical from the hypothetical imperative, and this happens in the third formula of the principle, namely the idea of the will of every rational being as *a universally legislative will*.

[Ak 4:432]

For if we think of such a will, then although a will *that stands under laws* may be bound by means of an interest in this law, nevertheless it is impossible for a will that is itself supremely legislative to depend on any interest; for such a dependent will would need yet another law, which limited the interest of its self-love to the condition of a validity for the universal law.

Thus the *principle* of every human will as *a will legislating universally through all its maxims*,* if otherwise everything were correct about it, would be quite *well suited* for the categorical imperative by the fact that precisely for the sake of the idea of universal legislation, it *grounds itself on no interest* and hence it alone among all[73] possible imperatives can be *unconditioned*; or still better, by converting the proposition, if there is a categorical imperative (i.e., a law for every will of a rational being), then it can command only that everything be done from the maxim of its will as a will that could at the same time have as its object itself as universally legislative; for only then is the practical principle and the imperative it obeys unconditioned, because it cannot have any interest at all as its ground.

Now it is no wonder, when we look back on all the previous efforts that have ever been undertaken to bring to light the principle of morality, why they all had to fail. One saw the human being bound through his duty to laws, but it did not occur to one that he was subject *only to his own* and yet *universal legislation*, and that he was obligated only to act in accord with his own will, which, however, in accordance with its natural end, is a universally legislative will. For if one thought of him only as subject to a law (whatever it might be), then this would have to bring with it some interest as a stimulus or coercion, because as a law it did not arise from *his*

[Ak 4:433]

[Ak4:432]   *I can be exempted here from providing examples to elucidate this principle, since those that first elucidated the categorical imperative and its formula can all serve here for precisely that end.

72. 1785: "just as little as this still cannot happen"

73. This word added in 1786

will, but rather this will was necessitated by *something else* to act in a certain way in conformity with the law. Through this entirely necessary consequence, however, all the labor of finding a supreme ground of duty was irretrievably lost. For from it one never got duty, but only necessity of action from a certain interest. Now this might be one's own interest or someone else's. But then the imperative always had to come out as conditioned, and could never work at all as a moral command. Thus I will call this principle the principle of[74] the *autonomy* of the will, in contrast to every[75] other, which on this account I count as *heteronomy*.

The concept of every rational being that must consider itself as giving universal law through all the maxims of its will in order to judge itself and its actions from this point of view, leads to a very fruitful concept depending on it, namely that of *a realm of ends*.[76]

By a *realm*, however, I understand the systematic combination of various rational beings through communal laws. Now because laws determine ends in accordance with their universal validity, there comes to be, if one abstracts from the personal differences between rational beings, as likewise from every content of their private ends, a whole of all ends — (of rational beings as ends in themselves, as well as of their own ends, which each may set for himself) in systematic connection, i.e., a realm of ends — can be thought, which is possible in accordance with the above principles.

For rational beings all stand under the *law* that every one of them ought to[77] treat itself and all others *never merely as means*, but always *at the same time as end in itself*. From this, however, arises a systematic combination of rational beings through communal objective laws, i.e., a realm that, because these laws have as their aim the reference of these beings to one another[78] as ends and means, can be called a 'realm of ends' (obviously only an ideal).

But a rational being belongs as a *member* to the realm of ends if in this

---

74. 1785: "Thus I will call this the principle of"

75. The editors suggest *jenem*, which would translate: "in contrast to that other, which."

76. The obvious source for Kant's conception of a "realm of ends" is Leibniz's conception of the "city of God" as the "realm of minds," and the relationship of the "realm of nature" to this "realm of grace." Gottfried Wilhelm Leibniz (1646–1716), *Discourse on Metaphysics* (1686), § 36; *Principles of Nature and Grace Based on Reason* (1714), § 15; *Monadology* (1714), §§ 85–90.

77. 1785: "may"

78. 1785: "as their aim their relation to one another"

realm it gives universal law but is also itself subject to these laws. It belongs to it *as supreme head*, if as giving law it is subject to no will of another.[79]

The rational being must always consider itself as giving law in a realm of ends possible through freedom of the will, whether as member or as supreme head. It can assert the place of the latter, however, not merely through the maxim of its will, but only when it is a fully independent being, without need and without limitation of faculties that are adequate to that will.

Morality thus consists in the reference of all action to that legislation through which alone a realm of ends is possible. But the legislation must be encountered in every rational being itself, and be able to arise from its will, whose principle therefore is: 'Do no action in accordance with any other maxim, except one that could subsist with its being a universal law, and hence only so *that the will could through its maxim at the same time consider itself as universally legislative*'. Now if the maxims are not through their nature already necessarily in harmony with this objective principle of the rational beings, as universally legislative, then the necessity of the action in accordance with that principle is called 'practical necessitation', i.e., *duty*. Duty does not apply to the supreme head in the realm of ends, but it does to every member, and specifically, to all in equal measure.

The practical necessity of acting in accordance with this principle, i.e., duty, does not rest at all on feelings, impulses, or inclinations, but merely on the relation of rational beings to one another, in which the will of one rational being must always at the same time be considered as *universally legislative*, because otherwise the rational being could not think of the other rational beings as *ends in themselves*. Reason thus refers every maxim of the will as universally legislative to every other will and also to every action toward itself, and this not for the sake of any other practical motive or future advantage, but from the idea of the *dignity* of a rational being that obeys no law except that which at the same time it gives itself.

In the realm of ends everything has either a **price** or a **dignity**.[80] What has a price is such that something else can also be put in its place as its *equivalent*; by contrast, that which is elevated above all price, and admits of no equivalent, has a dignity.

That which refers to universal human inclinations and needs has a *mar-*

79. See note 59 above (Ak 4:431).

80. The apparent source for this distinction is Seneca, *Epistles* 71.33. But it is an atypical passage in the Stoic literature, since typically both *pretium* and *dignitas* refer to the value of (preferred) indifferents rather than to virtue.

ket price; that which, even without presupposing any need, is in accord with a certain taste, i.e., a satisfaction in the mere purposeless play of the powers   of our mind, an *affective price*; but that which constitutes the condition under which alone something can be an end in itself does not have merely a relative worth, i.e., a price, but rather an inner worth, i.e., *dignity*.

Now morality is the condition under which alone a rational being can be an end in itself, because only through morality is it possible to be a legislative member in the realm of ends. Thus morality and humanity, insofar as it is capable of morality, is that alone which has dignity. Skill and industry in labor have a market price; wit, lively imagination, and moods have an affective price; by contrast, fidelity in promising, benevolence from principle (not from instinct) have an inner worth. Lacking these principles, neither nature nor art contain anything that they could put in the place of them; for the worth of these principles does not consist in effects that arise from them, in the advantage and utility that they obtain, but rather in the dispositions, i.e., the maxims of the will, which in this way are ready to reveal themselves in actions, even if they are not favored with success. These actions also need no recommendation from any subjective disposition[81] or taste, regarding them with immediate favor and satisfaction, and no immediate propensity or feeling for it:[82] they exhibit the will that carries them out as an object of an immediate respect, for which nothing but reason is required in order to *impose* them on the will, not to *cajole* them from it *by flattery*, which latter would, in any event, be a contradiction in the case of duties. This estimation thus makes the worth of such a way of thinking to be recognized as dignity, and sets it infinitely far above all price, with which it cannot at all be brought into computation or comparison without, as it were, mistaking and assailing[83] its holiness.

And now, what is it that justifies the morally good disposition or virtue in making such high claims? It is nothing less than the *share* that it procures for the rational being *in the universal legislation*, thereby making it suitable as a member in a possible realm of ends, for which it by its own nature was already destined, as end in itself and precisely for this reason as legislative in the realm of ends, as free in regard to all natural laws, obeying only those that it gives itself and in accordance with which its maxims can belong to a universal legislation (to which it at the same time subjects itself). For

81. *Disposition*

82. *dieselbe*, which would appear to refer to "morality"; some editors substitute the plural, so that this pronoun refers instead to "these actions."

83. "mistaking and assailing" = *vergreifen*

nothing has a worth except that which the law determines[84] for it. The legislation itself, however, which determines all worth, must precisely for this reason have a dignity, i.e., an unconditioned, incomparable worth; the word *respect* alone yields a becoming expression for the estimation that a rational being must assign to it. *Autonomy* is thus the ground of the dignity of the human and of every rational nature.

The three ways mentioned of representing the principle of morality are, however, fundamentally only so many formulas of precisely the same law, one of which unites the other two in itself. Nonetheless, there is a variety among them, which is to be sure more subjectively than objectively practical,[85] namely that of bringing an idea of reason nearer to intuition (in accordance with a certain analogy) and, through this, nearer to feeling. All maxims have, namely,

(1) a *form*, which consists in universality, and then the formula of the moral imperative is expressed thus: 'That the maxims must be chosen as if they are supposed to be valid as universal laws of nature';

(2) a *matter*,[86] namely an end, and then the formula says: 'That the rational being, as an end in accordance with its nature, hence as an end in itself, must serve for every maxim as a limiting condition of all merely relative and arbitrary ends';

(3) *a complete determination*[87] of all maxims through that formula, namely 'That all maxims ought to harmonize from[88] one's own legislation into a possible realm of ends as a realm of nature'.* A progression happens here, as through the categories of the *unity* of the form of the will (its universality), the *plurality* of the matter (the objects, i.e., the ends), and the *allness* or totality of the system of them.[89] But one does better in moral

---

*Teleology considers nature as a realm of ends, morality a possible realm of ends as a realm of nature. In the former, the realm of ends is a theoretical idea for the explanation of what exists. In the latter, it is a practical idea to bring about that which does not exist but what can become actual through our deeds and omissions and what we are to bring about in accord with precisely this idea.

84. 1785: "except the one the law determines"

85. This could also be translated "more subjective than objectively practical."

86. Kant's text reads *Maxime*; but editors universally correct this to *Materie*, as seems absolutely required by the second sentence of (3) below.

87. See *Critique of Pure Reason*, A571–83/B599–611.

88. 1785: "as"

89. See *Critique of Pure Reason*, A70–71/B95–96, A80/B106.

judging always to proceed in accordance with the strict method and take as ground the universal formula of the categorical imperative: *Act in accordance with that maxim which can at the same time make itself into a universal law.* But if one wants at the same time to obtain *access* for the [Ak 4:437] moral law, then it is very useful to take one and the same action through the three named concepts and thus, as far as may be done, to bring the action nearer to intuition.

Now we can end at the place from which we set out at the beginning, namely with the concept of an unconditionally good will. That *will* is *absolutely good* which cannot be evil, hence whose maxim, if it is made into a universal law, can never conflict with itself. This principle is therefore also its supreme law: 'Act always in accordance with that maxim whose universality as law you can at the same time will'; this is the single condition under which a will can never be in conflict with itself, and such an imperative is categorical. Because the validity of the will as a universal law for possible actions has an analogy with the universal connection of the existence of things in accordance with universal laws, which is what is formal in nature in general, the categorical imperative can also be expressed thus: *Act in accordance with maxims that can at the same time have themselves as universal laws of nature for their object.* This, therefore, is the way the formula of an absolutely good will is constituted.

Rational nature discriminates itself from the rest in that it sets itself an end. This would be the matter of every good will. But since, in the idea of a will that is absolutely good without a limiting condition (of the attainment of this or that end), every end to be *effected* has to be thoroughly abstracted from (as it would make every will only relatively good), the end here has to be thought of not as an end to be effected *but as a self-sufficient* end, hence only negatively, i.e., never to be acted against, which therefore has to be estimated in every volition never merely as means but always at the same time as end. Now this cannot be other than the very subject of all possible ends, because this is at the same time the subject of a possible absolutely good will; for this will cannot without contradiction be set after any other object. The principle:[90] Accordingly, 'Act in reference to every rational being (to yourself and others) so that in your maxim it is always valid at the same time as an end in itself' is, fundamentally, the same as the principle 'Act in accordance with a maxim that at the same time contains its own universal validity for every rational being'. For that I ought to limit my [Ak 4:438] maxim in the use of means to every end to the condition of its universality

90. 1785: "But the principle: . . ."

as a law for every subject, says just as much as that the subject of ends, i.e., the rational being itself, must be made the ground of all maxims of actions never merely as means, but as the supreme limiting condition in the use of all means, i.e., always at the same time as end.

Now it incontestably follows from this that every rational being, as an end in itself, would have to be able to regard itself at the same time as universally legislative in regard to all laws to which it may be subject, because precisely this suitableness of its maxims for the universal legislation designates it as an end in itself, just as the fact that this dignity (prerogative) before all mere beings of nature brings with it to have to take its maxims always from its own point of view but also at the same time from that of every other rational being as a universally legislative being (which is why they are also called 'persons'). Now in such a way a world of rational beings *(mundus intelligibilis)*[91] is possible as a realm of ends, and specifically for all persons through their own legislation as members. Accordingly,[92] every rational being must act as if it were through its maxims always a legislative member in a universal realm of ends. The formal principle of these maxims is: 'Act as though your maxim should serve at the same time as a universal law (for all rational beings)'. A realm of ends is thus possible only in accordance with the analogy with a realm of nature, but only in accordance with maxims, i.e., with self-imposed rules, whereas the latter is possible only in accordance with laws of externally[93] necessitated efficient causes. Regardless of this, even though nature as a whole is regarded as a machine, nevertheless one also gives to it, insofar as it has reference to rational beings as its ends, on that ground, the name 'realm of nature'. Such a realm of ends would actually be brought about through maxims, the rule of which is prescribed by the categorical imperatives of all rational beings, *if they were universally followed.* Yet although the rational being might punctiliously follow these maxims himself, he cannot for that reason count on everyone else's being faithful to them, nor on the realm of nature and its purposive order's harmonizing with him, as a suitable member for a realm of ends that is possible through him, i.e., on its favoring his [Ak 4:439]   expectation of happiness; thus the law 'Act in accordance with maxims of a universally legislative member for a merely possible realm of ends' still remains in full force, because it commands categorically. And precisely in this lies the paradox that merely the dignity of humanity as rational nature,

91. intelligible world
92. 1785: "Nevertheless"
93. 1785: "laws also of externally"

without any other end or advantage to be attained through it, hence the respect for a mere idea, ought nevertheless to serve as an unremitting precept of the will, and that the sublimity of the maxim consists in just its independence of all incentives, and the dignity of every rational subject consists in being a legislative member in the realm of ends; for otherwise it would have to be represented as subject only to the natural law of its needs. Although the natural realm, too, as well as the realm of ends, is thought of as united under a supreme head, and the latter thereby would no longer remain a mere idea but obtain true reality, so that through this the maxim would receive the accretion of a strong incentive; yet no increase of its inner worth would thereby come about; for irrespective of that, this sole unlimited legislator must always be so represented as judging the worth of the rational beings only in accordance with their selfless conduct as prescribed by itself merely through that idea. The essence of things does not alter through their external relations, and it is in accordance with that which alone constitutes the absolute worth of the human being, without thinking about such relations, that he must be judged by whoever it may be, even by the highest being. *Morality* is thus the relation of actions to the autonomy of the will, that is, to the possible universal legislation through its maxims. That action which can subsist with the autonomy of the will is *permitted*; that which does not agree with it is *impermissible*. The will whose maxims necessarily harmonize with the laws of autonomy is a *holy*, absolutely good will. The dependence of a will which is not absolutely good on the principle of autonomy (moral necessitation) is *obligation*. Thus the latter cannot be referred to a holy being. The objective necessity of an action from obligation is called *duty*.

From what has just been said one can now easily explain how it is that although under the concept of duty we think a subjection to the law, we at the same time represent to ourselves a certain sublimity[94] and *dignity* in a person who fulfills all his duties. For to be sure, to the extent that the person is *subject* to the moral law, there is no sublimity in him, but there is to the extent that he is at the same time *legislative* in regard to this law, and is only for that reason subject to them. Also we have shown above how neither fear nor inclination, but solely respect for the law, is the incentive that can give the action its moral worth. Our own will, insofar as it would act only under the condition of a possible universal legislation through its maxims, this will possible to us in the idea, is the authentic object of respect, and the

[Ak 4:440]

94. On the sublime, see *Critique of the Power of Judgment*, §§ 23–29, Ak 5:248–78; *Anthropology in a Pragmatic Respect*, § 68, Ak 7:243.

dignity of humanity consists precisely in this capacity for universal legislation, although with the proviso[95] that it is at the same time itself subject to this legislation.

Autonomy of the will
as the supreme principle of morality

Autonomy of the will is the property of the will through which it is a law to itself (independently of all properties of the objects of volition). The principle of autonomy is thus: 'Not to choose otherwise than so that the maxims of one's choice are at the same time comprehended with it in the same volition as universal law'. That this practical rule is an imperative, i.e., the will of every rational being is necessarily bound to it as a condition, cannot be proven through the mere analysis of the concepts occurring in it, because it is a synthetic proposition; one would have to advance beyond the cognition of objects and to a critique of the subject, i.e., of pure practical reason, since this synthetic proposition, which commands apodictically, must be able to be cognized fully *a priori*; but this enterprise does not belong in the present section. Yet that the specified principle of autonomy is the sole principle of morals may well be established through the mere analysis of the concepts of morality. For thereby it is found that its principle must be a categorical imperative, but this commands neither more nor less than just this autonomy.

[Ak 4:441]

Heteronomy of the will
as the source of all ungenuine principles of morality

If the will seeks that which should determine it *anywhere else* than in the suitability of its maxims for its own universal legislation, hence if it, insofar as it advances beyond itself, seeks the law in[96] the constitution of any of its objects, then *heteronomy* always comes out of this. Then the will does not give itself the law but the object through its relation to the will gives the law to it. Through this relation, whether it rests now on inclination or on representations of reason, only hypothetical imperatives are possible: 'I ought to do something *because I will something else*'. By contrast, the moral, hence categorical, imperative says: 'I ought to act thus-and-so even if I did not will anything else'. E.g., the former one says: 'I ought not to lie, if I want to retain my honorable reputation';[97] but the latter says: 'I ought not to lie, even if I did

95. *Beding*
96. 1785: "hence if it advances . . . , and seeks the law in"
97. *bei Ehren bleiben*

not incur the least disgrace'.[98] The last must therefore abstract from every object to the extent that it has no *influence* on the will, hence practical reason (will) does not merely administer some other interest, but merely proves its own commanding authority as supreme legislation. Thus, e.g., I should seek to promote someone else's happiness, not as if its existence mattered to me (whether through immediate inclination or any satisfaction indirectly through reason) but merely because the maxim that excludes it cannot be comprehended in one and the same volition as a universal law.

Division
of all possible principles of morality
from the
assumed fundamental concept of heteronomy

Here as elsewhere, human reason in its pure use, as long as it has gone without critique, has previously tried all possible incorrect routes before it succeeds in getting on the only true one.[99]

All principles that one may take from this point of view are either *empirical* or *rational*. The **first**, from the principle of *happiness*, are built on physical[100] or moral feeling;[101] the **second**, from the principle of *perfection*, are built either on the rational concept of it as a possible effect[102] or on the concept of a self-sufficient perfection (the will of God) as determining cause of our will.[103]

[Ak 4:442]

Empirical principles are everywhere unsuited to having moral laws grounded on them. For the universality, with which they are to be valid for all rational beings without distinction, the unconditioned practical necessity, which is imposed on these beings through them, drops out if the ground of these principles is taken from the *particular adaptation of human nature* or from the contingent circumstances in which it is placed. Yet the principle of *one's own happiness* is most reprehensible, not merely because it is false

98. *Schande*

99. Cf. *Critique of Pure Reason*, A xii.

100. Kant associates this with the hedonism of Epicurus (341–270 B.C.) (*Critique of Practical Reason*, Ak 5:40).

101. Kant associates this with the moral sense theory of Francis Hutcheson (1694–1727) (*Critique of Practical Reason*, Ak 5:40).

102. Kant associates this with the position of Christian Wolff and the Stoics (*Critique of Practical Reason*, Ak 5:40).

103. Kant associates this with the divine command morality of Christian August Crusius (1715–1775) (*Critique of Practical Reason*, Ak 5:40).

and experience contradicts the pretense that one's own welfare always accords with conducting oneself well; also not merely because it contributes nothing to the grounding of morality, since making a happy human being is something other than making a good one, and making him prudent and sharp-witted for his own advantage is something other than making him virtuous; but rather because it attributes incentives to morality that would sooner undermine it and annihilate its entire sublimity, since they put the motivations for virtue in the same class as those for vice and only teach us to draw better calculations, but utterly extinguish the specific difference between them; by contrast, moral feeling, this allegedly special sense* (however shallow the appeal to it may be, since those who cannot *think* believe they can help themselves out by *feeling* when it comes to universal laws, even though feelings, which by nature are infinitely distinguished from one another in degree, cannot yield an equal standard of good and evil, nor can one validly judge for others at all through his feeling) nevertheless remains closer to morality and its dignity by showing virtue the honor of ascribing to it *immediately* the satisfaction and esteem we have for it, and not saying directly to its face, as it were, that it is not its beauty, but only our advantage, that attaches us to it.

[Ak 4:443]

Among *rational* grounds[104] of morality, the ontological concept of *perfection* (however empty, indeterminate, hence unusable it may be for finding in the immeasurable field of possible reality the greatest suitable sum for us, and however much it has an unavoidable propensity to turn in a circle in order to distinguish the reality talked about here specifically from every other, and cannot avoid covertly presupposing the morality it ought to explain) is nevertheless better than the theological concept, of deriving morality from a divine, all-perfect will, not merely because we do not intuit his perfection, but can derive it solely from our concepts, of which morality is the foremost one, but because if we do not do this (which, if we did, would be a crude circle in explanation), the concept of his will that is left over to us, the attributes[105] of the desire for glory and domination, bound up

[Ak4:442]   *I count the principle of moral feeling to that of happiness, because every empirical interest promises a contribution to welfare through the agreeableness something affords, whether this happens immediately and without any aim to advantage or in regard to the latter. Likewise one must, with *Hutcheson*, count the principle of sympathetic participation in another's happiness under the same moral sense assumed by him.

104. *rationalen oder Vernunftgründe*

105. *Eigenschaften*

with frightful representations of power and vengeance, would have to make a foundation for a system of morals that is directly opposed to morality.

But if I had to choose between the concept of moral sense and that of perfection in general (both of which at least do not infringe morality, even if they are not at all suitable for supporting it as a foundation), then I would determine myself for the latter, because, since it at least transfers the decision of the question from sensibility to the court of pure reason, even if here it decides nothing, nevertheless it preserves unfalsified the indeterminate idea (of a will good in itself) for closer determination.

Besides, I believe I can dispense with an extensive refutation of all these doctrines.[106] It is so easy, and even those whose office it is to declare themselves for one of these theories presumably have such good insight into it (because their hearers would not tolerate a postponement of judgment) that it would be only superfluous labor. What interests us more here is to know that these principles everywhere set up nothing but heteronomy of the will as the first ground of morality and just for this reason must necessarily miscarry regarding their end.

[Ak 4:444]

Wherever an object of the will has to be taken as the ground in order to prescribe the rule determining that will, there the rule is nothing but heteronomy; the imperative is conditioned, namely: *if* or *because* one wills this object, one ought to act thus or so; hence it can never command morally, i.e., categorically. Now the object may determine the will by means of inclination, as with the principle of one's own happiness, or by means of a reason directed to objects of our possible volition in general, in the principle of perfection; then the will never determines itself *immediately* through the representation of the action, but only through the incentive, which the foreseen effect of the action has on the will; *I ought to do something because I will something other than that*, and another law in my subject must therefore be taken as ground, in accordance with which I necessarily will this other thing, which law once again needs an imperative that limits this

---

106. Kant's fuller taxonomy (*Critique of Practical Reason*, Ak 5:40) divides theories of heteronomy into four kinds. "Objective" theories are either (1) "internal" (the theory of perfection) or (2) "external" (divine command theory). (3) "Subjective internal" theories include both the theory of physical and the theory of moral feeling. This taxonomy makes a place for yet another classification not discussed in the *Groundwork*, namely (4) "subjective external" theories. These include the theory that morality is grounded on education, which Kant associates with Michel Montaigne (1533–1592), and the theory that morality is grounded on the civil constitution, which Kant associates with Bernard Mandeville (1670–1733).

maxim. For because the impulse that the representation of an object possible through our powers is supposed to exercise on the subject's will in accordance with its natural constitution, whether it be of sensibility (of inclination and taste) or of understanding and reason — which, in accordance with the particular adaptation of its nature, that faculty exercises with satisfaction in an object[107] — it is really nature that would give the law, which as such would have to be not only cognized and proven through experience, and hence is in itself contingent and thereby becomes unsuitable for an apodictic rule such as the moral rule has to be; but it is *always only heteronomy* of the will, the will does not give the law to itself, but rather an alien impulse gives it by means of the subject's nature, which is attuned to the receptiveness of the will.

The absolutely good will, whose principle must be a categorical imperative, will therefore, undetermined in regard to all objects, contain merely the *form of volition* in general, and indeed as autonomy, i.e., the suitability of the maxim of every good will to make itself into a universal law is itself the sole law that the will of every rational being imposes on itself, without grounding it on any incentive or interest in it.

How such a synthetic practical proposition a priori *is possible*, and why it is necessary, is a problem whose solution no longer lies within the boundaries of the metaphysics of morals, neither have we here asserted its truth, much less pretended to have a proof of it in our control. We showed only, through the development of the generally accepted concept of morality,[108] that it is unavoidably attached to, or rather is grounded on, an autonomy of the will. Thus whoever takes morality to be something, and not a chimerical idea without truth, must at the same time concede the stated principle of it. This section, therefore, like the first one, was merely analytical. Now that morality is no figment of the mind, which follows if the categorical imperative, and with it autonomy of the will, is true and absolutely necessary as a principle *a priori* — this requires a *possible synthetic use of pure practical reason*, upon which, however, we may not venture without preceding it with a *critique* of this very faculty of reason, which we have to exhibit in the last section as the main feature of this critique in a way sufficient for our aim.

[Ak 4:445]

107. Instead of "reason — which . . . object," 1785 reads: "reason takes in perfection in general, (whose existence either from itself or only depending on the highest self-sufficient perfection),"

108. *allgemein im Schwange gehenden Begriffs der Sittlichkeit*

Third Section

The concept of freedom
is the key to the definition[1] of autonomy of the will.

The *will* is a species of causality of living beings, insofar as they are rational, and *freedom* would be that quality of this causality by which it can be effective independently of alien causes *determining* it; just as *natural necessity* is the quality of the causality of all beings lacking reason, of being determined to activity through the influence of alien causes.

The proposed definition[2] of freedom is *negative*, and hence unfruitful in affording insight into its essence; yet from it flows a *positive* concept of freedom, which is all the more rich in content and more fruitful. Since the concept of a causality carries with it that of *laws* in accordance with which must be posited, through that which we call a cause, something else, namely its result; therefore freedom, even though it is not a quality of the will in accordance with natural laws, is not for this reason lawless, but rather it has to be a causality in accordance with unchangeable laws, but of a particular kind; for otherwise a free will would be an impossibility.[3] Natural necessity was a heteronomy of efficient causes; for every effect was possible only in accordance with the law that something else determined the efficient cause to causality; what else, then, could the freedom of the will be, except autonomy, i.e., the quality of the will of being a law to itself? But the proposition 'The will is in all actions a law to itself' designates only the principle of acting in accordance with no other maxim than that which can also have itself as a universal law as its object. But this is just the formula of the categorical imperative and the principle of morality: thus a free will and a will under moral laws are the same. [Ak 4:447]

Thus if freedom of the will is presupposed, then morality follows together with its principle from mere analysis of its concept. Nonetheless, the

1. *Erklärung*
2. *Erklärung*
3. *Unding*

latter is always a synthetic proposition: an absolutely good will is that whose maxim can always contain itself considered as universal law, for through analysis of the concept of an absolutely good will that quality of the maxim cannot be found. Such synthetic propositions, however, are possible only when both cognitions are combined with one another through the connection with a third in which they are both to be encountered.[4] The *positive* concept of freedom makes for[5] this third, which cannot be, as with physical causes, the nature of the world of sense (in whose concept the concepts of something as cause comes together in relation to *something else* as effect). What this third thing must be, to which freedom points and of which we have an idea *a priori*, still cannot be directly indicated here, and to make comprehensible the deduction of the concept of freedom from pure practical reason, with it also the possibility of a categorical imperative, instead still needs some preparation.

Freedom must be presupposed
as a quality of the will of all rational beings.

It is not enough that we ascribe freedom to our will, on whatever grounds, if we do not also have sufficient grounds to attribute the same quality also to all rational beings. For since morality serves as a law for us merely as for *rational beings*, it must also be valid for all rational beings, and since it must be derived solely from the quality of freedom, therefore freedom must also be proved as a quality of the will of all rational beings, and it is not enough to [Ak 4:448] establish it from certain alleged experiences of human nature (although this is absolutely impossible, and it can be established solely *a priori*); but rather one must prove it of the activity of rational beings in general, who are endowed with a will. Now I say: Every being that cannot act otherwise than *under the idea of freedom* is precisely for this reason actually free in a practical respect, i.e., all laws inseparably combined with freedom are valid for it, just as if its will had also been declared[6] free in itself and in a way that is valid in theoretical philosophy.* Now I assert that we must necessarily lend

*I take this route, of assuming freedom as sufficient for our aim only as rational beings ground it *on the idea* in their actions, so that I may not be obligated to prove freedom also in its theoretical intent. For even if this latter is left unsettled, these same laws that would obligate a being that is actually free are still valid for a being that cannot act otherwise than as

4. See *Critique of Pure Reason*, A7–10/B11–14.
5. *schafft*
6. *erklärt*

to every rational being that has a will also the idea of freedom, under which alone it would act. For in such a being we think a reason that is practical, i.e., has causality in regard to its objects. Now one cannot possibly think a reason that, in its own consciousness, would receive steering from elsewhere in regard to its judgments; for then the subject would ascribe the determination of its power of judgment not to its reason but to an impulse. It must regard itself as the author of its principles independently of alien influences; consequently it must, as practical reason or as the will of a rational being, be regarded by itself as free, i.e., the will of a rational being can be a will of its own only under the idea of freedom and must therefore with a practical aim be attributed to all rational beings.

Of the interest attaching to the ideas of morality

We have ultimately traced the determined concept of morality to the idea of freedom; but we cannot prove this freedom as something actual, not even in ourselves, nor in human nature; we saw only that we have to presuppose [Ak 4:449] it if we would think of a being as rational and as endowed with consciousness of its causality in regard to actions, i.e., with a will; thus we find that from precisely the same ground we have to attribute to every being endowed with reason and will this quality, to determine itself to action under the idea of its freedom.

From the presupposition of these ideas,[7] however, there also flowed the consciousness of a law of acting: that the subjective principles of actions, i.e., maxims, have always to be taken so that they can also be valid objectively, i.e., universally as principles, hence serve for our own universal legislation. But why ought I to subject myself to this principle, and specifically as a rational being in general, hence through this also all other beings endowed with reason? I will concede that no interest *drives* me to it, for that would yield no categorical imperative; but I must necessarily *take* an interest in it, and gain insight into how that happens to be; for this 'ought' is really a volition that would be valid for every rational being, under the condition that reason were practical in him without any hindrances; for beings, such as we are, who are also affected through sensibility, as with incentives of another kind, with whom what reason for itself alone would

---

under the idea of its own freedom. Thus we can free ourselves of the burden that pressures theory.

7. *diese Ideen*, which seem to refer to the "ideas of morality" mentioned in the subheading; because this yields a doubtful meaning for the sentence, some editors amend the text to read *diese Idee* (sc. the idea of freedom).

always do does not always happen, that necessity of action is called only an[8] 'ought', and the subjective necessity is different from the objective.

It therefore appears as if in the idea of freedom we really only presupposed the moral law, namely the principle of the autonomy of the will itself, and could not prove its reality and objective necessity for itself; and then we would still have gained something quite considerable, more than would have happened otherwise, by at least determining the genuine principle more precisely, but in regard to its validity and the practical necessity of subjecting ourselves to it, we would have come no further; for to someone who asked us why the universal validity of our maxim as a law has to be the limiting condition of our actions, and on what we ground the worth that we attribute to this way of acting — a worth that is to be so great that there can nowhere be any higher interest — and how it happens to be that the human being believes he feels his personal worth through it alone, and that over against it an agreeable or disagreeable condition is held to be nothing — to him we can give no satisfactory answer.

[Ak 4:450]

We indeed find that we can take an interest in a constitution of personality[9] that carries with it no interest at all in the condition, if only the former makes us susceptible to partaking in the latter just in case reason should effect the distribution of it, i.e., that the mere worthiness of being happy, even without the motive to partake in this happiness, could interest for itself: but this judgment is in fact only the effect of moral laws whose importance has already been presupposed (if we separate ourselves from all empirical interest through the idea of freedom), but that we ought to separate ourselves from this, i.e., consider ourselves as free in acting and thus nevertheless take ourselves to be subject to certain laws in order to find a worth merely in our person, and that this could compensate us for the loss of all the worth procured for our condition; and how this is possible, thus *from whence the moral law obligates* — in such a way we still gain no insight into this.

One must freely admit it[10] that a kind of circle shows itself here, from which, it seems, there is no way out. In the order of efficient causes we assume ourselves to be free in order to think of ourselves as under moral laws in the order of ends, and then afterward we think of ourselves as subject to these laws because we have attributed freedom of the will to ourselves, for freedom and the will giving its own laws are both autonomy,

8. 1785: "in the"
9. *persönliche Beschaffenheit*
10. This word added in 1786

hence reciprocal concepts, of which, however, just for this reason, one cannot be used to define[11] the other and provide the ground for it, but at most only with a logical intent to bring various apparent representations of the same object to a single concept (as different fractions with the same value are brought to the lowest common denominator).

But one way out remains for us, namely to seek whether, when we think of ourselves through freedom as *a priori* efficient causes, we do not take a different standpoint from when we represent ourselves in accordance with our actions as effects that we see before our eyes.

No subtle reflection is required to make the following remark, but rather one can assume that the commonest understanding might make it, even if in its own way, through an obscure distinction of the power of judgment that it calls feeling: that all representations that come to us without our choice (like those of sense) give us objects to cognize only as they affect us, so that what they might be in themselves remains unknown to us; hence that as regards this species of representations, even with the most strenuous attention and distinctness that the understanding might add to them, we can attain merely to the cognition of *appearances*, never to *things in themselves*.[12] As soon as this distinction is made (perhaps merely through the variation noted between the representations that are given to us from somewhere else, in which we are passive, and those which we produce solely from ourselves, and thus prove our activity), then it follows of itself that one must concede and assume behind the appearances something else that is not appearance, namely the things in themselves, even if of ourselves we are satisfied that since they never can become known to us except as they affect us, we can never come any nearer to them and can never know what they are in themselves. This[13] must yield a distinction, though a crude one, of a *world of sense* from a *world of understanding*,[14] of which the first, in accordance with the variations in sensibility of many ways of contemplating the world, can also be extremely varied, whereas the second, on which it is grounded, always remains the same. Even about himself and in accordance with the acquaintance that the human being has of himself through inner sensation, he may not presume to cognize how he is in himself. For since he does not, as it were, make himself and gets his concept not *a priori*

[Ak 4:451]

---

11. *erklären*

12. Cf. *Critique of Pure Reason*, B xv–xxii, A26–30/B42–46, A32–49/B49–73, A490–97/B518–25.

13. 1785: "They"

14. Cf. *Critique of Pure Reason*, A235–60/B294–315.

but empirically, it is natural that he can take in information even about himself through inner sense and consequently only through the appearance of his nature and the way his consciousness is affected, whereas he necessarily assumes about this constitution of his own subject, which is composed of sheer appearances, that it is grounded on something else, namely his I, however that may be constituted in itself, and must therefore count himself in regard to mere perception and the receptivity of sensations as in the *world of sense*, but in regard to whatever in him may be pure activity (what attains to consciousness not through the affection of the senses but immediately), he must count himself as in the *intellectual world*, of which, however, he has no further acquaintance.

[Ak 4:452]   A reflective human being must draw such a conclusion about all things that might come before him; presumably it is also to be encountered in the commonest understanding, which, as is well known, is very much inclined to expect behind the objects of sense always something invisible and for itself active, but is corrupted by the fact that it wants to make this invisible once again into something sensible, i.e., into an object of intuition, and thereby does not become by any degree the wiser.[15]

Now the human being actually finds in himself a faculty through which he distinguishes himself from all other things, and even from himself insofar as he is affected by objects, and this is *reason*. This as pure self-activity is elevated even above the *understanding* in the respect that although the latter is also self-activity and does not, like sense, contain mere representations that arise only when one is affected by things (hence passive), it can produce no other concepts from its activity except those that merely serve to *bring sensible representations under rules* and thereby to unite them in one consciousness, without which use of sensibility it would think nothing at all,[16] while by contrast, reason, under the name of the ideas, shows such a pure spontaneity that it thereby goes far beyond everything that sensibility can provide it, and proves its most excellent occupation by distinguishing the world of the senses and the world of the understanding from one another, thereby, however, delineating the limits of the understanding itself.[17]

On account of this, a rational being has to regard itself *as an intelligence* (thus not from the side of its lower powers), as belonging not to the world of sense but to the world of understanding; hence it has two standpoints, from which it can consider itself and cognize the laws for the use of its powers,

15. *klüger*
16. See *Critique of Pure Reason*, A84–130/B116–69.
17. See *Critique of Pure Reason*, A293–309/B349–66.

consequently all its actions: *first*, insofar as it belongs to the world of sense, under natural laws (heteronomy), and *second*, as belonging to the intelligible world, under laws which are independent of nature, not empirical, but rather grounded merely in reason.

As a rational being, hence one belonging to the intelligible world, the human being can never think of the causality of its own will otherwise than under the idea of freedom; for independence of determinate[18] causes of the world of sense (such as reason must always attribute to itself) is freedom. Now with the idea of freedom the concept of *autonomy* is inseparably bound up, but with the latter the universal principle of morality, which in the idea grounds all actions of *rational* beings just as the natural law grounds all appearances.

[Ak 4:453]

Now the suspicion has been removed that we aroused above, that there was a hidden circle contained in our inference from freedom to autonomy and from the latter to the moral law, namely that we perhaps took freedom as a ground only for the sake of the moral law in order afterward to infer the latter once again from freedom, hence that we could not offer any ground for the former, but rather only as begging a question,[19] which well-disposed souls might concede to us, but which we could never set up as a provable proposition. For now we see that if we think of ourselves as free, then we transport ourselves as members into the world of understanding and cognize the autonomy of the will, together with its[20] consequence, morality; but if we think of ourselves as obligated by duty,[21] then we consider ourselves as belonging to the world of sense and yet at the same time to the world of understanding.

How is a categorical imperative possible?

The rational being counts himself as intelligence in the world of understanding, and merely as an efficient cause belonging to this world does it call its causality a *will*. From the other side, however, it is conscious of itself also as a piece of the world of sense, in which its actions, as mere ap-

---

18. *bestimmten*; following Kant's formulation later at Ak 4:455, editors often emend this to *bestimmenden* ("determining").

19. *sondern nur als Erbittung eines Prinzips.* If there is a verb here, it is not obvious what it is; the clause might refer by parallel construction to *aufstellen könnten* ("could set up").

20. 1785: *seiner*, the most natural grammatical referent of which would have to be "will." 1786 changes this to *ihrer*, whose natural referent is "autonomy."

21. *verpflichtet*

pearances of that causality are encountered, but whose possibility from the latter, with which we have no acquaintance, is something into which we can have no insight, but rather in place of that we have to have insight into those actions as determined through other appearances, namely desires and inclinations as belonging to the world of sense. As a mere member of the world of understanding, all my actions would be perfectly in accord with the principle of the autonomy of the pure will; as a mere piece of the sensible world, they would have to be taken as entirely in accord with the natural law of desires and inclinations, hence with the heteronomy of nature. (The former would rest on the supreme principle of morality, the second on that of happiness.) But because[22] *the world of understanding contains the ground of the world of sense, hence also of its laws*, hence is immediately legislative in regard to my will (which belongs wholly to the world of understanding), and hence must also be thought of wholly as such,

[Ak 4:454] therefore as intelligence I will cognize myself, though on the other side as a being belonging to the world of sense, as nevertheless subject to the laws of the first, i.e., to reason, which in the idea of freedom contains the law of the understanding's world, and thus to autonomy of the will; consequently I must regard the laws of the world of understanding for myself as imperatives and the actions that accord with this principle as duties.

And thus categorical imperatives are possible through the fact that the idea of freedom makes me into a member of an intelligible world, through which, if I were that alone, all my actions *would* always be in accord with the autonomy of the will; but since I intuit myself at the same time as member of the world of sense, they *ought* to be in accord with it, which *categorical* 'ought' represents a synthetic proposition *a priori* by the fact that to my will affected through sensible desires there is also added the idea of precisely the same will, but one belonging to the world of understanding, a pure will, practical for itself, that contains the supreme condition of the first in accordance with reason; it is approximately in this way that concepts of the understanding, which for themselves signify nothing but lawful form in general, are added to intuitions of the world of sense and through that make possible synthetic propositions *a priori* on which rests all cognition of a nature.[23]

The practical use of common human reason confirms the correctness of this deduction. There is no one, even the most wicked scoundrel, if only he is otherwise accustomed to use his reason, who does not wish, if one lays

22. 1785: *But because* emphasized along with what follows
23. Cf. *Critique of Pure Reason*, B 162–65.

before him examples of honesty in aims, steadfastness in following good maxims, sympathetic participation, and general benevolence (and in addition combined with great sacrifices of advantage and convenience) that he might also be so disposed. But he cannot bring it about on account of his inclinations and impulses, while at the same time he wishes to be free of such burdensome inclinations. Thus through this he proves that with a will free of the impulses of sensibility, he transports himself in thoughts into entirely another order of things than that of his desires in the field of sensibility, since from that wish he can expect no gratification of desires, hence no condition that would satisfy any of his actual or even thinkable inclinations (for then the very idea that entices him to the wish would forfeit its superiority), but he can expect only a greater inner worth of his person. This better person, however, he believes himself to be when he transports [Ak 4:455] himself into the standpoint of a member of the world of understanding, to which the idea of freedom, i.e., independence of *determining* causes[24] of the sensible world, involuntarily necessitates him, and in which he is conscious of a good will, which constitutes by his own admission the law for his evil will as a member of the sensible world, the law with whose authority he becomes acquainted when he transgresses it. The moral 'ought' is thus his own necessary volition as a member of an intelligible world and is thought of by him as an 'ought' only insofar as he at the same time considers himself as a member of the sensible world.

Of the uttermost boundary of all practical philosophy

All human beings think of themselves, regarding the will, as free. Hence all judgments about actions come as if they *ought* to have *happened* even if they *have not happened.* Yet this freedom is no experiential concept, and also cannot be one, because freedom always remains even though experience shows the opposite of those requirements that are represented as necessary under the presupposition of freedom. On the other side it is just as necessary that everything that happens should remain unexceptionably determined in accordance with natural laws, and this natural necessity is also not an experiential concept, precisely because it carries with it the concept of necessity, hence of a cognition *a priori.* But this concept of a nature is confirmed through experience and must unavoidably be presupposed if experience, i.e., cognition of objects of sense connected in accordance with universal laws, is to be possible. Hence freedom is only an *idea* of reason, whose objective reality is doubtful in itself, but nature is a *concept of*

24. 1785: "to which the idea of freedom from determining causes"

understanding that proves its reality from examples in experience and necessarily must prove it.

Now although from this arises a dialectic of reason, since in regard to the will the freedom attributed to it appears to stand in contradiction with natural necessity;[25] and at this fork in the road, with a *speculative intent*, reason finds the route of natural necessity much more traveled and useful than that of freedom: yet with a *practical intent* the footpath of freedom is the only one on which it is possible to make use of one's reason for deeds and omissions; hence it is just as impossible for the subtlest philosophy as for the commonest human reason to ratiocinate freedom away. Thus the latter[26] must presuppose that no true contradiction is encountered between freedom and the natural necessity of precisely the same human actions, for it can give up the concept of nature just as little as it can that of freedom.

[Ak 4:456]

Nevertheless this seeming contradiction must be done away with at least in a convincing way, even if one could never conceive how freedom is possible. For if even the thought of freedom contradicts itself or the thought of nature, which is just as necessary, then it, as opposed to natural necessity, had to be[27] completely given up.

But it is impossible to escape this contradiction if the subject, which supposes itself free, were to think itself *in the same sense* or *in precisely the same relations* when it calls itself free as when it assumes it is subject to the natural law in regard to that very action. Hence it is an unremitting problem of speculative philosophy to show at least that its deception of a contradiction rests on the fact that we think of the human being in another sense and in other relations when we call him free than when we take him, as a piece of nature, to be subject to its law, and that both not only *can* very well stand side by side, but also that they have to be thought *as necessarily united* in the same subject, since otherwise no ground can be supplied why we should burden reason with an idea that, even if it can be united *without contradiction* with another that is satisfactorily confirmed, yet nevertheless involves us in an enterprise in which reason in its theoretical use is put in a very tight spot. This duty, however, lies merely on speculative philosophy, so that it can free the way for practical philosophy. Thus it is not put at the discretion of the philosopher whether he will remove this seeming conflict or leave it

---

25. Cf. *Critique of Pure Reason*, A532–58/B560–86.

26. *Diese*, which apparently refers to "the commonest human reason," but in the context of the entire paragraph could conceivably be taken to refer to "reason" earlier.

27. *mußte*; some editors read *müßte*, "would have to be."

untouched; for in the latter case the theory about it is *bonum vacans*,[28] and the fatalist can with grounds enter into possession of it and expel all morals from its supposed property as taken possession of without title.

Yet one can still not say that the boundary of practical philosophy begins here. For the settlement of that contest does not at all belong to it, but rather it only demands of speculative reason that it should bring to an end the disunity in which these theoretical questions involve it, so that practical reason can have tranquillity and security against external attacks that might contest the terrain on which it wants to build.   [Ak 4:457]

But the legal claim,[29] even of common human reason, on freedom of the will is grounded on the consciousness and the admitted presupposition of the independence of reason from all merely subjectively determined causes, which together constitute that which belongs merely to sensation, hence under the general term 'sensibility'. The human being who in such a wise considers himself as an intelligence sets himself thereby in another order of things, and in a relation to determinate grounds of an entirely different kind, when he thinks of himself as an intelligence with a will, consequently as endowed with causality, than when he perceives himself as a phenomenon in the world of sense (which he actually is too), and subjects his causality, regarding external determination, to natural laws. Now he soon becomes aware that both can take place at the same time, indeed even that they must. For that a *thing in its appearance* (belonging to the world of sense) is subject to certain laws, of which the very same thing *as thing* or being *in itself* is independent, contains not the least contradiction; but that he must represent and think of himself in this twofold way rests, regarding the first, on the consciousness of himself as an object affected through sense, and as far as the second goes, on the consciousness of himself as intelligence, i.e., as independent in his use of reason of sensible impressions (hence as belonging to the world of understanding).

Hence it comes about that the human being presumes to claim a will that lets nothing be put to its account that belongs merely to its desires and inclinations, and on the contrary thinks of actions through itself as possible, or indeed even as necessary, that can happen only by disregarding all desires and sensible stimuli. The causality of these actions lies in him as intelligence and in the laws of the effects and actions in accordance with principles of an intelligible world, of which he perhaps knows nothing further except that there it is solely reason, and indeed a reason that is pure

28. "vacant good," i.e., a piece of property belonging to no one

29. *Rechtsanspruch*

and independent of sensibility, that gives the law, and likewise, since in that world he himself only as intelligence is the authentic self (as human being, by contrast, only appearance of himself), those laws apply to him immediately and categorically, so that whatever inclinations and impulses (hence the entire nature of the world of sense) stimulates him to, they cannot

[Ak 4:458] infringe the laws of his volition as intelligence, even that he is not responsible to the first and does not ascribe it to his authentic self, i.e., his will, although he does ascribe to it the indulgence that it would like to bear toward them, if, to the disadvantage of the rational laws of the will, he were to concede them influence on its maxims.[30]

Through the fact that practical reason *thinks* itself into a world of understanding, it does not overstep its boundaries, but it would if it tried to *intuit* or *sense* itself *into it*.[31] The former is only a negative thought, in regard to the world of sense, which gives no laws to reason in determination of the will, and is only in this single point positive that that freedom, as a negative determination, is at the same time combined with a (positive) faculty and even with a causality of reason, which we call a 'will', so to act that the principle of the actions is in accord with the essential constitution of a rational cause, i.e., the condition of the universal validity of the maxim as a law. If, however, it were to fetch an *object of the will*, i.e., a motivation, from the world of understanding, then it would overstep its boundaries and presume to be acquainted with something of which it knows nothing. The concept of a world of the understanding is therefore only a *standpoint*, apart from appearances, which reason sees itself necessitated to take *in order to think of itself as practical*, which, if the influences of sensibility were determining for the human being, would not be possible, but which is necessary insofar as his consciousness of himself as intelligence, hence as a cause that is rational and active through reason, i.e., freely efficient, is not to be renounced. This thought obviously carries with it the idea of another order and legislation than that of the natural mechanism that pertains to the world of sense, and makes necessary the concept of an intelligible world (i.e., the whole of rational beings as things in themselves), but without the

---

30. In this sentence it is unclear whether some of the pronouns refer to "the human being" or to "his will." The present translation assumes the latter option. If one were to take the former, however, the end of the sentence should read: "i.e., his will, though he does ascribe to himself the indulgence he would like to bear toward them if, to the disadvantage of the rational laws of the will, he were to concede them influence on his maxims."

31. *wenn sie sich* hineinschauen, hineinempfinden *wollte*

least presumption here to think of them further than merely as regards their *formal* condition, i.e., the universality of the maxim of the will, as law, hence the will's[32] autonomy, which alone can subsist with freedom; whereas on the contrary, all laws that are determined to an object give heteronomy, which is encountered only in natural laws and can also pertain only to the world of sense.

But then reason would overstep all its boundaries if it undertook to *explain how* pure reason could be practical, which would be fully the same as the problem of explaining *how freedom is possible.*   [Ak 4:459]

For we can explain nothing unless we can trace it back to laws the object of which can be given in some possible experience. But freedom is a mere idea, whose objective reality can in no wise be established in accordance with natural laws, hence also not in any possible experience; for the same reason, because no example may ever be attributed to freedom itself in accordance with any analogy, freedom can never be comprehended, nor even can insight into it be gained. It is valid only as a necessary presupposition of reason in a being that believes itself to be conscious of a will, i.e., of a faculty varying from a mere faculty of desire (namely, of determining itself to action as an intelligence, hence in accordance with laws of reason, independently of natural instincts). But where the determination in accordance with natural laws ceases, there too ceases all *explanation*, and there is nothing left over except *defense*, i.e., aborting the objections of those who pretend to have looked deeper into the essence of things and therefore brazenly declare[33] freedom to be impossible. One can only show them that the presumed contradiction they have found in it lies elsewhere, since in order to make the natural law valid in regard to human actions, they necessarily have to consider the human being as appearance, and now when one demands of them that they should also think of him as intelligence, also[34] as thing in itself, they are still considering him as appearance, to which obviously the separation of his causality (i.e., of his will) from all natural laws of the world of sense in one and the same subject would stand in contradiction, but that contradiction goes away if they would keep in mind, and even

32. *als Gesetze, mithin der Autonomie des letzteren*; the referent of the last term would have to be "will" (singular), but the apparent antecedent is plural. Some editors therefore amend *Gesetze* to *Gesetz*.

33. *erklären*; so the clause could also be translated: "brazenly explain freedom as impossible."

34. 1785: "as intelligence, but"

admit, as is only fair,[35] that behind appearances things in themselves (though hidden) must ground them, and one cannot demand of their effective laws that they should be the same as those under which their appearances stand.

The subjective impossibility of *explaining*[36] the freedom of the will is the same as the impossibility of bringing to light and making comprehensible an *interest* * that the human being could take in moral laws; and nevertheless he actually does take an interest in them, the foundation of which in us we call 'moral feeling', which is falsely given out by some as the standard of our moral judgment, since it has to be regarded rather as the *subjective* effect that the law exercises on the will, for which reason alone provides the objective grounds.

In order for a sensibly affected rational being to will that which reason alone prescribes the 'ought', there obviously must belong to it a faculty of reason to *instill a feeling of pleasure* or satisfaction in the fulfillment of duty, hence a causality of reason to determine sensibility in accordance with its principles. It is entirely impossible, however, to gain insight, i.e., to make comprehensible *a priori*, how a mere thought that contains nothing sensible in it would produce a sensation of pleasure or displeasure; for that is a particular kind of causality, of which, as of all causality, we can determine nothing at all *a priori*, but rather we have to ask experience alone about it. But since experience can provide no relation of cause to effect except that between two objects of experience, but here pure reason, through mere ideas (which yield no object at all for experience), ought to be the cause of an effect

[Ak 4:460]

[Ak4:459]

[Ak4:460]

* 'Interest' is that through which reason becomes practical, i.e., becomes a cause determining the will. Hence one says only of a rational being that it takes an interest in something; creatures without reason only feel sensible impulses. Reason takes an immediate interest in an action only when the universal validity of its maxim is a sufficient determining ground of the will. Such an interest is alone pure. But if it can determine the will only by means of another object of desire or under the presupposition of a particular feeling of the subject, then reason takes only a mediated interest in the action, and since reason for itself alone without experience can bring to light neither objects of the will nor a feeling grounding it, the latter interest would be only empirical and not a pure rational interest. The logical interest of reason (to promote its insights) is never immediate but presupposes aims of its use.

35. *billig*

36. *erklären*, which could also be translated here as "defining"

which obviously lies in experience, it is entirely impossible for us human beings to have an explanation how and why the *universality of the maxim as a law*, hence morality, should interest us. Only this much is certain: that it does not have validity for us *because it interests* us (for that is heteronomy and dependency of practical reason on sensibility, namely a feeling grounding it, which could never be morally legislative), but rather that it interests us because it is valid for us as human beings, since it has arisen from our will as intelligence, hence from our authentic self; *but what belongs to the mere appearance is necessarily subordinated by reason to the constitution of the thing in itself.* [Ak 4:461]

Thus the question 'How is a categorical imperative possible?' can be answered to this extent: one can state the sole presupposition under which alone it is possible, namely the idea of freedom, and to the extent that one can have insight into the necessity of this presupposition, which is sufficient for the *practical use* of reason, i.e., for the conviction of the *validity of this imperative*, hence also of the moral law; but how this presupposition itself is possible, no insight into that can be gained through any human reason. Under the presupposition of freedom of the will, its *autonomy*, as the formal condition under which alone it can be determined, is a necessary consequence. To presuppose this freedom of the will is also not only (as speculative philosophy can show) entirely *possible* (without falling into contradiction to the principle of natural necessity in the connection of appearances in the world of sense), but it is also without any further condition *necessary* to impute[37] to it practically all its voluntary[38] actions, i.e., necessary as condition in the idea, to a rational being, who is conscious of its causality through reason, hence of its will (which is distinguished from desires). But now *how* pure reason can for itself be practical, without any other incentive that might be taken from anywhere else, i.e., how the mere *principle of the universal validity of all its maxims as laws* (which obviously would be the form of a pure practical reason), without any material (object) of the will in which one might previously take any interest, should for itself yield an incentive and effect an interest that would be called purely *moral* — or in other words, *how pure reason could be practical* — all human reason is entirely incapable of explaining that, and all the effort and labor spent in seeking an explanation are lost.

It is precisely the same as if I sought to get to the ground of how freedom

37. *unterzulegen*
38. *willkürlich*

[Ak 4:462] itself, as the causality of a will, is possible. For there I forsake the philosophical ground of explanation and have no other. Now of course I could enthuse about[39] in the intelligible world that is left over to me, in the world of intelligences; but although I have an *idea* of it, which has its own good ground, I still have not the least *acquaintance* with it and also can never reach one through every striving of my natural faculty of reason. It signifies only a 'something' that is left over if I have excluded everything from the determining grounds of my will that belongs to the world of sense, merely in order to limit the principle of motivation from the field of sensibility, by setting boundaries to it and showing that it does not embrace all in all, but that outside that principle I am still more; but I am not any further acquainted with this 'more'. Of pure reason, which thinks this ideal, there is left over to me to be thought, after the separation of all matter, i.e., the cognition of objects, only the form, namely the practical law of the universal validity of maxims, and in accord with this, reason in reference to a pure world of understanding as possible efficient cause, i.e., as determining the will; here the incentive has to be entirely lacking; it would have to be this idea of an intelligible world itself that is the incentive, or that in which reason originally would take an interest; but to make this comprehensible is precisely the problem that we cannot solve.

Now here is the supreme boundary of all moral inquiry; to determine it, however, is already of great importance, so that, on the one side, reason, in a way harmful to morality, does not look around in the world of sense for the supreme motivation and for a comprehensible but empirical interest, but on the other side, so that, in what for it is the empty space of transcendent concepts, under the name of the intelligible world, it does not beat its wings powerlessly, without moving from the spot and losing itself among figments of the mind. Besides, the idea of a pure world of the understanding, as a whole of all intelligences, to which we belong as rational beings (though on the other side at the same time members of the world of sense) is always a usable and permissible idea on behalf of a rational faith,[40] even if at its boundary all knowledge has an end, in order to effect a lively interest in the moral law in us through the splendid ideal of a universal realm of *ends in themselves* (rational beings), to which we can belong as members only when [Ak 4:463] we carefully conduct ourselves in accordance with maxims of freedom as though they were laws of nature.

---

39. *herumschwärmen*
40. *Glaubens;* see *Critique of Pure Reason*, A820–31/B848–59.

Concluding remark

The speculative use of reason, *in regard to nature*, leads to the absolute necessity of some supreme cause *of the world*; the practical use of reason, *in regard to freedom*, also leads to absolute necessity, but only *of the laws of actions* of a rational being as such. Now it is an essential *principle* of every use of our reason to drive its cognition to the consciousness of its *necessity* (for without this it would not be cognition of reason). But it is also just as essential a *limitation* of precisely the same reason, that it can gain no insight either into the necessity of what exists or what happens, or into that which ought to happen, unless grounded on a *condition* under which it exists, or happens, or ought to happen. In this wise, however, the satisfaction of reason is always deferred through the constant questioning after the condition.[41] Hence it seeks restlessly the unconditionally necessary and sees itself necessitated to assume it, without any means of making it comprehensible; it is fortunate enough if it can only discover the concept that is compatible with this presupposition. Thus it is no fault of our deduction of the supreme principle of morality, but only an accusation that one would have to make against human reason in general, that it cannot make comprehensible an unconditioned practical law (such as the categorical imperative must be) as regards its absolute necessity; for we cannot hold it against reason that it does not will to do this through a condition, namely by means of any interest that grounds it, because otherwise it would not be a moral, i.e., a supreme, law of freedom. And thus we indeed do not comprehend the practical unconditioned necessity of the moral imperative, but we do comprehend its *incomprehensibility*, which is all that can be fairly required of a philosophy that strives in principles up to the boundary of human reason.

41. Cf. *Critique of Pure Reason*, A310–40/B366–98, A408–20/B435–48, A497–515/B525–43.

Rethinking
Groundwork
for the
Metaphysics
of Morals

Why Study Kant's Ethics?

J. B. SCHNEEWIND

Kant's *Groundwork for the Metaphysics of Morals* is a very hard book to understand. Those of us who have put this volume together plainly think it's worth trying to do so. Why? There are three reasons.

First, Kant created a dramatically new way of thinking about morality and about ourselves as moral beings. He held that all previous attempts to spell out the principles of ethics had been mistaken. In the *Groundwork* he presented the fundamentals of a different vision of morality. And in later writings he showed how to work out the details of morality using his new formulation of its basis. To understand Kant's ethics historically is to come to see the emergence of a major new option in Western thought.

Second, Kant's ethical thought has been profoundly influential. It is one of the two or three most important contributions that modern moral philosophers have made to our culture. The *Groundwork* has always been the main text used to learn about Kant's ethics. Anyone who wants to understand the history of nineteenth- and twentieth-century moral philosophy and its importance for society has to understand this book.

Third, the positions Kant took in the *Groundwork* are very much alive in moral philosophy today. A renewal of scholarship, commentary, and philosophical discussion concerning the book began around the middle of the last century.[1] Many misunderstandings have been cleared away, and Kant's other writings on ethics have been brought in to illuminate this one. New philosophical insights from recent work are being used to show the depth and importance of what Kant said. Kantian views of morality are a central topic of contemporary moral philosophy. In developing Kant's positions to bring out their pertinence today, advocates of Kantian views depart more or less from what he himself actually said. But an understanding of the *Groundwork* is indispensable for anyone who wants to take part in current discussions of ethics.

These are strong claims about the importance of a short book. It would take another book, and a longer one, to support them all. Here I will try first to sketch Kant's epoch-making break with the past and then to indicate some of the developments underlying his importance for contemporary moral philosophy.

I. Kant's Historical Revolution

Two quotations will get us going. The first comes from St. Thomas Aquinas, the great thirteenth-century synthesizer of Roman Catholic doctrine. The second is from Kant.

> Law directs the actions of those that are subject to the government of someone. Hence, properly speaking, none imposes a law on his own actions.   (*Summa Theologiae* IaIIae 93.5)

> The rational being must always consider itself as giving law in a realm of ends . . . Morality thus consists in the reference of all action to that legislation through which alone a realm of ends is possible. But the legislation must be encountered in every rational being itself, and be able to arise from its will.   (G 4:434)

Aquinas and Kant agree that morality centrally involves law and obedience to law. Both could agree with an important passage in St. Paul's Epistle to the Romans (2:14–15): "when the Gentiles, which have not the law, do by nature the things contained in the law, these, which have not the law, are a law unto themselves: Which shew the works of the law written in their hearts, their conscience also bearing witness." The gentiles do not have the written Jewish law, but they find an unwritten law in their hearts or consciences. For Aquinas, the law is put there by God. He finds it unthinkable that human beings might legislate the moral law that we are all to obey. Kant thinks that our own reason gives us the law. Morality can be understood only if we see that each of us is equally a lawgiving member of the group of those who must also obey the moral law. He holds that each of us is both to legislate the law and to obey it.

Kant's remark comes from a part of the *Groundwork* in which he introduces the term 'autonomy' to indicate what is distinctive about his own view. The word had long been current in political discussions. An autonomous state was one that ruled itself. It could make its own laws without asking permission from rulers of other states. Kant took the term from political discourse and changed its meaning. He applied it to individuals and to the morality that ought to govern the relations of persons to themselves and to one another, regardless of the political laws under which they lived. He said that morality is a human creation. It is the legislation that comes from our own rational will.

We can see what a radical innovation this was by looking briefly at the history of moral philosophy. Ancient thought about ethics from Socrates to the time of St. Augustine centered on the question of human flourishing (a translation of the Greek *eudaimonia*). What is the best life for a human? Classical philosophers all thought that having good relations with others constituted a major part of the kind of life anyone would want to live. Consequently they held that in pursuing a good life for ourselves we would not only have to control our own passions and desires; we would also have to act thoughtfully and justly toward others. On this view virtue and happiness are inseparable.

Christianity gave a new twist to the search for a good life. Our ultimate good, theologians held, is to be found in a loving union with God. God made us so that we all seek such a union. We may not realize that that is what we want. But we are always dissatisfied with earthly goods. And this dissatisfaction shows that the pagans were wrong to think that we might find happiness in the present life. Moreover we are deeply flawed and sinful beings. We ought to live in loving friendship with other people. But we are dominated by selfish desires. Morality teaches us what we ought to do, but we find in ourselves a stubborn resistance to doing it. Instead we seek what we misguidedly think is our own individual good. We must be made to obey God's laws by threats of punishment. Morality thus becomes something external to our own nature — at least to our fallen nature. It does not come from within us, emerging as our own concern in the course of our natural development. It has to be imposed on us.

What is God's relation to the laws he imposes on all human beings — the laws of nature, as they came to be called? Aquinas held that God's intellect is the source of these laws. God commands us to obey them because he knows that they contain the core of justice and virtue. Two other medieval thinkers, Duns Scotus and William of Ockham, proposed an alternative. God is inscrutable and beyond human understanding, and he imposes on us whatever laws he chooses. The laws of nature contain the core of justice and virtue simply because God wills that we obey them. Later historians labeled these positions "intellectualism" and "voluntarism." Both positions were very much a part of arguments about morality with which Kant was familiar. Martin Luther's teaching derived from the thought of the medieval voluntarists, and Kant was raised a Lutheran. The German philosopher

Leibniz and his follower Christian Wolff were strongly opposed to voluntarism, and Kant learned Wolff's views from his first philosophy teachers.

Luther puts his view bluntly and forcefully: "God is he for whose will no cause or ground may be laid down as its rule and standard; for nothing is on a level with it or above it . . . What God wills is not right because he ought or was bound so to will; on the contrary, what takes place must be right, because he so wills."[2] This side of Lutheran teaching has a prominent place in the thought of Samuel Pufendorf, whose work on natural law was studied throughout Europe for over a century after its publication in 1672. His central point is simple. Christianity, as St. Paul shows, teaches that morality is obedience to law. Law is the command of a superior, and only God's commands can establish a morality for all humans. But then there cannot be moral requirements binding God, because — obviously — God can have no superior. It follows that there can be no morality common to God and humans. Pufendorf ridicules the very idea. "For who," he asks, "dare reason thus? Pay your debts, because God pays his. Be grateful, because God is kind to them that serve him . . . Honor your parents, because God honors his. Are not these reasonings manifestly absurd?"[3]

Pufendorf expresses what was then a widespread Christian feeling: we should humbly adore and obey God even if we do not understand him. Morality is simply obedience. There were many other Christians who found this position deeply disturbing. It puts God in the position of a tyrant and makes us into servile subjects. But Christ taught that the essence of the law is love: we are to love God above all and our neighbor as ourselves. And a Pufendorfian God, who lays down arbitrary laws and gives no rationale for them, is not, the critics said, a God who can be loved. If we are to love God we must understand his moral commands as expressions of his love for us. It must be possible for us to understand morality as common to God and ourselves, however mysterious other aspects of God's activity may be. If we govern ourselves by following laws that we see are just and right, we will be acting as nearly in God's way as we can. This is what it means to say that we are made in God's image. It seemed impossible for the voluntarists to explain how this could be so.

In Kant's time there were very few atheists. Most people not only believed in God but also agreed that he was somehow indispensable for morality. The Scots philosopher David Hume was an exception. He developed a view of morality in which God played no role. He saw human feelings as the source of morality. Purely natural explanations could be given of those feelings. And there is nothing about us that takes us out of the realm of nature. We must see ourselves and our morality as causally determined parts of a causally determined nature.

Hume's view avoided the problems of the relation of God to morality, but it seemed to many people to deprive humans of any special dignity or worth. For Hume, we are only a kind of animal — cleverer than the rest, but otherwise not very different from them. Religious believers could not see morality in this way. They could not accept the idea that the natural world is the only world there is. We must belong to a supernatural spiritual world, they held, in which God is supreme. They therefore had to face the problem of how to preserve human dignity in a universe governed by the kind of God they could not give up.

The intellectualists thought that the voluntarists could not solve the problem but that they themselves could. If we can know the eternal truth about morality and are able to bring ourselves to follow its directives just from concern for righteousness, then we are self-governed. We have a special relation to God. We are the only part of his creation that can obey his laws just because we know what they are. It is because of our knowledge — especially our moral knowledge — that we are entitled to think that we are made in God's image.

Some intellectualists held that there are eternal self-evident principles governing morality. They compared such principles to the axioms of geometry. God knows the moral axioms and so do we. God necessarily governs himself by them. When we have an intuitive grasp of the moral axioms and work out how they apply to the case at hand, we are self-governed when we act as they direct. Other intellectualists made no appeal to such intuitively evident axioms. They held that God always acts for the best. He created the most perfect possible universe, and we are to be like him. We are to bring about the most perfect results we can. To do so we need to know which of the options before us will bring about the greatest increase in perfection. We are self-governed when we know what is best and decide to bring it into existence. Both sorts of intellectualists rejected purely naturalistic theories of the world and used their moral philosophies as part of their defense of a religious outlook.

Kant rejected Hume's naturalism and insisted that we are not merely natural beings, like the animals. Morality itself shows us that we have free will. Kant shared the intellectualists' aim of defending human dignity and argued that free will gives it to us. But he feared that the intellectualists were all too likely to think that only people with superior minds could be morally good. The moral feelings that Hume saw as central could be shared equally by everyone, but plainly some people are much smarter than others. Does it follow that moral knowledge is not equally available to everyone alike? It is hard to understand geometry; it may be equally hard for many to understand morality. It would also be difficult for most people to calculate which among the choices before them will bring about the greatest increase in perfection. In either case not everyone can be self-governed. Most people will have to obey the few who knew the truth about morality. This was a view that Christian Wolff held. Kant found it abhorrent. Hume's reliance on sentiment was part of a naturalistic view that Kant rejected. A purely intellectualist morality apparently led to an elitism that he also found unacceptable. He thus seemed to be forced into a voluntarist view. But Kant rejected the servile attitude that seemed to go with that theory. His new idea of the autonomy of the will gave him a way to resolve this complex problem. He accepted the voluntarist claim that morality stems from will, but he transformed the conception of will by making it into a special form of rationality —practical rationality. He could then say that because the will is itself rational it contains a law within it, governing all its activities. We do not need to grasp eternal truths or to calculate complex consequences. A simple formula governs our legislative activity. It enables us to test our plans for action and to reject some and accept others. And just as we can think out for ourselves what we ought to do, so we can motivate ourselves to do it. We do not need rewards or threats from others to make us act morally. God's will and ours are alike in these respects. What God necessarily wills is what we ought to will. We and God are fellow legislators of a single moral community. We are equal to God, not merely his servile subjects, because of our moral autonomy.

II. Kant's Current Importance

The conception of morality as autonomy was Kant's fundamental innovation in moral philosophy. In working out his vision of humans as autonomous agents Kant developed new ideas about freedom and the nature of action that are still being discussed. His view also had important implications for longstanding positions about the structure and content of morality. One of these implications accounts for much of the significance of Kantianism in current discussions. It is that no principle of human happiness can be the foundation of morality or show its point. Utilitarianism is the label most commonly applied to views that make happiness central to morality. Kantianism is opposed to all such views.

Kant never denied the importance of happiness. He criticized the Stoics for thinking that the pleasure of self-approval arising from awareness of living a virtuous life was happiness enough for human beings. Happiness is the satisfaction of desire, he held, and he insisted that finite beings such as we are need to have our desires satisfied. He held it to be an important duty for each of us to help others achieve happiness as they understood it. But he denied that morality is simply the set of virtues or directives that lead to happiness, either our own or that of everyone affected. He held that morality has a different role in our lives. Morality's function is to set the limits within which it is permissible for us to seek our own happiness and to help others pursue theirs.

Kant had several reasons for rejecting a morality of happiness. One of them is this. We have little if any control over what desires we have. To say that what we ought to do is determined by what people want is to subordinate ourselves to our causally determined nature. It is, in other words, to abandon our autonomy. But the moral law forbids us to do so. More generally, Kant thinks that we cannot accept any morality holding that the goods relevant to deciding what to do are made good, and can be known to be good, without any appeal to what is morally right or obligatory. Kant holds, against this, that only pleasures and pains that are allowed by the moral law are morally relevant. In order for a pleasure to count as relevant in deciding what to do, it must be one that can be obtained by a morally permissible act. So there must be a way of determining what acts are permissible or impermissible prior to knowing what goods in the situation are morally relevant. And Kant thought, of course, that there is such a way. The categorical imperative tells us whether or not we may act on any plan of action, and from this we can learn what acts we may or may not do.

Kantianism is thus an alternative to utilitarianism. It is not the only one. Various forms of intuitionism hold that we can grasp a number of self-evident moral truths by which to guide our actions. One of these truths tells us to be benevolent, or to help others attain happiness, but that is not the only principle. We are also to tell the truth, keep promises, and be just. Principles like these may come into conflict with the principle that tells us to increase the happiness of others. And it is far from self-evident that in cases of such conflict benevolence ought always to win out.

Intuitionism often seems to be the best account available of the commonsense morality that most of us share. We don't come to philosophy with some single universal principle that we use to get answers to all our moral questions. And we do seem to think that it's just obvious that we should keep promises, tell the truth, help others in need, be just, and so on. Yet intuitionism has defects. It doesn't suggest any mode of reasoning for settling controversies with other people about what to do. And it doesn't give us any way of criticizing our pretheoretical moral convictions. Yet we know that people in the past have thought it "just obvious" that women should obey men, that people of color were inferior to white people, and that gay and lesbian practices were abhorrent and unnatural. It's hard to escape the thought that some of our "obvious" beliefs might be as benighted as these. But how can we tell?

One appeal of utilitarianism and of Kantianism is that each promises a way of arguing about moral disagreements and of criticizing socially accepted moral beliefs. During much of the nineteenth century British and American philosophers took utilitarianism and intuitionism to be the major alternatives in moral theory. Kant played little if any role in English-language ethics. And during much of the twentieth century English-language moral philosophers did not discuss the substantive issues of morality. They were concerned rather with whether moral beliefs were susceptible of rational proof. Was morality, as Hume held, simply a matter of sentiment? If it was rational, in what way? Was moral language used to express thought that could be true or false, or was it, rather, used just to express emotions?

These debates took place against the background of a widely shared assumption that utilitarianism captured the content or substance of morality, whether morality rested on reason or on feeling. Many philosophers were convinced, however, that utilitarianism led to morally unacceptable conclusions. But to oppose it they had little but intuitions or strong convictions. The first major effort to go beyond intuitionism and provide a systematic alternative to utilitarianism was John Rawls's *A Theory of Justice* (1971). Rawls presented a way of arguing in support of principles of justice that did not derive them from the good consequences that would follow from obeying them. Instead his principles could be used to determine the relevance of alleged goods and harms to moral decisions. He asserted what is now called "the priority of the right to the good," and he linked this strongly with Kant's moral views.

Rawls's work led to a great deal of constructive philosophical interest in Kant's ethics. Building on the scholarly work that had been published since the 1940s, American and British philosophers produced a substantial body of work influenced strongly by Kant's moral thought. New interpretations of almost every aspect of Kant's ethics were soon followed by important works applying Kant's insights to contemporary problems, such as world hunger. The English-language moral philosophy of the past decades has revolved to a large extent around controversies concerning Kantian moral philosophy. Kant's views continue to vitalize discussions. And their source is largely in the text of this volume.

NOTES

1. H. J. Paton's *The Categorical Imperative* (London: Hutchinson, 1947) is a landmark in the modern revitalization of Kant scholarship. It was preceded by a few German contributions. John Rawls's *A Theory of Justice* (Cambridge, Mass.: Harvard University Press, 1971) showed how much some Kantian ideas could be used to help with current issues. Much of the current discussion of Kantian ethics reflects developments of Rawls's ideas.

2. *Martin Luther: Selections from His Writings*, ed. John Dillenberger (Garden City, N.Y.: Doubleday, 1962), pp. 195–96.

3. Quoted in J. B. Schneewind, *The Invention of Autonomy* (New York: Cambridge University Press, 1998), p. 140.

Acting from Duty

MARCIA BARON

Readers of the *Groundwork* are often taken aback by Kant's discussion of acting from duty and moral worth. This reaction is not new. In 1796 Friedrich Schiller wryly expressed his distaste for what he took to be Kant's position:

> Scruples of Conscience
> I like to serve my friends, but unfortunately I do it with inclination
> And so often I am bothered by the thought that I am not virtuous.
> Decision
> There is no other way but this! You must seek to despise them,
> And do with repugnance what duty bids you.[1]

Schiller apparently read Kant as holding that if one does something nice for someone, and does it with inclination, one is not virtuous. This is an extension of a more understandable misreading of the First Section of the *Groundwork*. Kant definitely does hold that actions have moral worth only if they are done from duty, and if one thinks that he also holds that an action does not count as "done from duty" if the agent had (at the time of the action) an inclination so to act, one will conclude that he holds that an action can have moral worth only if the agent acted against her inclinations.

Because Kant discusses only instances of acting from duty that are contrary to inclination (or at least unsupported by inclination), it is easy to think that only acts that are contrary to inclination can be done from duty. But the reason he discusses only these cases of acting from duty is that he needs examples in which it is as evident as it can be that the person *is* acting from duty. It is evident if the action lacks any other incentive. It is not in the person's interest, and he lacks any inclination so to act, so he must be acting from duty. In the *Critique of Practical Reason* Kant likens the philosopher who arranges an experiment to "distinguish the moral (pure) determining ground from the empirical" to the chemist (KpV 5:92). "The purity of the moral principle," he writes, "can be clearly shown only by removing from the incentive of the action everything which men might count as a part of happiness" (KpV 5:156). This is precisely what he has done in his examples at G 4:397–99. He has "arranged an experiment" to distinguish the moral determining ground from the empirical.

Intuitively this makes sense. Think about when it is clearest that someone's motivation is purely moral: it is when the person is under pressure to act in a way that she sees to be immoral. Insofar as we believe that she has no incentive to do x other than the belief that it would be wrong not to do x, we regard her as acting morally (in the strong sense, meaning not only that she is not acting wrongly, but also that her motivation is purely or quintessentially moral).

In thinking about Kant's examples at G 4:397–99, we need to keep in mind the context of his discussion of acting from duty. Kant embarks on that discussion in order to develop the concept of a good will.[2] The concept of duty "contains that of a good will, though under certain subjective limitations and hindrances."[3] To explicate this concept he puts before us examples in which it is absolutely clear that the agent is acting from duty, and to this end he constructs the examples in such a way that other explanations of the agent's conduct — self-interest, a desire to please others, or just a warmhearted desire to lessen another's unhappiness — are not available. In a more typical case it would be less clear whether the agent is acting from duty or from some inclination, but his aim is not to present typical cases. Once we understand his aim, the impression that he was saying that acting from duty precludes having an inclination to the action begins to fade.

Further evidence that acting from duty does not preclude having an inclination to act accordingly (and doesn't require that, on balance, one's inclinations favor acting contrary to duty) comes from Kant's remarks at G 4:397 on the difficulty of discerning whether an action was done from duty if the subject has an inclination so to act.[4] If having an inclination to do x were incompatible with doing x from duty, how could there be any difficulty? It would be clear from the fact that the agent had this inclination that the action was not done from duty. That it is not clear, according to Kant, indicates that acting with such an inclination is compatible with acting from duty.[5]

I

Even if they acknowledge that Kant is not saying that only acts contrary to inclination can be done from duty, many readers will nonetheless find

Kant's position on acting from duty troubling. For what he clearly *does* hold is that acting from inclination, no matter how laudable the inclination, is in some important way not as good — not as morally worthy — as acting from duty. This seems strange, and it is disturbing to many people, even though they fully understand that one can act from duty without gritting her teeth, hating what she is doing, resenting having to do it, and so on. It is disturbing for two reasons.

First, surely it is better to enjoy helping the needy than not to. Yet the reader of the *Groundwork* is left with the impression that it does not add anything at all, that it does not make it better. As long as one acts from duty, it doesn't seem to matter to Kant whether one does it with gritted teeth or does it with pleasure. This is disturbing. Surely helping from duty with pleasure is better than helping from duty with gritted teeth. Yet it seems that on Kant's view — at least as it comes across in the *Groundwork* — it makes no difference.

The second reason why it is disturbing is this. Compare two people. One helps because she wants to; the other helps from duty and also wants to. To many readers it seems that there is nothing superior about the conduct of the second person. Yet Kant undeniably holds that the conduct of the second person has moral worth, while that of the first person does not. Why? What is so great about acting from duty?

II

Let us consider these two concerns in turn. To make the first concern clearer, let me offer an example. I recently helped an acquaintance by taking care of her child for a few afternoons when she was undergoing chemotherapy. When she thanked me, I didn't say, "Think nothing of it. We all have to do our duty," but something more along the lines of "I was glad I could help." Why does the first seem inappropriate, and what, if anything, does the fact that it seems inappropriate tell us?

One reason it would be inappropriate to say "We all have to do our duty" in response to an expression of thanks has to do with how we usually understand the word 'duty'. We think of duty as something imposed on us, something that we may well not endorse. We associate the word 'duty' with legal requirements, requirements of one's role (e.g., as a parent) or one's office (e.g., treasurer), requirements of one's job (to hold office hours), requirements of those who are members of a club (to pay dues), and expectations, which may not quite rise to the level of requirements, of members of a club or an academic department, or residents of a neighborhood. If I live in a town in which it is required by law that we remove the snow from the sidewalk in front of our homes, it is my duty to shovel my walk (or arrange for someone else to do so); if I live in a neighborhood in which we all do this and expect one another to do so, here, too, I may regard it as my duty. In each case I need not endorse it. I may think the law silly, or wish that I lived in a neighborhood in which a more laissez-faire attitude toward snow removal prevailed. To say "We all have to do our duty" in reply to an expression of gratitude suggests that this is something I did not exactly choose to do but felt pressured to do.

It is important to understand that 'duty' *(Pflicht)* in Kant's ethics is tied not to social expectations or laws, but to rationality. 'Duty' for Kant means, roughly, what one would do if one were fully rational. We are rational beings, but we are to be contrasted with those beings — if we can imagine such creatures — with "holy wills." Beings with holy wills cannot do other than what reason prescribes.[6] We, by contrast, feel the tug of inclinations, which not infrequently are at odds with reason. Hence we — rational beings whose wills are not and cannot be holy — experience the sense of duty as a constraint, because we are pulled toward what reason demands and toward what our inclinations urge. To do our duty is not to give in to social expectations but to do what reason requires (which may or may not be the same thing).

One reason, then, why it is inappropriate to say "We all have to do our duty" in response to an expression of gratitude has to do with connotations of 'duty' in ordinary speech, connotations that have no bearing on Kant's conception of duty.

A related reason why it is inappropriate is that in general when one does a favor for another and is thanked for it, it is inappropriate to draw attention to the effort one expended on behalf of the other, or to dwell on it if the other draws attention to it. If someone thanks me for a present and says, "That's too generous!" it wouldn't do to say, "It was a lot of money and a lot of effort and I was horribly busy then so didn't really have the time, but after all you are a good friend." Or if a friend comes to visit and I throw a party for her and she thanks me and says, "I really appreciate it. I can see it must have taken a lot of work," I should not say in reply (unless perhaps in pure and clear jest), "It sure did, and I'm utterly exhausted, so I'm glad you appreciate it." We can see from reflecting on these exchanges that the inappropriateness of saying, "We all have to do our duty" tells us nothing at all that indicates that acting from duty is in some way objectionable. It only reflects the fact that a certain graciousness, even modesty (in the form of not drawing attention to or dwelling on the effort to which one went for one's friend), is in order in such situations.

But this only partly answers the worry. The issue is not only what the benefactor *says* to the recipient, but also the benefactor's *attitude* (even if not conveyed to the recipient). It is not just that it is undesirable that one *disclose* to the recipient that she found it to be quite a burden. That she found it to be such a burden is itself not good. And so the point remains: it is preferable that the person who does us a favor does it with pleasure rather than simply because she sees it to be her duty. This need not mean unalloyed pleasure or pleasure free of ambivalence. We might prefer that, too — that a friend do us a favor with unalloyed pleasure — but that is not a preference that moral theory should strive to accommodate. (Why shouldn't my friend be ambivalent about spending two hours driving me to the airport, or giving up a delicious stretch of free time to visit me in the hospital? I would have to be extremely self-centered to think that she is wanting as a friend — or, even more implausibly, as a person — if she is ambivalent.) But a preference that people aid us with pleasure rather than without does not seem petty or self-centered or in any other way an unreasonable or unworthy preference. There is no getting around it: the character of someone who helps with pleasure — and, more generally, who acts from duty with pleasure — seems clearly to be better, *ceteris paribus*, than the character of one who acts from duty without pleasure. Can Kant recognize this, or is his view of moral motivation and character at odds with it?

To determine this we need to look at Kant's other works. There is nothing in the *Groundwork* that suggests that he does not or cannot recognize this (that is, nothing that suggests that his view of moral motivation and character is at odds with it), but there is also nothing to suggest that he does. The work to look at is the *Metaphysics of Morals*, for which the *Groundwork for the Metaphysics of Morals* was, as the title indicates, intended to be the foundation.

Kant indicates at a number of points in the *Metaphysics of Morals* that a person who acts from duty would ordinarily act with pleasure. Certainly a virtuous person would.

> The rules for practicing virtue . . . aim at a frame of mind that is *valiant* and *cheerful* in fulfilling its duties. . . . What is not done with pleasure but merely as compulsory service has no inner worth for one who attends to his duty in this way and such service is not loved by him;

instead, he shirks as much as possible occasions for practicing virtue. (MS 6:484)

The context in which the passage occurs bears mention. The quotation is from a section of the *Metaphysics of Morals* titled "Ethical Ascetics," in which Kant argues that the picture of the cultivation of virtue that takes as its motto the Stoic saying "Accustom yourself *to put up with* the misfortunes of life that may happen and *to do without* its superfluous pleasures" is defective. Kant explains: "This is a kind of *regimen* . . . for keeping a man healthy. But *health* is only a negative kind of well-being. . . . Something must be added to it . . . This is the ever-cheerful heart, according to the idea of the virtuous *Epicurus*" (MS 6:484–85).[7] It is part of being virtuous that one takes pleasure in life and in living as one does, i.e., takes pleasure in helping others, developing one's talents, and so on.

When we turn to Kant's discussion of specific virtues and vices, there, too, it is evident that he does not regard the sentiments with which we act as a matter of indifference. We have a duty, he says, to cultivate our compassionate impulses (susceptibility to which "Nature has already implanted" in us [MS 6:456]).[8] We also have duties of gratitude (MS 6:455)[9] and duties not to be envious (MS 6:459) and not to gloat over others' misfortunes (MS 6:460). "To rejoice immediately in the existence of such *enormities* destroying what is best in the world as a whole, and so also to wish for them to happen, is secretly to hate human beings; and this is the direct opposite of love for our neighbor, which is incumbent on us as a duty" (MS 6:460). It is also a duty to be forgiving (but not to tolerate wrongs meekly or to renounce rigorous means for preventing the recurrence of wrongs by others [MS 6:461]).

Reading only the *Groundwork*, it is easy to get the impression that sentiments do not matter (or, worse, that they matter only negatively, as obstacles to acting as we should). We need to bear in mind that the aim of *Groundwork for the Metaphysics of Morals* is simply to lay the groundwork for the later work. My point is not only that the *Metaphysics of Morals* presents the final form of Kant's ethics, the fully developed theory — although I think it does.[10] Given the particular task of the *Groundwork*, it is no wonder that we find little there about sentiments, and that what we do find underscores their irrelevance, or their lack of "standing." The main task of the *Groundwork* is to seek out and establish the supreme principle of morality and to show that it can and must have a purely nonempirical foundation. Hence the insignificance of emotions and sentiments to morality is much more apparent in that work than is their significance. They do not play any role in grounding morality,[11] and so we hear little about them in that work — except what they do not do.

Before turning to the second objection to Kant's discussion of acting from duty, I want to mention a common misunderstanding, related to the one noted above, that may lie behind the view that Kant is unable to recognize that acting from duty with pleasure is better than acting from duty with gritted teeth. It is sometimes supposed that as Kant sees it, someone who acts from duty has as his purpose simply "duty" (whatever that would mean). On this mistaken view, whereas the person who helps another just because he wants to cares about the other's happiness, the person who helps from duty is indifferent to it, caring only about doing his duty. The first is seen as having as his purpose to help the other; the second is seen as having as his purpose only to do his duty. The temptation to draw a sharp division between caring about doing one's duty and caring about the content of that duty can be explained only by an error noted earlier, that of thinking that duty *(Pflicht)* in Kantian ethics is something imposed on us from without. That error may lead us to think that to care about doing one's duty is to care about pleasing an authority figure, getting "brownie points," or maintaining social respectability. But since duty is something that the agent rationally endorses, it would hardly make sense for someone to care about doing his duty but to be indifferent to the content of the particular duty.

A careful reading of the text makes it plain that someone who helps from duty does not care only about doing his duty. Kant emphasizes that what distinguishes an action done from duty from an action done from inclination is not its purpose, but the maxim by which it is determined — that is, why the person chose so to act (G 4:399). Both the agent who acts from duty and the agent who acts from inclination want to help the person they are helping, but only the former sees the person's needs as making a moral claim on him.[12]

Still, one might think that because one person is drawn to the action by emotion, and the other is not, only the former will help another with pleasure. But the fact that what led the agent to the action was not emotion or feeling does not mean that one will lack emotion and feeling when she acts. As Christine Korsgaard explains,

> Once you have adopted a purpose and become settled in its pursuit, certain emotions and feelings will naturally result. In particular, in ordinary circumstances the advancement or achievement of the purpose will make you happy, regardless of whether you adopted it originally from

natural inclination or from duty. So a dutiful person, who after all really does value the happiness of others, will *therefore* take pleasure in making others happy.[13]

Once again, the *Metaphysics of Morals* brings out more sharply than the *Groundwork* does that conducting oneself as one morally ought usually brings with it certain sentiments. The happiness of others is an obligatory end. We have a duty, that is, to make others' ends our own.[14] Someone lacking in sympathy for others, someone unmoved by the plight of human suffering, would seem — without some special explanation — not to have adopted as an end the happiness of others. At the very least, the person seems not to have integrated that end into her life in a way that develops the kinds of feelings that Kant thinks are part of having, and seeking to promote, the end.[15]

Now in unusual circumstances one's ability to enjoy helping may be marred. This is the situation of the man whose mind is so "clouded over with his own grief" that "the distress of others does not touch him" (G 4:398). But as noted above, this is not typical, and Kant constructed the example as he did in order to isolate the moral incentive and to make it absolutely clear that the man was acting from duty. Even in this case, however, there is reason to hope that having torn himself "out of this deadly insensibility" (G 4:398), the man now does take pleasure in helping others. If he doesn't yet, he very likely soon will (if he doesn't relapse into his insensibility and cease to help others). Kant says of beneficence that if "someone practices it often and succeeds in realizing his beneficent intention, he eventually comes actually to love the person he has helped" (MS 6:402).

III

I turn now to the second reason why Kant's account of acting from duty and moral worth is troubling even to those who understand that acting from duty does not require that one lack an inclination so to act or that one not take pleasure in what one does from duty. To recap, the first was that surely it is better to enjoy helping the needy than not to; yet Kant shows no signs in the *Groundwork* of recognizing this. We have seen, though, that when he discusses virtues and vices and duties to cultivate certain qualities of character, it becomes clear that he does not take the sentiments and attitudes with which one acts to be a matter of indifference, and that he regards taking pleasure in doing what is morally required to be a part of virtue. The second objection is that as long as one acts with the right sentiments, does it really add anything if the person acts from duty? If one helps others and does it not for gain but from the kindness of his heart, why think that there is something wanting if he does not act from duty?

One reason to think that acting with the right sentiments — compassion, sympathy, eagerness to help — is not full virtue is suggested by the following quotation from Lord Shaftesbury, a philosopher writing before Kant's time (and not someone usually thought of as displaying Kantian colors):

> If a Creature be generous, kind, constant, compassionate; yet if he cannot reflect on what he himself does, or sees others do, so as to take notice of what is *worthy* or *honest*; and make that Notice or Conception of Worth and Honesty to be an Object of his Affection; he has not the Character of being virtuous.[16]

This strikes a chord with Kantians, calling to mind the opening paragraphs of the First Section of the *Groundwork*. The good qualities of temperament alone are only conditionally good; for "without the principles of a good will they can become extremely evil" (G 4:394). Only the good will is unconditionally good. Without a good will one may be generous without any sense of when or to whom one should be generous, or of the importance of generosity. One may be self-controlled without a good sense of the importance of self-control — and to what ends one should control or redirect one's emotions. Generosity in the form of helping others to carry out their robbery is not virtuous; nor is self-control in a situation in which, in order not to jeopardize one's social standing, one controls one's impulse to speak out against injustice.

Shaftesbury's point is similar.[17] A person who enjoys — even loves — helping others (and who does help, even at great cost to her well-being) does not exhibit virtue if she does not reflect on her conduct — and the conduct of others — and care about its ethical character. For her conduct to count as virtuous, it has to matter to her that she acts virtuously.

Part of virtue, Lord Shaftesbury suggests, is having a sense of virtue. The virtuous person has a sense of the moral (or, as many virtue ethicists would prefer to say, ethical) dimensions of her conduct, and cares not only about the welfare of others but also about virtue itself. Is Lord Shaftesbury saying, then, that the virtuous person must have (and act from) a sense of duty? Not quite. Let's distinguish three conceptions of virtuous persons. First, imagine someone who has all the right sentiments but no sense of duty — no sense of being under a constraint to act as she does.

(1) The virtuous agent just does what is virtuous without any sense of constraint about it. She does what is virtuous effortlessly, naturally, without having to give any thought to the matter. This is simply her way of doing things. If asked, "Why do you do that?" she would be at a loss. "That is just what I do," she would say.

Both Lord Shaftesbury and Kant would reject this conception of a virtuous person.[18] This would not constitute virtue.

Here is another picture of the virtuous person, one that contrasts with (1) and does justice to Lord Shaftesbury's point.

(2) The virtuous agent acts virtuously with an understanding that what she is doing is virtuous, and she does so out of a recognition of the importance of so acting. She sees it as making a claim on her; it is not all the same to her whether she acts virtuously or not.

But there is still another way of thinking of the virtuous person, which arguably also does justice to Lord Shaftesbury's point.[19]

(3) The virtuous agent wants to be virtuous. She sees virtue to make a claim on her but only because she wants to be virtuous, or cares about virtue. Its making a claim on her is conditional on her caring about it.

Both (2) and (3) are consistent with Shaftesbury's point, but only (2) is a Kantian position. Why? *Duty involves constraint.* It is not just that one *wants* to do what is right, wants to do her duty; one feels and recognizes herself to be under a constraint. In (2) we see that constraint: she recognizes virtue to make a claim on her, and to do so unconditionally. Its making a claim on her is not conditional on her wanting to be virtuous or caring about virtue. In (3), there is no such constraint; for virtue makes a claim on her only conditionally on her caring about virtue.

Duty is not a matter of "affection" but of commitment. That is why I said that it is not quite right to understand Lord Shaftesbury as saying that the virtuous agent must have and act from a sense of duty. One acts from duty not by virtue of doing what is right because one wants to do what is right; rather, one does what is right because rightness makes a claim on one. One recognizes that one should.

We are now in a position to see what is missing — part of what is missing, anyway — in someone who acts with good sentiments but not from duty: a commitment to doing what morality requires. One's attitudes, emotions, and desires are shaped and moderated by one's commitment to doing what morality requires. They—especially the emotions and desires—are not always in harmony with it, even in the most virtuous person; and because of this, even the most virtuous person needs such a commitment. The virtuous person, like everyone else, needs a sense of duty.

It is instructive to see what, on Kant's view, distinguishes good people from others. This is elaborated in *Religion within the Boundaries of Mere Reason*. The difference between the good man and one who is evil cannot, Kant says, lie in the incentives that they incorporate into their maxims. Rather, it "must lie in their *subordination*," i.e., which of the two incentives he makes the condition of the other (R 6:36). The good and the evil alike adopt into their maxims the moral law as well as other incentives. The difference between them is that the good person subordinates the other incentives to the moral law, while the evil person does just the opposite. The good man makes pursuing what he fancies conditional on its being morally permissible to do so, whereas the evil man makes abiding by morality's requirements conditional on this squaring with what he fancies.

We may want to take issue with Kant's characterization of the evil person. It seems too generous and benign a portrayal. My reason for drawing attention to this passage, however, is simply to bring out that what is crucial to a person's moral goodness is that he or she puts morality first, giving it priority over any competing considerations. This is the heart of acting from duty.

Since Kant introduced the notion of duty to explicate that of a good will, this should not surprise us. The goodness of good qualities of temperament, talents of the mind, and gifts of fortune is conditional on the possessor's having a good will. As noted earlier, without a good will, such qualities as courage and resoluteness can become "extremely evil and harmful" (G 4:393). Similarly, one's conduct needs to be undergirded and shaped by a commitment to doing what is right. Kindhearted acts, generous acts, acts of loyalty and fidelity are good only insofar as they are guided and supported by a sense of duty.

This brings us to the second component that is missing in someone who acts with good sentiments but not from duty: recognition that the fact that an act is kindhearted, or generous, or loyal does not ensure that it is right. In addition to lacking a commitment to put morality first, the person who acts with good sentiments but not from duty is not attuned to the possibility that the benevolent act might happen to be impermissible.

Here is another way of getting at the same point. To suppose that someone could be fully virtuous simply by having whatever affections, desires, and affective responses are ideal (including an affection for virtue), but without any sense of duty, overlooks the fact that acts that issue from ideal desires may nonetheless be morally imperfect. Compassion may lead us to help when help is unfair to another, or when what we are helping the other to do is morally wrong for some other reason.

To see the importance of both components, contrast the Kantian view to a view that acting from duty is of value only as a backup, as a second best. Ideally (according to the backup model), one would act from a desire, unmediated by any sense of duty, to do the act in question or to bring about the good result. It is only when someone is deficient in sympathy or fellow feeling that the motive of duty is of value. It needs to "kick in," on this view, when the real thing, the feeling we would like everyone to act from, is missing (or eclipsed by conflicting feelings, such as resentment or annoyance). If I weren't so easily annoyed, if I didn't nurse old grudges and thus feel unwarranted resentment, if I weren't lazy and self-centered and thus inclined just to put myself first, I would have no need for the motive of duty. I would act as I should without any sense of constraint, any sense that whatever I might prefer to do, this is what I must do, for morality requires it.

This view could take either of two slightly different forms. In one form, it holds that only those lacking in virtue need to act from duty. Virtuous people do not. Their emotions, feelings, and desires — more generally, their affective natures — are exactly what they should be. Always. So simply by acting from their desires, virtuous people act as they should. In its other (more modest and more plausible) form, the position is that even the most virtuous sometimes are in need, motivationally, of a sense of duty. Even the most virtuous became weary or afraid, and do not always act as they should without the help of the thought "I really should do this."

The Kantian view is closer to the second, more modest position, but still is in fundamental disagreement with it. It takes issue with the idea that it is only because of a deficiency — only because even the best of us are sometimes weary or afraid — that purely moral motivation is of value. The person who just wants to do x (which is morally required) and does not recognize that she ought to do x, fails to acknowledge the moral importance of x, and specifically, that x *makes a moral claim on her.*

In addition, there is an implicit assumption in the view that acting from duty is of value only as a backup that needs to be challenged. The assumption is that a perfect affective nature would guarantee perfect conduct. An example will illustrate why this is not the case. Imagine someone tempted to favor someone close to him, but who refrains from doing so because under those circumstances it would be unfair to others. The circumstances might be that one's child is upset about something and wants a great deal of attention over several days, and asks not to have to go to day camp in order to spend more time with her parents. The parents, however, have obligations to students and colleagues (and let us imagine that what is owed to the students — attendance at dissertation orals, preparation for the orals, consultation with the students — cannot be postponed without detriment). In some situations it might be possible to grant the child her wish and still do right by the students and colleagues, but let us imagine that this is not the case. My claim is that it may well be the case that a perfect affective nature would pull one in a direction different from rightness: one's emotional leaning is toward one's child (depending on her age, and perhaps on why she is upset), but one acts against that leaning because on reflection it seems clearly to be wrong to request that the dissertation orals be postponed, or simply not to prepare for the orals (and to take the child along to them).

The same point emerges if we picture the situation a bit differently: it might be the case that one thinks that the child should not rely on the parent so much for comfort, and is better off attending the day camp; here, too, affect, in one with an ideal affective nature, might be at odds with one's better judgment. Affect might incline one toward granting the child's request, while reason says, "No, the child is using this as a crutch." Arguably it is part of love — at least love for one's children — to want to protect and to soothe; someone who never felt this in a situation in which she or he saw that protecting or soothing was not possible or was contraindicated would probably be a rather cold individual. Yet in some situations in which everyone except the cold and unfeeling will want to soothe and to shelter, it will be right to refrain from sheltering (and to take care not to overdo the soothing). The point here is that there is no reason to assume that affect in one with an ideal affective nature will never be at odds with what is (and what one sees to be) right. One need not be affectively less than perfect in order for one's emotions and feelings not to line up perfectly with what is, and what one sees to be, right. For the same reason, a perfect affective nature does not guarantee perfect conduct. Hence the need for a sense of duty — for a concern to do what is right, even if one's desires are impeccable.

IV

I have argued that acting from duty is compatible with having an inclination so to act and with acting with pleasure. Furthermore, although Kant doesn't say so in the *Groundwork*, it is clear in the *Metaphysics of Morals* that he holds that acting with pleasure is not only compatible with acting from duty, but is a part of being virtuous. But although it is part of being virtuous, there is still something for Schiller to find objectionable. *Virtue in Kant's theory involves overcoming obstacles.* One need not despise one's friends or despise what one is doing in order for one's conduct to count as an action done from duty. And one needn't despise one's friends in order for one's beneficent actions toward them to be virtuous. Nonetheless, virtue involves constraint and the recognition of constraint. Only those beings capable of acting contrary to reason (i.e., all human agents) are subject to moral constraints. 'Oughts' apply, indeed make sense, only for such beings. "[F]or a *holy* will, no imperatives are valid; the *ought* is out of place here, because the *volition* is of itself already necessarily in harmony with the law. Hence imperatives are only formulas expressing the relation of objective laws of volition in general to the subjective imperfection of the will of this or that rational being, e.g., to the human being" (G 4:414). Virtue, Kant writes in the *Metaphysics of Morals*, "is the strength of a human being's maxims in fulfilling his duty. — Strength of any kind can be recognized only by the obstacles it can overcome, and in the case of virtue these obstacles are natural inclinations, which can come into conflict with a human being's moral resolution" (MS 4:394).

Should we be troubled by this? Should we prefer Aristotle's conception of the virtuous person as free of inner conflict, free of contrary inclinations?[20] There is something appealing about the Aristotelian conception. We admire the person who would never be tempted to act wrongly; we regard such a person as a saint, as possessing some remarkable inner goodness.[21] But there is greatness in those who had to overcome obstacles — obstacles coming from within the personality of the individual — to become the exemplary people they became. (Think of Eleanor Roosevelt. Would we admire her more if she had not had a fear of public speaking and other obstacles from within that she had to overcome in order to carry out her extraordinary work against social injustice?) Of course, whether we admire people more or less for inner struggles that they had to overcame — and in some instances never fully overcome — depends in part on what those obstacles are. Someone seems less, not more, virtuous, if to be virtuous he has to struggle against a desire to torment others. (And the point is even clearer if the desire he had to overcome was a desire to rape, mutilate, murder for the thrill of it, and so on.) We are very glad that he overcame it, and we may admire him for having overcome it or, if the desire remains, for never giving in to it (although it seems a bit odd to speak of admiration here), but surely it would be a very rare person who saw him as more virtuous for having had those obstacles. This complication can be addressed by stipulating that although virtue is exhibited only when the agent finds it hard to do the virtuous act in question, it matters what makes it hard. Not every obstacle qualifies.

Setting aside that complication, suppose we do hold that virtues are exhibited only when the person finds it very hard to do the act in question. We would hardly hold — nor does logic require us to hold — that people who do not find it hard should try to bring it about that they do.[22] If it is the case, in other words, that virtue is shown only by overcoming obstacles, it does not follow that we should try to put obstacles in our path in order to be able to qualify as virtuous.[23] This brings into relief another error in Schiller's reasoning. If it is true that I do not act virtuously if I have no contrary impulses to overcome when I serve my friends, it does not follow that I should try to despise them in order to qualify as virtuous. It might seem to be the right thing to do if my goal were to earn as many moral brownie points as possible, i.e., to qualify as acting virtuously as often as possible, but that would be self-defeating. By making that my goal, I would be making myself less virtuous. In any event, Kant does not take the position that we are to perform as many morally worthy acts as possible. Nor is virtue additive. It is not a function of how many morally worthy acts we perform (or of the proportion of our actions that are morally worthy). We are to strive to perfect ourselves morally — to make the thought of duty an all-sufficient motive, so that we never think to ourselves, "It is wrong, but should I do it anyway?" or "I see it is what I morally ought to do, but even so, what about the tempting alternative?" Perfecting ourselves morally also involves setting ends for ourselves, ends that are subsidiary to the two obligatory ends (the happiness of others and our own perfection) as well as cultivating our characters so that we lack, as far as possible, the various vices Kant lists and have, as far as possible, the virtues.

I see no reason to be troubled by Kant's conception of virtue. Others may prefer the Aristotelian paradigm, but this "no inner conflict" model seems to me to require us to swallow a lot harder. Virtue, on the Aristotelian model, would have far less to do with personal effort and accomplishment, and thus seems to reflect very little on the agent. It reflects, instead, either luck or an upbringing in which one has been conditioned to take pleasure in exactly what one should take pleasure in, and not in anything else. In addition, the model of virtue is an otherworldly one: to strive to be virtuous is to strive to be something a human cannot be, a being that either has no affective nature at all, or whose affects are invariably in accord with reason (with what duty requires). On Kant's view, we are to aim to be virtuous humans, not to be divine. This is as it should be.[24]

NOTES

1. Friedrich Schiller, *Xenien* "The Philosophers," in Goethe, *Werke*, vol. 1, ed. Erich Trunz (Munich: Beck, 1982). I am using, with very slight modification, Allen Wood's translation of the passage in his *Kant's Ethical Thought* (Cambridge: Cambridge University Press, 1999), p. 28.

2. And to understand the structure of the entire First Section, keep in mind that through explicating the concept of a good will, "to be esteemed in itself and without any further aim," Kant introduces the idea of a categorical imperative (although he does not introduce that terminology until the Second Section). "Since I have robbed the will of every impulse that could have arisen from the obedience to any law, there is nothing left over except the universal lawfulness of the action in general which alone is to serve the will as its principle, i.e., I ought never to conduct myself except so *that I could also will that my maxim become a universal law*" (G 4:402).

3. I should clarify that "subjective limitations and hindrances" qualify the concept of the will, not the way this concept is contained in the concept of duty. Thanks to Dieter Schönecker for pointing out the need to clarify this point. To understand why the concept of duty contains that of a good will, see G 4:413–14, bearing in mind that a duty is what one ought to do or (equivalently for Kant) what one would do if one were fully rational.

4. The passage I am citing is obscure, however, and no interpretation I have thought of or read seems quite satisfactory. Because of its obscurity, this piece of textual evidence seems to me less decisive than it did when I wrote *Kantian Ethics Almost without Apology* (Ithaca: Cornell University Press, 1995), p. 150. For a different reading of the passage, see Wood, *Kant's Ethical Thought*, chap. 1.

5. In *Kantian Ethics Almost without Apology* I argue that on Kant's view, acting from duty is not compatible with acting *from* inclination, but is compatible with the agent's *having* such an inclination, provided that the inclination is not part of the ground of the agent's action. Presence of inclination is consistent with the action's being done from duty, and thus having moral worth, but an action cannot qualify as an action done from duty if it is done from inclination. This view is also taken by Henry Allison in *Kant's Theory of Freedom* (New York: Cambridge University Press, 1990).

6. See G 4:414.

7. For other discussions of Stoicism and Epicureanism, see *The Critique of Practical Reason* (KpV 5:116) and *Religion within the Boundaries of Mere Reason* (R 6:57–59).

8. It is "not in itself a duty to share the sufferings (as well the joys) of others," but "it is a duty to sympathize actively in their fate; and to this end it is therefore an indirect duty to cultivate the compassionate . . . feelings in us, and to make use of them as so many means to sympathy based on moral principles and the feeling appropriate to them" (MS 6:457).

9. Of gratitude Kant writes that it requires that one not regard "a kindness received as a burden one would gladly be rid of" but instead take "the occasion for gratitude as a moral kindness, that is, as an opportunity given one to unite the virtue of gratitude with love of man, to combine the *cordiality* of a benevolent disposition with *sensitivity* to benevolence (attentiveness to the smallest degree of this disposition in one's thought of duty), and so to cultivate one's love of man" (MS 6:456).

10. See Allen Wood, "The Final Form of Kant's Practical Philosophy," *Southern Journal of Philosophy* 36, suppl. (1997), 1–20.

11. However, as Kant explains in the *Metaphysics of Morals*, in one important way some of them do "lie at the basis of morality": "*moral feeling, conscience, love* of one's neighbor, and *respect* for oneself . . . are *subjective* conditions of receptiveness to the concept of duty." They are not "objective conditions of morality," but "every man has them, and it is by virtue of them that he can be put under obligation" (MS 6:399).

12. See Christine Korsgaard, *Creating the Kingdom of Ends* (New York: Cambridge University Press, 1996), p. 58.

13. Ibid. p. 59. I have altered the text to correct a typographic error. Although the original publication in the *Monist* 72 (July 1989) has "advancement or achievement," instead of "or" we find "of" in the more recent publication.

14. See MS 6:385–88.

15. I am grateful to Lara Denis for encouraging me to bring out this point.

16. Anthony Ashley Cooper, Earl of Shaftesbury, "An Inquiry concerning Virtue or Merit" (1699; reprinted 1732), in *British Moralists*, ed. L. A. Selby-Bigge (1897; reprint, Indianapolis: Bobbs-Merrill, 1964).

17. But there are also dissimilarities. In addition to the one noted just below in the text, there is another, depending on how much rests on Shaftesbury's choice of the word 'reflect'. If Shaftesbury has in mind philosophical reflection of a sort that only the well-read, well-educated, or intelligent could engage in, Kant would disagree with the quoted passage. As Allen

Wood reminds me, Kant is very reluctant to think of well-educated, philosophical people as having any moral advantage over those who lack the occasions and tools for moral reflection. Recall G 4:404: "it needs no science and philosophy to know what one has to do in order to be honest and good, or indeed, even wise and virtuous."

18. So would Aristotle. See *Nicomachean Ethics* II.6 as well as *Eudemian Ethics* VII.15. Jennifer Whiting emphasizes the similarity between Aristotle and Kant on this and related points in her "Self-Love and Authoritative Virtue: Prolegomenon to a Kantian Reading of *Eudemian Ethics* viii 3," in *Aristotle, Kant and the Stoics,* ed. Whiting and Stephen Engstrom (New York: Cambridge University Press, 1996).

19. I say "arguably" because I might be putting too fine a point on Shaftesbury's choice of the word 'Affection'. Since my concern is with Kant, not with Shaftesbury, I will not pursue that possibility here.

20. Aristotle, *Nicomachean Ethics* VII.

21. This may exhibit a misapprehension, on our part, of saintliness. See R. M. Adams, "Saints," *Journal of Philosophy* 81 (1984): 392–401. Adams takes issue with the characterization of moral excellence in Susan Wolf', "Moral Saints," *Journal of Philosophy* 79 (1982): 419–39. He suggests that there is considerably more depth and complexity in saints than Wolf supposes, and, most relevant for my purposes, more inner struggle.

22. As Allen Wood observes in *Kant's Ethical Thought,* "Needless to say, Kant does not advocate that we cultivate hatred of our friends or other contra-moral desires in order to give ourselves opportunities to resist them. (That would make about as much sense as putting your loved ones in needless danger so as to give yourself the opportunity to display your courage by rescuing them)" (p. 29). We should not, however, be all that surprised if some readers think that Kant holds this; indeed, some might not even regard it as an absurd view. After all, some people try to justify the existence of evil — i.e., explain why an omnipotent, benevolent deity would have created a world with so much human suffering and other evil, or allowed such evil and suffering to arise — by saying that were it not for the existence of evil, there would be no opportunity for us to exhibit (heroic) virtue in battling it; likewise, were there no human suffering, there would be no opportunity to show one's moral mettle by seeking to ameliorate it.

23. I once met an erstwhile rescue worker who told me there was nothing he had loved so much as the excitement of emergency calls. He spoke rapturously about the adrenalin rush he had felt when hurrying to the scene, not knowing what it would hold. It would be silly for him to rid himself (even if he could) of this thrill in going to accident scenes, even though it

probably is true that it is more admirable — inspires more esteem — if someone takes part in rescue efforts despite finding them distressing, and takes pleasure only in actually helping.

24. I am very grateful for helpful comments from Lara Denis, Dieter Schönecker, Allen Wood, and Santiago Zorzo.

Kantianism for Consequentialists

SHELLY KAGAN

Kant's moral philosophy represents one of the most significant approaches to the foundations of ethics. For obvious reasons — including the simple fact that Kant offered no distinctive name for his general approach to ethics — views of this same, basic sort are typically known as Kantian. But this common practice, natural as it is, carries with it an obvious danger as well: there is a temptation to assume that Kant himself is the last word on Kantianism, rather than merely being an important advocate of this *sort* of view. This can lull us into overlooking the possibility that in various places Kant may have been mistaken about the implications of Kantianism; and it can also make us feel needless pressure to reconstruct Kantianism in precisely the terms in which Kant himself presented it. As a result, we may narrowly focus on the details of Kant's particular views, at the expense of appreciating the fuller significance and general interest of Kantianism. (In contrast, we are quite used to thinking of Bentham, Mill, and Sidgwick as merely being leading representatives of the general *utilitarian* approach, without thinking that any one of them has the last word on utilitarianism itself.)

In this paper I want to discuss one significant strand of Kantianism in ethics. I focus, in particular, on certain ideas put forward in the *Groundwork for the Metaphysics of Morals*. But I must emphasize the point that the ideas I will be discussing are primarily put forward here as being Kantian, rather than Kant's. The position I will be discussing is certainly inspired (at a minimum) by Kant's own discussion in the *Groundwork*, and I will periodically turn to the text of the *Groundwork* itself for guidance and comparison. But this essay is not intended as a piece of Kant scholarship. Rather, it is intended as a contribution to understanding Kantianism. Indeed, because of this, I will hereafter refer to *k*antianism (rather than *K*antianism) where the lower case "k" is intended to mark the idea that I am primarily interested in the *type* of approach that Kant represents, rather than Kant exegesis per se. What I want to do, then, is to sketch the basic elements of a possible kantian approach, and indicate why I think the view has abiding significance for moral philosophy.

My primary goal is expository. I hope to say enough to make it clear why kantianism is worth taking seriously — even by those who may, at the end of the day, choose not to accept it. It is not my intention to offer anything like a *full* presentation of kantianism (we will only be considering a few of the main ideas discussed in the *Groundwork*), nor is it my intention to offer anything like a full *defense* of kantianism. While I hope to say enough to show why one might find kantianism attractive and plausible, the arguments I offer are only rough sketches, and many important objections will go unanswered (or unmentioned).

I have a secondary goal as well, reflected in my choice of title. Kant himself believed that kantian foundations supported a deontological rather than a consequentialist normative theory.[1] Since most philosophers have assumed that he was right about this, those sympathetic to consequentialism have typically had little interest in understanding kantianism. But in fact it is far from clear whether Kant *was* right about this.[2] So I hope to offer an account of kantianism that consequentialists may find congenial. In any event, if I am right in thinking that kantian foundations are themselves fairly plausible, then it behooves those who want to reject those foundations to identify exactly where they think those foundations go wrong. (Of course, given the obscurity of much of Kant's writing, it may not be surprising that few consequentialists have actually attempted to do this.) Accordingly, I want to offer a guide to kantianism that may be of particular use to consequentialists.

But this further goal is indeed only secondary. My primary purpose is to sketch the main lines of a potentially attractive version of kantianism. Questions about the particular normative implications of kantian foundations can be put aside until we have a better handle on the kantian foundations themselves.

I. Autonomy and the Formula of Universal Law

Where then should we begin? Kantianism begins with freedom. More particularly, it begins with the fact that we are free, and with an account of that freedom. So we must begin with that account. (It is worth noting, however, that the *Groundwork* itself does not begin with the idea of freedom, but rather works backward toward it, arguing in the first two sections that if there is to be such a thing as morality, then we must be free — that freedom is the basis of morality. Unfortunately, in the *Groundwork* itself Kant says rather little explicitly about how exactly we are supposed to be able to move from the assumption of freedom back "up" to morality (see G 4:446–47). Thus we must depart from Kant exegesis almost immediately.)

Kantianism begins with freedom. But I think we will better understand the relevant notion of freedom if we begin instead with rationality. What, exactly, is it to be rational?

Suppose we start with theoretical rationality. As a theoretically rational being, I am capable of examining my various beliefs and seeing whether it makes sense for me to hold them. Thus, in the first place, I have *standards* for evaluating beliefs, in the light of which I can ask whether or not I am justified in holding a given belief. I might, for example, appeal to various principles of logic, discovering that some of my beliefs commit me to accepting still other beliefs; or I might appeal to various rules of scientific methodology, finding that, given the available evidence, I am unjustified in accepting some further belief. But rationality in the theoretical domain goes beyond the mere *evaluation* of my beliefs: I can *change* my beliefs in light of my judgments concerning the extent to which they meet (or fail to meet) the relevant standards. Normally, that is, when I see that the evidence better supports one claim rather than another, my beliefs change accordingly. Roughly, then, theoretical rationality consists in my ability to evaluate my beliefs in light of the standards relevant for evaluating beliefs, and to alter my beliefs in the light of those evaluations.

Practical rationality is similar. As a practically rational being I am capable of examining my various desires, goals, intentions, actions, and the like, so as to see which of these make sense in the circumstances. Here too, then, I have standards in terms of which my plans can be evaluated, goals assessed, actions endorsed or criticized. Nor are these various practical elements merely subject to evaluation; I can *change* my goals, my intentions, and the like, in light of my judgments concerning the extent to which these meet (or fail to meet) the relevant standards. Thus practical rationality consists in my ability to evaluate actions, intentions, and so forth, in light of the standards relevant for these, and to alter these elements in light of those evaluations.

Generalizing, then, we can say that rationality — whether practical or theoretical — consists in the ability to evaluate beliefs and acts (and so forth) with an eye to whether they meet the relevant standards, and to alter our beliefs and acts in light of those evaluations.

In this way rationality goes beyond mere intelligence. Nonhuman animals, I presume, also have beliefs and desires, and act in a way that is often appropriate to their circumstances. Some animals may well be extremely adept at achieving goals and forming appropriate beliefs about their environment. Thus they display varying (and perhaps considerable) degrees of intelligence. We could say that *intelligence* consists in the ability to produce beliefs and actions that in point of fact are appropriate (that is, conform to the relevant standards); animals are often intelligent in this sense. But only rational creatures are capable of *articulating* the standards against which beliefs and actions are to be evaluated, and only rational creatures are capable of consciously *comparing* beliefs and actions (real or imagined) against those same standards (G 4:412, 427).

It is worth emphasizing as well the point that as rational beings we are capable of *rejecting* the beliefs and actions (and the like) that don't meet what we take to be the relevant standards. We modify our behavior and our beliefs in light of what we think appropriate. For example, we are not normally *forced* to act on desires that we happen to have, when we conclude that such desires don't make sense, or that acting on them in present circumstances would be inappropriate (by whatever standards we here take to be relevant). In this way, too, rational beings are different from merely intelligent animals. For it seems plausible to view animals as mere "playthings" or "puppets" of their desires — incapable of evaluating them, and thus incapable of rejecting them. In contrast, rational beings are in an important sense *free*: if we conclude that a given desire makes no sense (perhaps we recognize that it was based on what we now see to be a mistaken belief) or that a given intention is inappropriate, we are free to step back from that desire or intention, and to refuse to act on it.

Of course, the simple fact of the matter is that humans are not *perfectly* rational. At times we misapply our own standards and fail to see that a belief cannot be justified (given the relevant standards). Or we may find ourselves incapable of *abandoning* certain beliefs, even though we can see that these beliefs are not in fact justified. Similarly, at times we may find ourselves giving in to desires, even though we see full well that acting on this desire, in this situation, doesn't actually make sense, or is otherwise inappropriate. Thus we are, at best, only imperfectly rational. Still, it would be implausible to suggest that we are not rational at all (in this sense), for we clearly are capable of articulating standards for evaluating beliefs and actions, and we are typically capable of evaluating our beliefs and actions in the light of those standards; and often, at least, we are capable of modifying our behavior and beliefs in the light of those evaluations. Humans may not be perfectly rational, but we are rational nonetheless, even if only imperfectly so.

The account of rationality that I have been sketching is, indeed, only a sketch. But even so, it remains significantly incomplete, in that I have not yet drawn attention to an important further fact: not only are we capable of articulating relevant standards, and evaluating and modifying beliefs and actions in light of those standards; the standards *themselves* are things that we can evaluate and modify. That is, for any given standard that I might use to evaluate a belief or an act (or an intention, and so forth), I can ask of the standard itself whether *it* makes sense, whether *it* is indeed an appropriate standard to be used in this way in these circumstances. In effect, I can ask whether the given standard itself meets the standards (whatever they are) relevant for evaluating *standards*. And armed with these evaluations, I can in turn reject any given standard, modify it, or replace it. Thus, as a rational being I am free not only to reject, modify, or endorse my various beliefs and actions — I am also free to reject, modify, or endorse the standards I appeal to in evaluating beliefs and actions. I am not forced to accept and appeal to standards that do not make sense to me or that seem unjustified or inappropriate. I am free to alter the standards as I see fit.

And the same is true, of course, with regard to the "second order" standards that I may use to evaluate the "first order" standards. These higher order standards can themselves be subject to critical evaluation: I can ask whether the standards I use for evaluating standards are themselves appropriate, whether they themselves meet the relevant ("third order") standards (whatever I may take these to be) for evaluating such (second order) standards. And I can modify these higher order standards as seems appropriate in light of these further evaluations. And so on, and so forth, all the way up (or all the way down): no standard is itself forced upon me, no standard is immune to potential criticism or evaluation. I am free, in principle, to evaluate any standard whatsoever, to ask whether it makes sense to me, whether it is indeed an appropriate standard to use. The principles or standards by which I evaluate beliefs and actions are themselves subject to rational assessment and open to modification or rejection. Put another way, the rules of rationality are not forced upon me (against my will, as it were): I need only appeal to standards that make sense to me, that seem appropriate in light of whatever principles, rules, or standards I endorse.

Our examination of the nature of rationality has thus led us to an important insight. The rules or standards to which I appeal in rationally assessing beliefs and actions are themselves subject to rational assessment, and at no point need I simply accept a relevant rule or standard as simply given — from "out there," as it were, forced upon me despite its making no sense. On the contrary, the relevant rules or standards need only be accepted if they, too, make sense in light of whatever rules and standards I reasonably accept. We could put the point this way: the laws of rationality are not forced upon reason from the outside. Rather, reason is free to reject those standards (at whatever level) that do not make sense to itself. Reason is its own last court of appeal. It chooses what standards to obey. In short: reason is *autonomous* (G 4:440).

The fact that reason is autonomous in this way is certainly not altogether obvious. Indeed, Kant believed that previous moral philosophers had failed to recognize the autonomy of reason, and certainly had failed to appreciate the implications of reason's autonomy for ethics (G 4:432–33). Most moral philosophies have been founded in heteronomous conceptions of reason, where some ultimate principle of reasoning is simply taken as "given" (from outside reason's control) and beyond question (G 4:441–44). But kantians believe that since we are autonomous (insofar as we are rational), all such approaches to ethics must fail. If there is to be any hope for a sound foundation for ethics, it must take account of our autonomy.

In the account I have been sketching, the ideas of reason, freedom, and autonomy are tightly connected. Clearly, much more needs to be said, both in defense of the general kantian picture I have been presenting, and by way of further clarification of the three related concepts. But I am going to restrict myself here to two quick remarks.

First, our analysis of rationality has led us to a picture of rational beings as free. So eventually the kantian must confront the question of whether the freedom that we take ourselves to have (as rational beings) is genuine or a mere illusion. Kant himself postpones the discussion of this issue until the third section of the *Groundwork*, and even there the discussion is cursory. In this essay I shall make no attempt whatsoever to pursue this question.[3] I believe it plausible to hold that we are free, in the relevant sense, but I won't attempt to defend this claim here. And so, along with Kant in the first two sections of the *Groundwork*, we can view the rest of our discussion as taking the form of a conditional: if we *are* free, what follows?

Second, I want to say a word more about the concept of autonomy. Kant typically expresses the thought that reason is autonomous by saying that reason is the *author* or *source* of the rules and standards used by reason (e.g., G 4:431). But it is not clear that our concept of rationality can take us quite this far. Suppose we grant the kantian that the freedom involved in rationality means that there are no sound or valid standards for rational assessment that cannot themselves withstand the scrutiny of rational assessment. This would mean that there are no valid rules of reasoning that reason doesn't itself "accept," or "will," or "approve." We might capture this idea by saying that reason must itself "sign off" on any purported rules of rationality that are themselves to be binding upon reason. (There are no rules binding upon reason that reason wishes itself free of, no rules that it considers unreasonable rules.) But is it also true that we must think of reason as the *author* of these rules (the *ground* of their validity)? Kant apparently thinks so, though it is not clear why. Perhaps (and this is sheer speculation) he believes that it is inexplicable how reason *could* have this kind of veto power over rules of reasoning (so that no rule it disapproves of is valid) unless reason is itself the *source* of the validity of the (valid) rules of reasoning. This claim is not completely unattractive, and so I shall follow Kant here in speaking of reason as the source or author of its own rules. I believe, however, that this further claim is not strictly needed by the kantian. So long as it is conceded that reason's autonomy means that reason must "sign off" on any principles of rationality if they are indeed to be sound — that no standard for rational assessment is valid unless reason itself can approve of it — the kantian has, I believe, all that he needs.

Now kantians believe that *given* the autonomy of reason, certain implications fall out concerning the rules or standards that reason can give to itself. In particular, they believe that once we recognize the autonomy of reason, we are committed to accepting a certain fundamental rule — the *universal law* formulation of the categorical imperative (FUL). Here is a possible reconstruction of the main line of thought.

Whenever I act, my acting presupposes that there is reason to do whatever it is that I am doing, that my act makes sense in the given circumstances. In effect, each action presupposes some rule or principle (though not necessarily the same rule from act to act) that endorses the act, a rule in the light of which the act can be seen as reasonable. Typically, of course, these underlying principles or rules will only be implicit, but were we to make them explicit, they might say something along the following lines: under such and such circumstances, given such and such desires or such and such goals, there is reason to act in such and such a way. As I say, we rarely make such rules explicit (and even less frequently attempt to state them fully and with care), but whenever I act, I presuppose some such rule — a rule which, if sound, would validate my action, by showing why it is that I have reason to do whatever it is that I am doing. (In many cases, of course, one acts spontaneously, or simply "goes with the flow." But in such cases, presumably, the principle implicit in one's act is precisely one that endorses acting spontaneously in circumstances of this sort.)

So when I act, I presuppose a rule or principle that claims that I have reason to do what I do (given the circumstances, and so forth). But which rules should I act on? This much seems clear: I should only act on rules that are themselves *valid*. (The precise term of commendation used here isn't important for our purposes. We could equally well talk of those rules that are sound, or legitimate, or good, or reasonable.) I should only do what it truly makes sense for me to do; so I should only act on those rules that are themselves correct in their claims about what it is that I have reason to do. I should only act on those principles that are valid.

But given that I am autonomous, the rules are up to me. Valid rules are valid by virtue of my signing off on them, by virtue of my approving of them as a rational being.

So this means: I should only act on rules that I can sign off on. I should only act on rules that I can rationally choose to be rules. Put in slightly different terms: I should act only upon rules that I can (rationally) *will* to be rules.

But rules are *laws*. They tell everyone what to do (or believe, or intend, and so on) in relevant circumstances. They say, for example, that in such and such circumstances, given such and such desires, one has reason to perform an act of such and such a type. But this means (if the given rule is valid) that *everyone* has such a reason — provided that they have the relevant desires and find themselves in the relevant circumstances. Of course not everyone will necessarily find themselves in the relevant circumstances, or with the relevant desires — but it is true of everyone that *if* they were in the relevant circumstances (and so forth) then they *would* have reason to perform an act of the relevant sort. Rules are *universal*, providing the same reasons (under the relevant circumstances) to everyone.

So we can restate our earlier conclusion. Instead of saying that I should act only upon rules that I can (rationally) will to be rules, we can say: I should act only on those rules that I can (rationally) will to be universal laws.

This is Kant's formula of universal law, though his own favored statement of it makes use of a piece of jargon. Kant typically talks about *maxims*, which for our purposes we can take to be first person statements of intentions ("I will perform such and such an act in such and such circumstances, given such and such goals"). Each such maxim corresponds to an implicit principle ("if one is in such and such circumstances, with such and such goals, then one has reason to perform such and such an act"), and so we could restate the formula at which we have arrived as follows: I should act only on those maxims, where I can (rationally) will that the corresponding principle be universal law. Simplifying a bit further still, we can say: act only on those maxims that I can will to be universal laws. And this is exactly what Kant tells us. Here is his own statement of the formula of universal law:

> FUL: "Act only in accordance with that maxim through which you at the same time can will that it become a universal law" (G 4:421).

Kant's decision to state FUL in terms of maxims rather than the corresponding principles carries certain risks, for one can normally state one's intentions in a way that only gives a partial indication of what one takes oneself to be doing, and why it seems to make sense. Thus, for example, if my intention is to close the door to keep out the person attacking me, so as to save my life, it will normally be correct to say, as well, that I intend to close the door. But if we then focus on "I will close the door" as a statement of my maxim, we will have no idea (or at best a poor idea) of why I think it makes sense to do this in the present circumstances, and thus no idea (or at best a poor idea) of just what the corresponding principle is supposed to be that I am to examine so as to see whether I can indeed will it to be universal law. These problems could have been avoided had Kant stated FUL directly in terms of examining complete statements of the underlying principles. But so long as we bear in mind that the real question is always whether a purported reason-giving principle is indeed one that we can rationally will to be universal law, we should be able to make use of Kant's own formulation without too much confusion.

Now the argument I have just sketched moves from our autonomy to FUL, a requirement to act only on certain types of maxims (in Kant's formulation). But if this argument is sound, then the resulting requirement should apply equally to *everyone*, that is, to every rational being. For if reason is autonomous, and autonomy yields FUL, then FUL is binding upon all rational beings. That is to say: all rational beings should obey FUL; they *must* do it if they are to act rationally. We can express this point in kantian jargon by saying that FUL is a *categorical imperative* (one binding upon all rational beings; see, e.g., G 4:432). Of course this does not mean that all rational beings *will* obey FUL. As we have already noted, humans, at least, are only imperfectly rational, and thus may often fail to conform to FUL, sometimes knowingly. But everyone *should* obey FUL: they have reason to do so, based on the mere fact that they are rational. If the argument is sound, then FUL is a categorical imperative.

Kant says there is exactly one categorical imperative, though it has several equivalent formulations (G 4:420–21, 436). FUL is supposedly only one of the different ways of stating this single imperative. Another of the formulations, the formula of autonomy (FA), goes like this:

FA: "the idea of the will of every rational being as a will giving universal law" (G 4:431).

Note that Kant doesn't even bother to state this version in the form of an imperative at all! Presumably, however, what he is most concerned to impress upon us here is the idea that it is autonomy (the fact that reason is the source of its own laws) that provides the basis for FUL: given the former, we are led to the latter. The argument I have been sketching tries to make good on this thought. (To get full equivalence, of course, we would also need to go on to argue as well that given FUL we can derive an imperative along the lines of "Act autonomously!" or "Act in keeping with your autonomy!" I won't attempt to argue that here.)

But is the argument sound? Can we actually derive FUL from the mere assumption of reason's autonomy? I am not sure. Doubtless several steps of the argument could be questioned, but the most important issue, I believe, is this. Is it really true that the only rules or standards that I could autonomously will are *universal*? Must the reason-giving principles I endorse be principles that would equally give *everyone* a reason? Putting the same point in a slightly different way, is it really true that the only rules that I could freely give to myself are rules that make similar prescriptions for everyone? Unless something like this is true, then all that autonomy will demand is that I act on maxims that I can (autonomously) will. We won't have a requirement that I act only on maxims that I can will to be universal law. And so we won't have made it all the way to FUL. So we need to ask: is it really true that the only principles I can autonomously give myself are universal?

Now it might seem that the answer to this question is obvious. For it seems obvious that I can (and should!) endorse principles that recognize that what *I* have reason to do normally differs from what *you* have reason to do. For example, I may have reason to eat right now, while you do not.

In thinking about this question, however, it is important to bear in mind the point, already noted, that the requirement that the reason-giving principles be (ones that I can will to be) universal laws only amounts to a requirement that people *in the same circumstances* have the same reasons. Thus, universality here only amounts to the requirement that *if* someone else were in the same circumstances (that is, whatever the principle takes to be the relevant circumstances) then they too would have reason to perform the same kind of act. (And it should be noted that, depending on the given principle, the relevant circumstances may well include a specification of the person's desires or goals as well as more "external" circumstances.) So even if the principles I give myself are universal, this doesn't mean that everyone has reason to do the same specific types of acts, for people will still find themselves in differing circumstances.

In typical cases, at least, when we find ourselves thinking that one person has reason to do something that another person does not, this will be because we think there is some relevant difference in their circumstances — and a full specification of the relevant reason-giving principles will take note of these circumstances. Thus, for example, I may believe that I should eat, while you should not, but this may be because I believe that only hungry people should eat, and I recognize that you are not hungry. (Or perhaps I believe that people on diets shouldn't eat between meals, and you are on a diet and it is between meals; or that you need to get to a class, and I do not, and so on.) Despite initial appearances to the contrary, then, the underlying principle will actually be universal: anyone who is similarly situated (with regard to hunger, dietary needs, availability of food, more pressing demands, and so forth) will have similar reason to eat (or not). If this is right, then at the very least most of the principles I can actually sign off on will indeed be universal laws in the relevant sense.

But is it truly *impossible* for me to autonomously will principles that are not in this way universal? Can't I simply endorse a rule that says that *I* (but not others) should do such and such an act in *this* case (but not in other cases that are otherwise similar)?

Here I can only reply that when I honestly contemplate such irreducibly person specific or irreducibly case specific principles I find them virtually unintelligible. I cannot fathom the idea that I might have reason to do something in a certain kind of case, while you do not — even though there is not a single relevant difference between us. This is not to say that I can't imagine someone "stating" such a principle, nor do I mean to claim that I wouldn't understand what someone affirming such a principle would be attempting to do. Rather, I simply find that I cannot take seriously the possibility that such a principle would be one that merits endorsement. If in the circumstances someone has *reason* to act in a given way, then it seems to me that anyone at all who genuinely found themselves in relevantly *identical* circumstances would have reason to act in the same way. Which is to say, when I ask myself what sorts of reason-giving principles I can truly imagine autonomously giving to myself — fully accepting upon complete rational reflection — the only such principles are ones that are universal.

In my own case, then, if I am indeed to restrict myself to maxims that I can autonomously will, then I must restrict myself to maxims that I can will to be universal laws. Perhaps others differ from me in this regard. The idea seems just barely possible, though, again, I find that I can't take the thought seriously. As far as I can see, *any* rational being would find that the only maxims he could autonomously will would be maxims that he could will to be universal laws. And if this is indeed correct, then given the autonomy of reason something like FUL may well follow for all rational beings whatsoever. In short, FUL may indeed be a categorical imperative.

To be sure, other questions about this step of the argument could be pressed, and other stages of the argument could be challenged as well. So I would not want to claim that the validity of the derivation of FUL (from the assumption of autonomy) has now been established. But I hope that I have said enough at this point to make it clear why the kantian's appeal to FUL is a position worth taking seriously. The claim that reason is autonomous is, I think, a plausible one, and the further claim that autonomy yields FUL is not, I believe, one that can be easily dismissed. If nothing more, these claims are sufficiently plausible (even if one ultimately rejects one or the other of the pair) that what I have said should make it clear why many people have found FUL so compelling.

II. Understanding the Formula of Universal Law

Suppose, then, that we grant the kantians the validity of FUL (if only for the sake of argument). Even if we do this, it is hardly obvious how FUL is to be applied, how it is to be put to work. Nor is it the least bit obvious whether — as kantians believe — FUL has sufficient "bite" that it can be used to generate concrete moral guidance. So let us put aside further questions about the derivation of FUL, and turn instead to the question of what follows from it. Granted that I must only act on maxims that I can will to be universal law, how exactly am I to decide what to do?

The first thing to notice is that FUL itself doesn't actually provide us with maxims; it only serves to rule some of them out. We bring candidate maxims *to* FUL, to see whether they are acceptable. The point here is easy enough to grasp if we recall that maxims are, in effect, statements of what one intends to *do* in a given situation. What we should imagine then is that faced with the given situation, I have come up with some tentative plan of action, something that I propose to do (perhaps to serve some desire or goal I have). Armed with this tentative plan, then, I turn to FUL to see if it is legitimate to act on it. FUL is, in effect, a *test* of maxims: it tells me to act only on maxims that have a certain feature.

For the moment, let's leave the details of that test aside, and focus on the negative form of the imperative. FUL tells me to act only on maxims that pass a certain test. Thus, if some maxim *fails* the test, FUL commands me not to act on it. Notice, however, that although FUL tells me to act *only* on maxims that pass the test, it does not require me to act on all the maxims that *do* pass the test. Apparently, then, if a maxim passes the relevant test you *may* act on it (FUL, at least, won't rule this out); but absent any further argument, it seems, there won't be any *requirement* to act on the maxim. We must restrict ourselves to acting on maxims that pass the test, but among the maxims that do pass, which we choose to act upon is up to us.[4]

Suppose, then, that some maxim fails the FUL test (whatever, exactly, it turns out to be). What can we conclude? If FUL is indeed a categorical imperative, binding upon all rational beings, then we must conclude that it is forbidden to act on that maxim. But what follows in the alternative case, where the given maxim passes the test? Here we have to be more cautious. Obviously enough, if a given maxim passes FUL, then as far as FUL itself is concerned there is nothing objectionable about acting on the maxim. But we cannot yet safely conclude that it is indeed *permissible* to act on the maxim in question, because, for all that we have said so far, there might be some other imperative — beyond FUL — that must be taken into account as well. After all, even if kantians are right in thinking that reason's autonomy supports FUL, it doesn't yet follow that this is the only fundamental principle supported by our autonomy. Perhaps there are *additional* tests that must be passed as well. If so, then passing FUL will be necessary for permissibility but not sufficient.

Presumably Kant means to put this possibility aside with his insistence that FUL is the *only* categorical imperative. (Because of this belief, he typically refers to it simply as "the" categorical imperative, though as we have noted Kant also believes that this imperative can be stated in several different, though equivalent, ways.) But even if Kant *could* prove that FUL (in its various formulations) is indeed the only categorical imperative,[5] that wouldn't necessarily put the worry to rest. For what if there were additional, basic principles (that is, principles not derived from FUL) that, although not categorical, nonetheless validly applied in particular cases? Even if FUL is the only *categorical* imperative, nothing yet rules out the possibility that a maxim might pass FUL but nonetheless fail to pass these further (noncategorical) principles.

What the kantian needs to claim then (*regardless* of whether FUL is the only categorical imperative) is that even if there are any further valid principles (not themselves derived from FUL), it is not actually possible for a maxim to pass FUL but to violate these further principles. Happily, this may not be an implausible claim for the kantian to make. Imagine that a given maxim violates some such principle, P. Now given the autonomy of reason, any valid principle of reasoning, including P, must be one that I rationally favor. But if I truly continue to endorse P (even in light of its ruling out the maxim in question) then I cannot rationally favor any principle incompatible with P — including, in particular, the underlying principle corresponding to the maxim. Thus, given my acceptance of P, I cannot in fact rationally will the maxim to be universal law. That is, if the maxim violates P, it fails FUL as well.

What this means, then, is that even if there *are* additional principles (not themselves derived from FUL), so long as a given maxim does pass FUL it will pass those additional principles (if any) as well.[6] Thus, provided that a maxim passes FUL, it is indeed permissible to act upon it.

I think, therefore, that we can put aside the potential complications that threatened to arise from the existence of additional tests beyond that provided by FUL. We can say, straightforwardly, that if a maxim passes FUL then it is permissible to act on it. And we can combine this result with a point already made, that if a maxim *fails* FUL it is *forbidden* to act on it. Summing all of this up then we can conclude, quite simply, that it is permissible to act on a maxim if and only if it passes FUL.

It would, however, be easy to become confused about what we have shown so far. Suppose that in some situation I consider a maxim, M, that would permit me to perform an act, A, in those circumstances. And let us suppose, as well, that this maxim fails FUL. It would be natural to think that what this shows me is that it is forbidden to do A (at least, in these circumstances). But in point of fact this doesn't actually follow at all. From the mere fact that M fails FUL, all that immediately follows is that one should not act on M. That is, one should not do A for the particular *reasons* given by M. The maxim M, after all, corresponds to a particular reason-giving principle, and that principle picks out certain features of the situation, and tells me that by virtue of these features I have reason to do A. The fact that M fails FUL shows me that this particular claim about what I have reason to do (and why) is mistaken. Thus, if I *do* have reason to do A it is not for *those* (purported) reasons. But all of this is still compatible with the possibility that there may be other (genuine) reasons to do A — even in this very situation. For there may still be some other reason-giving principle which *is* sound — a principle that focuses on different features of the very same situation, and tells me that by virtue of *those* features I have reason to do A. In short, even though M fails FUL, some other maxim that would permit me to do A may still pass.

Thus, even though M fails FUL, we cannot yet conclude that it is forbidden to do A (in this situation). To reach that conclusion we would need to examine various other maxims as well, that is, the various other maxims that would also instruct me to do A. It is only if *all* such "permission giving" maxims fail FUL as well that we can conclude that doing A is forbidden. (Since I may only act on maxims that do pass FUL, if *all* such permission giving maxims fail, then I am indeed forbidden to do A.)

This is not to say, of course, that before concluding that a given type of act is forbidden in a certain situation one must literally examine a huge (perhaps infinite) number of maxims. It is possible that when a particular maxim fails FUL we will be able to see precisely why it fails, and generalize to other, relevant maxims. In effect, we may be able to test large classes of maxims at (more or less) the same time. But logically speaking the point remains, that the failure of a single maxim does not suffice to establish that a given act is forbidden; that requires, rather, the failure of all maxims that would permit the act (in those circumstances). (Similarly, of course, to establish that a given type of act was forbidden under *all* circumstances, we would need to show that all such permission giving maxims would fail, regardless of what circumstances the maxims specify as relevant.)

In the last few paragraphs I have been freely talking about actions as permissible or forbidden. What kind of permissibility is this? So far, the answer is *rational* permissibility. FUL provides a test for reason-giving principles, allowing us to conclude, in certain cases, that an action is rationally forbidden (say) because no genuinely adequate reason supports doing it. But the kantian believes that FUL captures a central *moral* idea as well. It serves to sort the morally permissible from the morally forbidden. If this is right, then rationality meets morality here: if the autonomy of reason requires you to conform to FUL, and acts forbidden by FUL are morally forbidden, then reason requires you to obey morality.

To understand why the kantian thinks FUL can plausibly be taken not only as a requirement of rationality but also as the basic principle of morality, it may be helpful to turn to a concrete example. Kant asks us to consider a case where I attempt to borrow some money, promising to pay it back, even though I know full well that I will be unable to keep such a promise. (The same basic example is discussed at two different places — G 4:402–3 and 422 — though only the second discussion makes explicit that the case involves money.) Kant supposes that my maxim here tells me that "when I am in a tight spot" I will "make a promise with the intention of not keeping it" (G 4:402). And here is part of Kant's discussion of whether this maxim passes FUL:

I ask myself: would I be content with it if my maxim (of getting myself out of embarrassment through an untruthful promise) should be valid as a universal law (for myself as well as for others), and would I be able to say to myself that anyone may make an untruthful promise when he finds himself in embarrassment which he cannot get out of in any other way? Then I soon become aware that I can will the lie but not at all a universal law to lie.   (G 4:403)

Several details of this argument will require more careful discussion later. Here I only want to draw attention to the plausibility of the idea that FUL is indeed concerned with fundamental moral aspects of the situation. In effect, Kant is telling us that immorality is a matter of cheating — making an exception of oneself (cf. G 4:424). When I tell a lie, or make a promise I don't intend to keep (or butt in line, or kill someone for personal gain, and so forth), I am playing by rules that I don't favor others acting on as well. After all, it is not as though someone who is immoral wants others to act in the same way! On the contrary, what I want when I act immorally is that everyone else should play by one set of rules (the moral rules) while I alone get to act on a *different* set of rules. Here I am, then, proposing to act in a certain way, in a certain situation, but it is perfectly clear that I cannot rationally will that everyone act in the same way in similar situations. There is a (purported) reason-giving principle that I propose to act on, but I can't reasonably favor that others act on it as well. This is the telltale sign of immorality, says the kantian. I want to treat myself differently than every-one else gets treated; I want one set of rules for myself, and another set of rules for everyone else. When I violate FUL, acting on a principle that I cannot will to be universal law, I try to make an exception of myself, even though I see full well that there is nothing at all that I consider a relevant difference between myself and others; and that is the mark of immorality.

That is why FUL is a requirement, not only of rationality, but of morality as well. And so we can conclude: if an act is forbidden by FUL, it is morally forbidden. But can we similarly conclude that if an act is permitted by FUL, it is morally permissible? As before, however, this conclusion assumes that FUL is not only one test among many, but is indeed the only fundamental principle — now, the only fundamental *moral* principle. This, too, is a claim that Kant appears to make (though it is not clearly distinguished from the earlier claim that FUL is the only fundamental rational principle), and for the sake of argument, at least, let us grant it as well (we'll consider its plausibility later). Then we can say that an act is morally permissible if and only if it is permitted by FUL.

Once again, it is important to avoid misunderstanding. We have just concluded that an act will be morally permissible if and only if it is permitted by FUL. And as we have already discussed, an action will be permitted by FUL provided that there is some maxim that passes FUL that permits the action in the circumstances. Note, however, that nothing that we have said requires that this maxim be the one that the person is actually acting upon. Provided that there is *some* permission giving maxim that passes FUL, it will be morally permissible to perform the act in question, even if the person is acting on some *other* maxim, and that maxim *fails* FUL!

Of course, if the person *is* acting on another maxim, and that maxim fails FUL, there will be plenty that is amiss. The person will be acting on a maxim that is unsound, both rationally and morally. That is to say, she will be performing the action for the *wrong* reasons — for "reasons" that are not actually adequate reasons for action at all. What's more, she will be performing the action for reasons that are not morally legitimate. As such, the person may well be open to moral condemnation of one sort or another. But this is not to say that what she is doing is morally *forbidden*. Rather, we will have a case of someone who is doing an action that is perfectly permissible morally, but is doing so for the wrong reason. In kantian jargon we can say that such a person is conforming to the moral law, but not acting for the sake of the moral law (G 4:390).

The distinction being drawn here is a perfectly familiar one. We all have the idea of someone doing the morally right thing, but for the wrong reasons. For example, Kant discusses a shopkeeper who gives correct change to his customers, but does so only out of fear of being caught and having business suffer (G 4:397). Presumably, we will all agree that giving correct change is a morally permissible (indeed morally obligatory) thing to do. And so we would agree that when the shopkeeper does this his action is morally permissible; he is conforming to the moral law. This is true even though he acts out of fear — acts for the morally wrong reasons. Thus, despite the fact that the maxim he acts on is unsound, that it would (as we may suppose) fail FUL, it remains true that the action he performs is morally permissible. And what *makes* it morally permissible is the very fact that some *other* maxim that enjoins giving correct change *would* pass FUL. In short, an act is morally permissible if and only if some permission giving maxim passes FUL, whether or not the person in question is actually acting on that maxim.

Let us now return to the question, earlier set aside, of how exactly we are to determine whether or not a given maxim does pass FUL. The basic idea, of course, is clear: a maxim passes FUL just in case I can will it to be a universal law. But how, exactly, can I tell whether or not I can "universalize" a maxim in this way? What, exactly, do I do when I try to determine whether a maxim can be universalized?

On what I take to be the standard proposal here, I should begin by trying to imagine a world where everyone *does* in fact conform to the reason-giving principle corresponding to the maxim being tested. If the maxim enjoins me to perform an act of type A, in such and such circumstances, then I am to imagine a world in which *everyone* performs acts of type A when in circumstances of that sort. I attempt to imagine a *full compliance world*, as we might call it, and then I ask myself two questions about this world. First, is such a world truly possible, or does something go wrong in trying to imagine it? Second, assuming that such a world is indeed possible (that nothing goes wrong in the relevant sense), can I rationally will it? The first question, in effect, is supposed to tell me whether the principle corresponding to the maxim could actually *be* a universal law; the second, whether I can *will* it to be such. To pass FUL, I must be able to answer both questions in the affirmative.

According to this interpretation, then, there are two distinct ways in which a maxim could fail to pass FUL, corresponding to the two questions I've just distinguished. In effect, there are two distinct subtests. This seems to be Kant's own view of the matter, in any event: he says that some maxims "cannot even be *thought* without contradiction as a universal law," while other maxims that also fail FUL generate no such "internal impossibility"; for these other maxims, rather, the *will* would "contradict itself" if it attempted to will the maxims to be universal laws (G 4:424).

More significantly, Kant seems to think this distinction picks out something important, generating different types of moral requirements. These are obscure matters, and Kant says little about them in the *Groundwork*, but roughly the picture seems to be this: when maxims fail at the first step, this is supposed to generate "perfect" duties, while "imperfect" duties (which are, despite the name, perfectly genuine duties) are generated by maxims failing at the second step (cf. G 4:424). But it is far from obvious why the two subtests should be invested with anything like this kind of significance. FUL says that one should not act on maxims that cannot be willed to be universal law. It does *not* say that it matters *why* a given maxim cannot be so willed. So it is far from clear that the kantian should follow Kant in holding it significant at which step a given maxim fails.

For that matter, it must be admitted as well that it is far from clear what precisely we are supposed to be concerned with as we consider the two subtests. In a moment we will turn to an examination of some of Kant's own examples. At the very least this should help us get clearer about what Kant thought could lead to a maxim's failing FUL. Whether, at the end of the day, we agree with Kant that it makes a difference at which step a maxim fails (or whether, indeed, maxims can fail in only two basic ways) is a matter of less importance.

Kant discusses four main examples in the *Groundwork*. I am going to discuss only two of these, but I am going to do so in some detail. (In thinking about these examples, it is also worth bearing in mind the point that Kant is only human. In certain cases he may simply be wrong about what FUL entails. Kantians can embrace FUL while still rejecting one or more of Kant's own views concerning which particular moral requirements emerge from it.)

A. *The False Promise*

The first example I want to examine is Kant's second, a return to the false promise case that we have already had a look at. Recall that Kant claims that "I can will the lie but not at all a universal law to lie." Here is Kant's initial argument for this claim — that I cannot will the maxim to be a universal law:

> for in accordance with such a law there would properly be no promises, because it would be pointless to avow my will in regard to my future actions to those who would not believe this avowal, or, if they rashly did so, who would pay me back in the same coin; hence my maxim, as soon as it were made into a universal law, would destroy itself. (G 4:403)

And here is the argument the second time around, when Kant returns to the case as one of his four examples:

> Yet I see right away that it [my maxim] could never be valid as a universal law of nature[7] and still agree with itself, but rather it would necessarily contradict itself. For the universality of a law that everyone who believes himself to be in distress could promise whatever occurred to him with the intention of not keeping it would make impossible the promise and the end one might have in making it, since no one would believe that anything has been promised him, but rather would laugh about every such utterance as vain pretense. (G 4:422)

Now the basic line of argument here is clear enough. If we try to imagine a world in which everyone lies, or makes insincere promises, so as to achieve personal goals by deceiving others, we find that something goes wrong. No one would believe you when you tried to make such a promise.

But what, exactly, is it that goes wrong here? Some think that what we find is that it is *literally impossible* for there to be a world in which everyone lies or makes insincere promises. Perhaps in a world where promises are so routinely broken, the very institution of promising would disappear (or, alternatively, would never have come into being). So there cannot be a world in which everyone makes promises they do not intend to keep. The maxim of lying to get out of a tight spot could not be a universal law, because there literally could not be a world in which everyone complies with this maxim. This interpretation sits nicely with Kant's saying that in such a world "there would properly be no promises," that the universality of the law would make such promises "impossible" — that (as he later puts it) the maxim "cannot even be *thought* without contradiction" to be a universal law (G 4:424). If there literally cannot *be* a world in which everyone acts on the maxim, I cannot will it to be universal law, and the maxim fails FUL.

Others interpret the argument somewhat differently. Taking their cue instead from Kant's remarks that making the promise in such a world would be "pointless," that it would be impossible to achieve "the end one might have" in making the promise, they conclude that what actually goes wrong is this: in a world in which promises are routinely broken, it is much more difficult, and perhaps even impossible, to achieve the *goal* specified in the maxim (getting out of a tight spot by deceiving others) by performing the *action* specified in the maxim (making an insincere promise). Insincere promising works more effectively (and perhaps only at all) against a general background in which people keep their promises. Thus, making the maxim be a universal law — one that everyone has reason to act on — undercuts the effectiveness of the maxim itself. And this involves a kind of practical contradiction: if I will my maxim to be universal law, I make it harder to achieve the very goal specified by the maxim by acting on that maxim. From the point of view of someone willing the maxim, then, it is irrational of me to will it to be universal law. So I cannot will the maxim to be universal law, and it fails FUL.[8]

This second interpretation, it should be noted, assumes that it is not rational for someone who accepts the maxim to *will* that everyone act on the maxim, since this makes it harder to achieve the goal specified in the maxim (in the specified manner). The argument thus presupposes some principle to the effect that it is not rational to favor things that make it harder to achieve one's goals. This is not an objection to the argument, of course, for presumably we would indeed want to endorse *some* such principle of instrumental reasoning (although the details of the principle might be a matter of debate). Kant himself, for example, earlier in the *Groundwork* (G 4:417), defends the claim that "Whoever wills the end, also wills (insofar as reason has decisive influence on his actions) the means," and it looks as though, on the second interpretation, this principle, or some near relative of it, is assumed.

Again, this observation is not intended as an objection to the second argument. If we are to sometimes reject maxims on the grounds that we cannot autonomously will them to be universal laws, then presumably one reason this may happen is because we find that willing the maxim to be universal law would be an act that would fall short in terms of one or another standard that we rationally endorse. Thus, if we do rationally endorse some principle of instrumental reasoning, it is not problematic for the kantian to appeal to that principle when arguing that one cannot will a particular maxim to be universal law.

Regardless of which interpretation we accept, it is worth drawing attention to the fact that the argument makes use of various contingent, empirical facts. The argument assumes, for example, that people have memories, and will recognize the fact that promise breaking has become widespread, and that this will result in either a breakdown of promising (on the first interpretation) or a disinclination to trust the promises of others (on the second interpretation). I note this point only to put to rest the widely held belief that kantians think that morality is entirely *a priori*, something that can be established without appeal to empirical facts.[9] At best, FUL itself has this kind of status. As we can see, however, more specific moral conclusions — such as a prohibition against lying or making insincere promises — are derived from FUL through the use of empirical truths.[10]

Suppose we grant, if only for the sake of argument, that Kant has successfully shown that the maxim in question cannot pass FUL. For reasons we have already discussed, however, it won't yet follow that it is morally forbidden to make an insincere promise in this case. To reach that conclusion, after all, we must argue that not only this maxim, but any other maxim that would permit lying here, would fail as well. Kant doesn't try to generalize his argument, to cover the other relevant maxims, but it is easy to see how the attempt might go. The features of the maxim that seem relevant to its failure are ones that would appear in any permission granting maxim relevant to the case at hand. Thus if one maxim that would permit lying here would fail, others should as well. (We'll consider an objection to this claim below.)

Can the argument be generalized even further? Can we derive not only a prohibition against lying in this particular case, but a general prohibition against all lying whatsoever? Kant thought so, and notoriously claimed that it is never morally permissible to tell a lie. But this is a point at which many kantians part company from Kant himself. To take the standard case, many kantians believe it permissible to lie to a would-be murderer so as to protect his innocent victim hiding in your basement. And it seems at least possible that a maxim that would permit this act could pass FUL. After all, the existence of at least some insincere promising is compatible with the continued existence and effectiveness of promising (for there are, let us admit, insincere promises made in the real world, yet promising has not been rendered impossible or ineffective). Thus it seems possible that a maxim that enjoined promise breaking or lying in sufficiently rare or special circumstances (for example) might yet pass FUL. Perhaps a maxim that permitted lying to the would-be murderer is one such.[11] Kant may have thought that FUL supported an absolute prohibition against lying, but the kantian need not follow him in this regard.

B. The Maxim of Nonaid to Others

Kant's fourth example involves a person who has a chance to aid another in need, but is tempted to pass him by without offering assistance. Kant imagines the person's maxim to be one of complete refusal to provide aid ("I will not take anything from him or even envy him; only I do not want to contribute to his welfare or to his assistance in distress"), and he says of this case:

> But although it is possible that a universal law of nature could well subsist in accordance with that maxim, yet it is impossible *to will* that such a principle should be valid without exception as a natural law. For a will that resolved on this would conflict with itself, since the case could sometimes arise in which he needs the love and sympathetic participation of others, and where, through such a natural law arising from his own will, he would rob himself of all the hope of assistance that he wishes for himself.   (G 4:423)

Once again, the basic line of argument is fairly straightforward. Kant says that although there could be a world in which everyone acts on the maxim in question — a world where no one helps others — you cannot will this maxim to be universal law. You cannot rationally will that indifference to the needs of others be universal law, for you might find yourself in a situation where you *need* the help of others. The maxim thus fails at the second subtest: it cannot be willed to be universal law.

The first thing to notice about this argument is that it, too, appeals to empirical facts, here the fact that each of us has needs that we cannot always meet on our own. The second thing to notice is that it, too, makes use of something like the principle of instrumental reasoning. The thought is that each of us has goals of some sort, goals that we will want to achieve. But this makes it irrational to favor things that would make it more difficult to achieve those goals. Yet this is precisely what we will have done, in at least certain logically possible scenarios, if we will that it be *universal law* that no one help another. Once I recognize that I, too, can be in need of the aid of others, I cannot rationally favor a principle that would mean that I not get the help I need.

Notice, as well, that the relevant question is not particularly what I *would* will, *were* I in the situation where I needed help. That is no more relevant than the question of what I would will in the case where I don't need help. Rather, the question is what I am rationally prepared to will *here and now* as a principle to govern the case where I need help. Presumably, it is not rational of me (here and now) to be indifferent to my own need in that possible case. So I cannot (here and now) favor a rule that would mean that that need would go unmet (were it to arise). That is why I cannot will the maxim to be universal law. Thus it fails FUL.

Being clear about this point helps us to understand why it is irrelevant for someone to object that in the actual world they simply do not need anyone's help. Even if that were the case, it would remain a live possibility that the situation could be different: for anyone other than a deity, one *could* find oneself in need. And the thought, then, is that it cannot be rational to will, with regard to such a situation, that one not get the aid one would need.

Sometimes it is thought that whatever the force of this argument, it fails against an imagined "rugged individualist" who truly favors getting by completely on his own. Such a person, it is suggested, can will that the maxim of nonaid be universal law — for when he contemplates the possibility that he would himself be in need of the aid of others, he insists that even in such a case he (here and now) prefers that he die (in the given case) rather than be helped by others. (Of course, were he actually in a position of extreme need, he might lose his resolve and desire help. But as we have seen, that is strictly irrelevant. What matters is that here and now he wills that he not be aided, even in that case.)

I believe, however, that the kantian may have an answer to this objection available to him. For even the rugged individualist wants help of a particular kind — namely, to be left alone. This is easily seen if we imagine someone else bent on "aiding" him, despite his protests. The individualist wants the cooperation of others, just as the rest of us do; it is just that aid and cooperation take an unusual form in his case: leaving him to do things completely by himself. If this is right, then not even the individualist can favor a principle that would enjoin everyone to refuse to provide each with the particular aid that they need, for that would strip the individualist of what he most needs — to be left alone. If this is right, then none of us — not even the rugged individualist — can will a maxim of nonaid to be universal law.

Of course, as always, even if this is right it doesn't yet show us that it is morally forbidden to refuse to aid others. Doing that would require showing that not only this particular maxim but other, similar maxims would fail FUL as well. Once again, Kant doesn't attempt to generalize the argument, but here too it is not difficult to see how that more general argument might go: all humans (at least) are finite in ability, capable, in principle, of needing help (of some sort) from others; thus for any maxim at all that would simply permit disregarding the needs of others, no one can rationally will the maxim to be universal law.

But there remains a further worry. It might be objected that no principle at all could avoid the objection being raised against a principle of nonaid. For if, as the argument claims, it is irrational for me to will a principle (such as a principle of nonaid) that might leave me unable, or less able, to achieve my goals, then won't it be similarly irrational for me to will a principle that *requires* providing aid to others? After all, acting on a requirement to provide aid can itself leave me unable, or less able, to achieve one or another of my goals. Thus, won't the very same principle of instrumental reasoning that supposedly makes it irrational to favor a principle of nonaid also make it irrational to favor a principle *requiring* aid to others? How, then, can any principle at all — whether requiring aid or not — pass FUL?

Presumably the kantian must claim that an adequate answer to this worry involves balancing the various needs and aims I might have that might go unmet under the differing principles. I am looking for a principle that I can will to be universal law. And since, logically speaking, I might find myself in either one of the relevant roles (aid provider or aid recipient), I have to ask myself which costs I would rather endure. But in at least some cases — for example, when the gain to the needy when aid is provided is significantly greater than the loss to the person who actually provides the aid — the answer to this question is clear. Presumably, then, the principle of instrumental reasoning can lead me (here and now) to favor principles that do require providing aid in cases of this sort. But if this is right, then FUL will indeed support some sort of requirement to provide aid after all.

Doubtless, further questions could be raised about both of these examples (and as I have already noted, Kant discusses two other examples in the *Groundwork* as well). But I hope I have said enough to give at least some sense of how FUL is supposed to be used as a test for maxims and for deriving moral obligations.

Our discussion should also put to rest one common objection to FUL, namely, that it has no "bite," that any maxim at all can pass. For as we have now seen, it's not implausible to think that certain maxims do indeed fail FUL. Thus, whatever its other shortcomings may be, at least FUL isn't altogether devoid of content.

There are, however, other general objections to FUL that merit further discussion. Let me quickly mention four. All of them concern the adequacy of FUL from the *moral* point of view. First, it is sometimes objected that FUL is raising a morally irrelevant concern when it asks us to consider a world where everyone acts on the maxim in question. After all (the objection notes), in the *real* world typically it simply isn't going to happen that *everyone* acts on a given maxim. From the moral point of view, then, why should we concern ourselves with such an unrealistic possibility?

Recall, however, that the kantian's position is that if a maxim passes FUL, then it is morally permissible to act on it, indeed, morally permissible for anyone at all to act on it. It hardly seems irrelevant, then, to consider a world in which everyone *does* act on the given maxim. This would simply be a world in which — in the relevant way at least — everyone is acting in a manner that is supposedly morally permissible. Surely it makes sense to insist that it must at least be *possible* for everyone to act in a morally permissible manner, and indeed, to insist further that it must be reasonable to *favor* a world in which everyone acts in a morally permissible manner. (It cannot be preferable, from the moral point of view, that some act in a morally forbidden manner.) A world in which everyone acts morally must be both possible and attractive. Thus, in directing our attention to a full compliance world, FUL is not at all directing our attention to a morally irrelevant possibility.

But this immediately suggests a second objection: even if the full compliance world is indeed a world worth considering when testing maxims from the moral point of view, it is quite another matter to suggest that this is the *only* world worth considering, or even the most important. After all, in the real world not everyone is going to act morally, and so it is important to know how one is permitted (or required) to act in the face of immoral behavior by others. It would seem that the relevant question with regard to such cases of *partial* compliance is what I can will with regard to a world in which *not* everyone is acting on the maxim in question. But FUL apparently never asks us to consider such worlds: it *restricts* our attention to asking whether I can will a given maxim in a world in which everyone is acting on the maxim. Thus FUL inappropriately disregards the very real possibility of immoral behavior (partial compliance). Worse still, because of this neglect, it can generate morally implausible guidance, since acts that might be perfectly attractive were everyone to be acting morally (ones that I can will for the full compliance world) might be catastrophic when done in the face of immoral behavior.

Presumably, this difficulty about how to properly evaluate maxims for dealing with partial compliance might not be particularly worrisome if there were further tests, beyond FUL, that needed to be passed as well before it was permissible to act on a given maxim. If there were such further tests, then they might do a better job of evaluating whether a maxim can properly handle cases of merely partial compliance. We could appeal to these further tests to rule out maxims passed by FUL that were inadequate in this regard. But as we have already noted, Kant believes that FUL (and its equivalent, alternative formulations) is the only fundamental principle needed, and kantians have typically followed him in this. So it is worth asking whether FUL has the ability to handle the problem of imperfect compliance on its own.

I believe that it does. The problem, I think, lies not with FUL itself, but with what I earlier called the "standard proposal" for interpreting FUL. According to this interpretation, recall, to see whether a maxim passes FUL I need only ask whether I can will that the principle corresponding to the maxim be one that everyone acts upon. That is, I need only consider the full compliance world — whether it is possible, and whether I can rationally favor it. But why should we take FUL to be so easily satisfied? According to FUL, after all, I should only act on maxims that I can will to be *universal* law. In particular, then, I have to ask whether the appropriate principle is one that I can rationally will for *all* cases to which it applies. Now one such case, to be sure, may well be the case of full compliance. But often enough the principle in question will apply to other cases as well, cases of imperfect compliance; and so I must ask whether I can rationally will that the principle govern *those* cases as well. Thus, contrary to the claim put forward by the objection (and reinforced by the standard interpretation), FUL does not actually disregard consideration of partial compliance worlds, worlds where not everyone is acting morally. On the contrary, it demands that we consider such worlds as well, before signing off on a principle. Only if we can will the principle for cases of imperfect compliance as well (assuming that it applies to such cases) is it really true that we can will the maxim to be universal law.

It may also be worth recalling, in this regard, that the principles we favor need not prescribe the same type of action regardless of circumstances. In particular, then, we might favor principles that tell us to act in one way when others are acting similarly, and in quite another way when they are not. Thus the principles that pass FUL may enjoin one kind of behavior when others are acting morally, and quite another in the face of immoral behavior. In short, there is no good reason to believe that FUL will be unable to generate appropriate moral guidance for dealing with cases of noncompliance.

A third objection complains that in point of fact *no* maxims (or perhaps only very few maxims) can actually pass FUL. In particular, perfectly harmless maxims — maxims that intuitively it ought to be permissible to act upon — fail. If this is correct, of course, then we have some reason to reject FUL: if it fails maxims that ought to pass, then it isn't a very good test of the validity of a maxim. Here is an example of the sort of problem that people have in mind when they raise this worry. Suppose that I form the intention of going to the local pizza house, and ask whether my maxim ("I will go to Naples for lunch") can pass FUL. I must ask whether I can will this maxim to be universal law; and apparently this involves trying to imagine a world in which *everyone* — at a minimum, all five billion humans — goes to Naples for lunch! But as soon as I do this I see that either this is literally not possible (not everyone could fit) or it would involve a practical contradiction (it would make it much more difficult to get lunch). Thus my maxim fails FUL. But this — the objection concludes — is absurd. Surely going to the local pizza house is morally permissible (special circumstances aside), and if FUL condemns my maxim, so much the worse for FUL.

In answering this objection, the first thing to remember is that even if this maxim does fail FUL, that doesn't entail that it is morally impermissible to have lunch at Naples. So long as another maxim that permits having lunch at Naples passes FUL, then it will be perfectly permissible to have lunch there. At worst, all that would follow is that the short maxim we are here testing — "I will go to Naples for lunch" — does not provide a completely accurate account of what I have reason to do. And this is not, in fact, an implausible claim. For as a moment's reflection makes clear, whether it makes sense for me to go to Naples depends on any number of factors not mentioned in the maxim as stated, for example, whether or not I am hungry, whether or not I want pizza, whether or not the restaurant is crowded, whether or not it is nearby, and so forth. Presumably I do *not* have reason to go to Naples regardless of how crowded it is, how inconvenient it is to get to it, and so on. Thus the simple maxim "I will go to Naples for lunch" cannot in fact be plausibly taken to be a complete account of what I have reason to do and why. That requires a much fuller statement, one that, for obvious reasons, I rarely have occasion to try to articulate fully. Normally, the relevant extra conditions are left implicit, and so the short maxim is perhaps best understood as a kind of shorthand for that fuller statement.

Once we keep this point in mind, and try to universalize an appropriately full statement of the maxim (or universalize the short maxim, understood to implicitly contain the various necessary qualifications), we find that the maxim can indeed pass FUL. I can certainly will that everyone go to Naples if it is convenient, if it isn't too crowded, if they want pizza, and so forth. After all, obviously enough, one or another of these conditions won't be met for almost any person we might consider (most, for example, are much too far away for it to be convenient). And so, when we imagine a world in which everyone acts on this maxim, we won't imagine a world with billions trying to crowd into the local restaurant. Rather, we imagine a world in which those who want pizza and are nearby (and so forth) go. And this is a world, it appears, that we can readily will.

In short, if we take the simple maxim to be a complete statement, it does fail FUL, but appropriately so, while the fuller maxim passes. And if we take the simple maxim to be shorthand for that fuller maxim, then of course it passes as well. Either way, there will indeed be a maxim that passes FUL that permits me to go to Naples (special circumstances aside), and so, contrary to the claim of the objection, FUL won't forbid this morally innocuous act.

The third objection claimed (albeit incorrectly) that too little passes FUL. The final objection that I want to consider, our fourth, makes the opposite complaint, that too much passes. For as we have just seen, a complete specification of one's maxim might include any number of clauses and conditions. (FUL does not restrict us to testing "simple" maxims: any maxim can be put forward for testing.) The worry, then, is that if one is sufficiently clever in formulating one's maxim, one can always arrive at a version that will pass FUL, no matter how morally unacceptable the act in question. For example, suppose I want to murder you. Even if (as we might suppose) the straightforward maxim "I will murder those I want dead" would fail FUL, I need only propose, instead, a maxim that includes, say, my proper name. Suppose, then, that I try the maxim "If I am named Shelly Kagan then I will murder those I want dead." If this maxim can indeed pass FUL, then I am permitted to murder you (whether or not this is in fact my maxim). But this would clearly be unacceptable. So if the rigged maxim does indeed pass FUL, we will simply have to reject FUL.

The objection then continues by insisting that this maxim does, in fact, pass FUL. After all, there is presumably no impossibility about having a world in which *everyone* named Shelly Kagan kills at will (indeed I may well be the only person named Shelly Kagan in the world), and it certainly seems that I (Shelly Kagan!) can be in favor of a principle that gives me this extra freedom. So it looks as though I can will the maxim to be universal law, and FUL unacceptably permits me to kill at will. (Similar results could presumably be achieved by replacing my name with a definite description that uniquely picks me out, for example, "If I am a professor of philosophy at a midsize university, with three children, and a wife who works as a midwife, etc., etc., . . . then . . ." For simplicity, however, I'll stick to introducing the proper name.)

In fact, however, I think it far from obvious that I can rationally will the maxim in question to be universal law. After all, although I believe that I am one of at best a handful of people named Shelly Kagan — perhaps, indeed, the only one — I could presumably be mistaken about this. Perhaps there is a vast extended clan, currently living peacefully in the jungle, all of whose members are named Shelly Kagan. I can hardly rationally favor a principle that would permit this vast group to kill at will. And even if (as certainly seems likely) this possibility is unrealized in the actual world, there *could* be such a world, and it simply isn't true that I (here and now) am prepared to will with regard to such a world that all the Shelly Kagans in that world be permitted to kill at will. Thus it isn't really true that I can rationally will that the maxim "If I am named Shelly Kagan then I will murder those I want dead" be a universal law. Accordingly, the fourth objection fails as well.

Generalizing from the failure of this particular example, it seems we can say the following. Although nothing in FUL, in and of itself, places restrictions on the content of the maxims that we bring for testing — we can add whatever silly clauses and conditions we'd like — proper application of FUL does have the result of ruling out maxims that introduce irrelevant conditions. If a maxim is couched in terms of conditions that are in point of fact rationally and morally irrelevant, we will discover that we are not genuinely prepared to will that the maxim be a universal law.

But the discussion of the third objection has already suggested a complementary point as well, namely, that proper application of FUL will also have the result of ruling out maxims that *lack* relevant conditions. If a maxim is overly simplistic, we will find that we are not genuinely prepared to will that either. Taking these points together, then, the kantian claims that FUL provides a sufficiently subtle and sophisticated test to guide us toward plausible moral principles, ones that are sensitive to the relevant features of acts and their circumstances while disregarding the irrelevant features.

III. Kantianism and Consequentialism

What would those moral principles look like? That is, given FUL, what kind of normative moral theory emerges? Putting the question like this appropriately emphasizes the fact that what we have been primarily discussing up to this point is the kantian account of the *foundations* of ethics. (In this regard we have been following the lead of Kant himself in the *Groundwork*, the very title of which, after all, reveals that its primary concern lies with foundational issues.) We have not yet much concerned ourselves with describing the particular *normative* principles (roughly, the more directly action guiding principles, such as those requiring promise keeping or aiding others) that would emerge from that account, except as a means of illustrating FUL at work.[12] I have, of course, tried to portray that kantian account of the foundations of ethics as attractive and worth taking seriously — and if I have succeeded in this endeavor, then my primary purpose in this essay is accomplished. Still, it is natural to wonder about the normative level as well. Given FUL, what kinds of normative principles are we led to?

We have, of course, already taken a quick look at two particular examples. FUL, we have seen, rules out moral principles that would permit me to be indifferent to the needs of others, or to lie (or make a false promise) simply because this would be personally convenient. Obviously enough, given the time, we could apply FUL to a variety of other cases as well, and doing this over a sufficiently wide range of cases would doubtless enhance our understanding of FUL's plausibility and adequacy. But instead of continuing to focus on particular cases, I want to step back and ask, in a general way, whether we can say anything helpful about the overall structure of the moral theory that would emerge from FUL.

I raise this question, of course, because most kantians have thought it fairly clear that FUL supports a deontological moral theory. Kant himself certainly believed this. Indeed, even those who reject deontology — consequentialists being the most prominent among this group — have typically accepted this claim as well, and thus concluded that avoiding deontology requires rejecting the kantian account of the foundations of ethics. Now it is certainly true that nothing that I have said in this essay constitutes a full defense of kantianism. One might reject the account of autonomy that I sketched at the outset, for example, or deny that autonomy leads to FUL. If one does this, of course, then even if it is true that FUL does support deontology, given a rejection of FUL this won't threaten, say, one's acceptance of consequentialism. On the other hand, some will find the kantian account of autonomy and its implications sufficiently attractive, and FUL sufficiently plausible in its own right, that they are prepared to accept the moral principles supported by FUL, even if this requires revising some of their previously held moral opinions. If FUL does indeed support deontology rather than consequentialism, this may then provide a powerful argument in favor of deontology.

But there is a third possibility as well, of course, which is that Kant and most kantians are wrong when they claim that FUL supports deontology. If it should turn out that FUL actually supports consequentialism instead, then to the extent that one finds the kantian account of the foundations of ethics attractive, this will actually provide an argument in favor of consequentialism, rather than deontology.

Of course, one point is certainly true. If the kantian account of the foundations of ethics is correct, then the *basis* of ethics looks rather unlike the accounts typically offered by consequentialists. For historically speaking, at least, most consequentialists (though certainly not all) have grounded their consequentialism in what we might call *foundational consequentialism* — the claim that the ultimate basis of the (valid) normative moral principles lies in an appeal to the significance of the overall good. In contrast, the kantian account that we have been sketching gives no particularly important role at the foundational level to the concept of the good at all. The ultimate basis of morality, for the kantian, is not the good, but rather freedom. For this reason, it is appropriate to say that the kantian account of the foundations of morality is foundationally deontological, rather than foundationally consequentialist.

But it is one thing to insist that the kantian account of the foundations of ethics is usefully classified as deontological; it is quite another to insist that the particular normative principles that emerge from that account are themselves deontological. For absent further argument, there is no particular reason to assume that deontological foundations must yield deontological moral principles.[13] When I claim, then, that FUL may well support consequentialism rather than deontology, I have in mind a claim not about the foundational level, but rather one about the normative level, the level that concerns the various action guiding principles themselves. FUL may itself be grounded in a nonconsequentialist account (this much certainly seems to be true), but what *emerges* from FUL may well be a consequentialist rather than a deontological normative theory.

Evaluating this claim, of course, requires at least a working account of the distinction between deontological and consequentialist theories (at the normative level). Simplifying somewhat, the following should do for our purposes. Consequentialism holds that an act is morally permissible if and only if it has the best overall consequences (of those acts available to the agent). Deontology rejects this simple account of right and wrong, insisting that certain acts are morally forbidden, even when they would lead to better results overall. Deontologists thus embrace *constraints* — prohibitions against performing the offensive types of acts, even when doing so would lead to better results. Typical examples of constraints include prohibitions against lying, harming the innocent, failure to keep one's promises, and so on.[14]

Deontologists normally also reject consequentialism on the further ground that it is too demanding, always requiring the agent to perform the act that would lead to the best results overall, no matter how great the sacrifice involved to the agent himself. Deontologists thus typically embrace *options* as well — permissions to avoid promoting the overall good when the cost to the agent would be too great. For example, deontologists typically don't believe we are required to sacrifice huge portions of our income to famine relief, even though if we did so a great many lives might be saved. Such sacrifice is doubtless praiseworthy (they say), but it is strictly optional: we are permitted, instead, to pursue our own individual projects — as well as going to concerts, eating at expensive restaurants, and so forth — even though our time and money could do much more good were it spent in other ways. Most deontologists do insist, of course, that sometimes sacrifices for others are morally required (for example, when I can rescue someone at minimal cost to myself); but consequentialism goes too far (they say) in putting no limits on the obligation to promote the overall good.

While most deontologists accept both constraints *and* options (thus holding that consequentialism sometimes permits what is actually forbidden, and sometimes requires what is actually optional), I think it fair to say that so long as a theory contains constraints, it would normally be considered deontological, whether or not it contained *options* as well. In contrast, the presence of options alone (that is, without constraints as well) would not suffice to render a theory deontological. For our purposes, then, in asking whether FUL supports deontology, the key question facing us is whether or not FUL supports constraints.

Nonetheless, it may be helpful if we begin with the question of whether FUL supports *options*. For even though deontologists need not accept options, all consequentialists reject them. Thus, if FUL is to generate a consequentialist normative theory, it must reject options as well. Let us therefore postpone, for the moment, the question of whether FUL supports constraints. Even if there *are* constraints, I might still be morally required to do as much good as I can by permissible means (that is, those means not forbidden by constraints). So in asking whether FUL supports options or not, we are asking whether FUL supports a requirement to do as much good as one can — *within* the limits of constraints (if any).

Now we already know, from the discussion of the aid example, that FUL generates a requirement to aid others; FUL does not allow us to be indifferent to the good that we can do. But many kantians have thought it plain that FUL does not require us to do as *much* good as we can (within constraints — a qualification that I will hereafter leave implicit). While FUL sometimes requires us to promote the good (such as helping to meet the needs of others), it does not require us to do *all* that we can in this regard. The claim of these kantians, then, is that FUL generates a requirement to aid, but a *limited* one; when the cost of providing aid to others is too great, I am not required to do it.

But it is far from obvious that FUL will actually support this kind of limitation on the requirement to provide aid. It is certainly true, of course, that a maximally demanding requirement to promote the good will potentially impose considerable costs upon me. Indeed, in the real world I might find myself required to make huge sacrifices, while benefiting little, or not at all, from the fact that others are similarly required to promote the overall good. But in evaluating alternative principles concerning aid I must bear in mind the fact that I am looking for a principle that I can rationally favor for *all* worlds to which it applies. I cannot restrict my attention to the costs and benefits that I actually expect; I must consider all possible costs and all possible benefits. And since I have no more reason to be concerned with the costs that I might have to pay (as benefactor) than with the benefits I might receive (as recipient), it seems reasonable to favor a principle that provides the best overall balance of costs and benefits. But this is precisely what is done by a requirement to promote the *overall good*: it requires sacrifices only in those cases in which an even greater amount of good overall is thereby achieved. Thus, when I ask myself what sort of requirement to provide aid I can rationally favor to be universal law, it may well be that I must favor a requirement to bring about the best possible results overall. Anything less demanding will be inadequate.

Indeed, this implication of the aid example may have been staring us in the face all along, even if we did not previously draw it. For any requirement to provide aid at all will impose costs on those who have to provide the aid. If, nonetheless, I cannot rationally favor a maxim that would allow me to remain indifferent to the needs of others — and this, after all, is what Kant and kantians have always claimed — this must be because when I bear in mind the logical possibility that I might be either benefactor or recipient, I am led to balance the potential costs and benefits, and thus come to favor a principle that *at a minimum* requires aid when the benefits to those in need are significantly greater than the costs to those providing the aid. This is what we argued when discussing the original aid example. But this line of thought, if it is sound at all, has no obvious stopping point short of a general requirement to promote the overall good. The same balancing that leads me to favor a principle requiring aid when the benefits are "significantly" greater than the costs will, it seems, similarly lead me to favor a principle requiring aid *whenever* the benefits are greater than the costs, period. Thus, if FUL supports any requirement to provide aid at all, it should support a requirement to promote the *overall* good.

As always, there are a variety of objections that might be raised against the argument I have just been sketching. But once again, my purpose is not to offer a full defense of the claim that FUL rejects options. I merely wanted to indicate one main line of thought that might lead one to hold that FUL supports a general requirement to promote the overall good — despite what many kantians seem to believe.[15]

So let us suppose, if only for the sake of argument, that FUL does rule out options. As we have already noted, this is still compatible with FUL generating a deontological system. For we have not yet considered the question of whether FUL supports *constraints*. If it does, of course, then despite the general requirement to do as much good as possible within the *limits* of those constraints, it will still be true that certain kinds of action will be forbidden even when performing acts of the given kinds would lead to better results overall. Thus, so long as FUL supports constraints — even if it does reject options — it will in fact generate deontology rather than consequentialism. Accordingly, our next question must be whether FUL supports constraints.

Now it might seem obvious, in light of our earlier discussion, that FUL does indeed support constraints. For our very first illustration of FUL at work seemed to show that it rules out making insincere promises, or, more generally, lying. But if FUL does support a moral prohibition against lying, doesn't it follow trivially that it supports constraints, and thus that it supports deontology?

In point of fact, however, this conclusion does not follow so readily, for consequentialists themselves will be among those who support a moral prohibition against lying. Normally, after all, lying leads to worse results overall (counting everyone's interests equally) and so lying will typically be forbidden — even by consequentialists. In particular, in a typical case of false promising the overall results would be better if one refrained from making the insincere promise. Consequentialists will thus join deontologists in forbidding me to make insincere promises on the mere grounds that I need the money, or am in a tight spot, and so forth. And this means, of course, that from the mere fact that FUL prohibits making the insincere promise in such a case, we cannot yet determine whether FUL supports a *constraint* against lying and making insincere promises — even when (unlike the normal case) lying would have better results overall. Thus we are not yet in a position to tell whether FUL supports deontology or consequentialism. (Similarly, of course, for normal cases of promise breaking, harming the innocent, and so forth.)

What is needed, rather, if we are to settle the matter, is a case where it is stipulated that lying would lead to *better* results overall. If FUL would forbid lying even in a case of this kind, then indeed it would be clear that FUL generates a deontological normative theory — since it would support a moral principle that forbids lying even when lying is necessary to achieve the best results overall. But we have not yet investigated whether FUL prohibits lying even in cases of *this* sort; and I don't think it obvious that it does.

Of course, as we have already noted, Kant himself believed that FUL (or its equivalent) rules out *all* cases of lying, no matter what the circumstances. Were he right about this, obviously enough, FUL would be the basis of a particularly strict form of deontology. But as we have also noted, many kantians refuse to follow Kant on this matter, holding that under the *right* circumstances FUL can indeed pass a maxim that would permit lying (for example, lying to a would-be murderer). So at a minimum, we shouldn't take it as *obvious* that FUL will pass no maxims that permit lying when this is necessary to promote the overall good.

Presumably, we might attempt to settle the matter by considering a particular case where lying is stipulated to lead to better results overall, and then testing various maxims that would permit lying in such a case — so as to see whether any of these lie permitting maxims could pass FUL. In principle an investigation of this sort could tell us whether FUL forbids lying even when such an act leads to better results overall. If it does, this would show that FUL supports a constraint against lying, and thus supports deontology rather than consequentialism.

But such an investigation would have a variety of drawbacks. First of all, suppose we took some such maxim — say, a maxim of the form "I will lie under such and such circumstances" — and found that it could not pass FUL. As we know, this would show that one should not act on that maxim. But it would not actually show that FUL *forbids lying* in such cases. It would only show that one should not act on *that* maxim, that *if* lying is permitted, the reasons why it is permitted are not adequately captured in the particular maxim being tested. It would still be possible that some other maxim would pass FUL, a maxim that would permit lying in the case at hand.

On the other hand, suppose we found a maxim that permitted lying in the particular case imagined. That would of course show that it was permissible to act on that maxim, and thus permissible to tell a lie in that case, and thus — by hypothesis — permissible to tell a lie in at least one case where doing so leads to better results. But this still wouldn't necessarily constitute a defense of consequentialism, for the fact that lying here leads to better results might be irrelevant (or inadequate, by itself) to explaining *why* the maxim passed FUL. There might well be other cases where lying would also lead to better results, yet where telling a lie would *not* be permitted by the particular maxim that permitted it in the original case. In short, even if lying is permitted in *some* cases where this happens to have the best results, we couldn't necessarily conclude that it was permitted in *all* cases where this had the best results. So even if we did find a maxim that permitted lying in our original case, we wouldn't necessarily have shown that FUL supports consequentialism. To do that, we will need to show that FUL permits lying in *all* cases where this has the best results overall.

But of course even this wouldn't suffice, for it might be that FUL permits *lying* in all cases where this leads to the best results but nonetheless rules out *other* types of actions, regardless of the results. Perhaps, for example, lying is permitted when this promotes the overall good, but there is, nonetheless, a constraint against bodily harm to the innocent, even when this is necessary to bring about the best results overall. If something like this were the case, then, of course, it would still be true that FUL supports deontology. So long as there is any constraint at all — any prohibition against performing an act with good results overall — FUL supports deontology rather than consequentialism. In short, focusing on maxims concerned with lying alone will be too narrow a method of investigation to settle the question of whether FUL supports deontology or consequentialism.

What we want to know, of course, is whether there are any actions at all, of any sort whatsoever, that are forbidden even when performing actions of that sort is necessary to bring about the greatest amount of good overall. If any act, of any kind, is forbidden even when the results would be better, then FUL supports deontology. What the consequentialist must insist, therefore, is that *any* act is permissible, so long as it leads to the best results overall. But since the permissibility of an act follows so long as there is a single maxim that passes FUL that permits the given act, what the consequentialist must claim is that for each act that has the best results, there is *some* maxim or the other that would permit the act, that passes FUL.

Now in principle, I suppose, it could be a different maxim in each case. But this hardly seems likely. For as we have seen, maxims that pass FUL are supposed to do so by virtue of referring to the various features of the situation that actually provide the agent with adequate reason for acting in the specified manner. A valid, fully specified maxim would pick out all and only those features of the situation that make it reasonable for the agent to act in the given way. According to consequentialism, however, what *ultimately* justifies an agent's performing a given act is always the very *same* reason, namely, that the act would lead to the best results overall. Thus the consequentialist believes that in any given case, the act that leads to the best results is the appropriate act to perform, and the ultimate *reason* why it is the right act to perform is the very fact that it leads to the best results. Thus we should expect the consequentialist to hold that the principle "act in the way that has the best results overall" is universally valid, and that the quite general maxim "I will act in the way that has the best results overall" will pass FUL (no matter what the particular case at hand).

So let us consider that maxim. If it passes FUL, then, of course, it is permissible to act on it, which means that it will always be permissible to perform the act that has the best results overall — *whatever* type of act that may be, and whatever the circumstances. In short, if the *consequentialist maxim* (as we might call it) passes FUL, then it is never forbidden to perform the act with the best results, FUL does not support constraints, and FUL does not support deontology.

Does the consequentialist maxim pass FUL? I believe it does. At the very least it must be admitted that if it fails FUL it is not obvious how and why it does so. Consider the sorts of difficulties that have plagued maxims in our previous examples. On at least one interpretation of the false promising example we literally cannot imagine a world in which everyone makes false promises. Is there any comparable impossibility with regard to a world where everyone acts in such a way as to produce the best results overall? Obviously not. A world where everyone promotes the overall good is, sad to say, highly unrealistic, but there is no conceptual impossibility involved in trying to imagine it.

On the alternative interpretation of the false promising example, the existence of a world where everyone makes false promises makes it more difficult to achieve the end specified in the maxim itself through the means specified by the maxim (that is, getting out of a tight spot by making a false promise is less likely in a world where everyone tries to do this). When one imagined the maxim as universal law, the maxim's course of action became a less effective means to the maxim's own end. This was a kind of practical contradiction. Is there any comparable practical contradiction involved in imagining a world where everyone promotes the overall good? Again, the answer is obviously not. A world where everyone promotes the overall good is not a world that makes it more difficult to bring about the best results overall. On the contrary, it is likely to be a world that makes it easier to bring about the best results overall. Thus, whatever our interpretation of the first step of the FUL test, there seems to be no reason to think that universalizing the consequentialist maxim leads to a "contradiction in thought."

Nor, so far as I can see, is there any reason to believe that universalizing the consequentialist maxim leads to problems at the second step, generating a "contradiction in will." When we imagined a world where no one aided others in need, this was indeed a coherent possibility, but we found we could not will the relevant maxim to be a universal law. Given that we ourselves could have needs (that we were unable to meet without aid from others), it violated a principle of instrumental reasoning to favor a maxim that if made a universal law would necessarily leave those needs unmet. But is there any comparable violation of instrumental reason involved with willing it to be a universal law that everyone is to bring about as much good as possible? It is far from clear that there is.

To be sure, if it is a universal law that everyone is to bring about as much good as possible, then there may arise cases in which I may have to make significant sacrifices for others. From the point of view of instrumental reasoning this is undesirable, and gives me some reason to oppose such a requirement. But we have, of course, already considered this point. Since I am asking what I can will to be universal law, I must also consider the possibility that I might be the *recipient* of the aid. In effect, I must weigh all the potential costs against all the potential benefits, and when I do this — or so I have argued — instrumental reasoning will lead me to favor a principle in which sacrifices are required precisely when the benefits are greater than the costs. That is to say, instrumental reasoning will lead me to favor a principle requiring each of us to act in the way that has the best results *overall*.

Are there other reasons to think that I cannot rationally favor its being a universal law that everyone is to act in such a way as to maximize the overall good? At the very least it is not obvious what they might be.

Of course, one might object to such a law on the very ground that it would permit violating *constraints!* Intuitively, after all, certain acts are simply morally forbidden, despite their results. But promoting the overall good might sometimes require performing acts of these intuitively unacceptable kinds. Isn't this adequate grounds for refusing to will the maxim to be a universal law?

In point of fact, however, it is not at all clear that such intuitions are even *relevant* in thinking about which maxims pass FUL. FUL, after all, was supposed to be the basis of morality, the source of the valid moral principles (whatever they turn out to be). It can't play this role if we are going to *presuppose* various moral principles (whether directly, or by relying on moral intuitions) in determining what can, and what cannot, pass FUL. Put another way, given the kantian account of the foundations of ethics, appeals to moral intuitions are logically beside the point, until we have confirmed their accuracy *independently*, through appeal to FUL (cf. G 4:408–10). Thus we cannot appeal to the intuitive plausibility of constraints, and use this as a reason for claiming that principles that violate such constraints must fail FUL. Rather, we must first decide what passes FUL — and we must do this on independent grounds. And what this means, of course, is that despite the intuitive appeal of constraints, we don't yet have reason to think that FUL *generates* constraints.

For all that, of course, there might well be further arguments available to those who want to claim that I cannot rationally will it to be a universal law that everyone do the act with the best results overall. If such further considerations were offered, and found to be compelling, then it would indeed turn out that the consequentialist maxim cannot pass FUL. I certainly haven't attempted to discuss all possible arguments along these lines. But it must be admitted, I think, that it isn't obvious what these further arguments might look like. And so I think we should conclude — even if only tentatively — that our maxim can indeed pass FUL. Or, at a minimum, we should at least admit that this possibility is not one that can be readily dismissed.

But if the maxim passes FUL then it is always permissible to act on it. It is always permissible to do the act that will have the best results overall. Thus, if the consequentialist maxim passes, there are no constraints. FUL simply doesn't generate them.

Putting together the results of these various arguments, we can say, at a minimum, that it should not be taken to be obvious that FUL supports a deontological normative theory. On the contrary, there is at least some reason to believe that FUL yields no constraints at all, despite what Kant and most kantians have assumed. Indeed, there is some reason to believe that FUL supports a normative theory with neither constraints nor options. On such a theory, each of us is simply required to do as much good as possible. But this, of course, is consequentialism.

Here is a slightly different way to see how consequentialism is supported by FUL (assuming that the arguments we have been considering are sound). We have just argued that despite what kantians have typically thought, it may well be the case that kantian foundations support the claim that it is always *permissible* to do the act that will have the best results overall. By itself, of course, this result (even if correct) wouldn't yet show that we are *required* to do the act with the best results. But this further conclusion would indeed follow given the earlier claim that we are required to do as much good as possible within the limits of whatever constraints there may be. For if we are always *permitted* to do the act with the best results, there *are* no constraints. Thus the requirement to do as much good as possible *within* the limits of constraints reduces to the simple requirement to do as much good as possible. Each of us is required to do the act with the best results overall. But this, again, is precisely the claim of consequentialism.

These same basic ideas (if they are accepted) can be rearranged once more, into an even more straightforward "proof" that FUL supports consequentialism. To begin with, since the consequentialist maxim passes FUL, agents are always *permitted* to perform the act with the best results overall. But in point of fact, contrary to what most people have thought, no *other* maxim will pass FUL as well[16] (since any maxim that permitted doing less, or required doing something different, would run afoul of the principle of instrumental reason, and thus could not be willed to be universal law). Thus agents are actually *required* to do the act that would best promote the overall good. In short, given FUL — and assuming, of course, that the arguments we have been considering are correct — everyone is required to do the act with the best results overall, just as consequentialism claims.

Once again, it is worth emphasizing that I do not take these remarks to constitute a full defense of the claim that kantian foundations support a consequentialist normative theory rather than a deontological one.[17] But I hope I have said enough to show that this possibility is one that must be taken very seriously indeed, despite the fact that Kant and almost all kantians after him have rejected it (as have indeed almost all those who have studied kantianism, whether sympathetic to it or not).

If one were to attempt to complete the project of grounding consequentialism on a kantian basis, much would still need to be done. Beyond the obvious point, that the various arguments sketched here would need to be developed more fully (and a host of objections would need to be considered in greater detail), the most important remaining task would be this. A consequentialist theory is incomplete until combined with a theory of the good. Knowing that we are required to do as much good as possible does not yet generate determinate guidance until we know what makes one outcome better or worse than another. What we need, then, is an account of the intrinsic goods for the sake of which we should act. If the kantian account of the foundations of morality is correct, of course, then the intrinsic goods must be ones that we can autonomously set for ourselves as ends. Kantians believe there are such goods, however, and so the possibility of erecting a complete consequentialist theory on kantian foundations remains, I believe, both appealing and important. But I won't attempt to sketch here what an adequate kantian theory of the good might look like. That must be left for another occasion.

Let me return, finally, to a point noted much earlier, when we first introduced FUL. Kant, it will be recalled, claims that FUL is itself only one way of stating the same basic imperative. That is, he held that there are other ways of formulating the very same categorical imperative in quite different language. For example, at one point in the *Groundwork* Kant claims that the categorical imperative can also be stated like this (the formula of humanity):

> FH: "Act so that you use humanity, as much in your own person as in the person of every other, always at the same time as end and never merely as means" (G 4:429).

And at a different point he claims that the categorical imperative can also be stated like this (the formula of the realm of ends):

> FRE: "That all maxims ought to harmonize from one's own legislation into a possible realm of ends as a realm of nature" (G 4:436).

It certainly must be admitted that it is far from obvious that these different formulas are truly equivalent, generating the very same guides to action. Indeed, not all kantians agree with Kant about the supposed equivalence. Of course, for that matter, it is also far from obvious how these alternative formulas are best understood, and how they are to be applied. Unfortunately, pursuing these related issues would involve considerable further discussion, and so we cannot consider them here.[18]

I do, however, want to address one final question that might naturally arise at this point. If there are different formulations of the categorical imperative, is there any particular justification for focusing, as I have, on FUL, as opposed to some of the alternative formulations? Perhaps not. After all, if they are genuinely equivalent, then they must all support the same moral principles. And if I am right in thinking that FUL may lead to consequentialism, then if they are equivalent the other formulas should lead to consequentialism as well. I find that a plausible claim as well, but I won't attempt to defend it here.[19]

But Kant himself, in surveying the alternative formulations of the categorical imperative, makes an interesting remark. With regard to some of the other formulas, Kant suggests, it might well be the case that they are more intuitive and accessible. But if we want a strict accounting of what to do, he says, then we should turn to FUL (G 4:436–37). I have followed Kant's lead in this regard, and focused on FUL itself. Of course, I have also argued that Kant may well be mistaken about where, precisely, FUL takes us. Kantianism, I have argued, represents a significant account of the foundations of ethics. But contrary to the claims of most kantians, and Kant himself, these foundations may well lead us to consequentialism.

NOTES

1. I mean here to distinguish between foundational theories and more "normative" theories — theories involving basic moral requirements such as those concerning harm doing, promise keeping, and so forth. For the distinction between these two levels of theory, see Shelly Kagan, "The Structure of Normative Ethics," *Philosophical Perspectives* 6 (1992): 223–242, or *Normative Ethics* (Boulder: Westview Press, 1998). I will have more to say about the distinction between deontological and consequentialist normative theories below.

2. Two important precedents for challenging this widely held view are David Cummiskey, *Kantian Consequentialism* (Oxford: Oxford University Press, 1996); and Richard Hare, "Could Kant Have Been a Utilitarian?" in his *Sorting Out Ethics* (Oxford: Oxford University Press, 1997). The former is particularly sensitive to the details of Kant's own position. But insofar as *Kantian Consequentialism* is primarily concerned with the formula of hu-

manity rather than with the universal law formulation of the categorical imperative, the present essay is perhaps best viewed as being complementary to that work rather than simply duplicating it. I should perhaps note explicitly that while I have qualms about various details of Cummiskey's arguments, I am, of course, in broad agreement with his main conclusions. The same is largely true for Hare's discussion as well, though I am unconvinced that it is precisely *utilitarianism* — rather than some other consequentialist theory with a more complicated theory of the good — that emerges from Kant's account.

3. I will note, however, that Kant's own discussion of freedom is made complicated by his unargued assumption of incompatibilism — the claim that freedom is incompatible with determinism (see, e.g., G 4:446–47 or 455–56) — and that this is a view that the kantian need not accept.

4. Might the line of thought that leads from autonomy to FUL support an even stronger conclusion? If autonomy requires that I restrict myself to acting on reason-giving principles that I can autonomously will to be universal law, does it also require that I act on all those principles that I *can* so will? This is an important question, but I won't pursue it here (except to note that the distinction between what I can will, and what I do will, will be relevant). For simplicity, let's continue to follow Kant's lead and consider FUL only in its familiar, "negative" formulation.

5. His reasons for claiming this are not altogether clear or persuasive. At G 4:402 and 420–21 he seems to have in mind something like the following disjunctive argument: (1) the validity of imperatives must be based either on their content or on their form. But (2) considerations of content yield no categorical imperatives, and (3) the only categorical imperative based on form is FUL. So (4) the only categorical imperative is FUL. Now one worry about this argument is that it is difficult to see how to reconcile (2) with the later search (at G 4:428–29) for a formulation of the categorical imperative based on its inevitable content, a search that supposedly successfully results in the derivation of the formula of humanity. But since Kant holds that the formula of humanity is itself simply another way of formulating the same imperative as FUL, perhaps (2) could be replaced with (2'): the only categorical imperative derivable from considerations of content is equivalent to FUL. He could then still conclude with (4') — that the only categorical imperative is FUL or its equivalent. The more serious difficulty with the argument, however, is that even if we grant (1) (and it is not clear that we should) neither (2) (or (2')) nor (3) seems adequately defended or obviously correct.

6. Are there any such additional principles — valid, but not derived from

FUL? I don't see why the kantian should deny their existence. Indeed, as we will note later, many applications of FUL seem to make use of some sort of principle of instrumental reasoning. Kant defends his own favored version of this principle, but it is noteworthy that this defense doesn't make reference to FUL at all (see G 4:417). So there may be at least one such further principle, and I don't see why there shouldn't be others.

7. Kant speaks here of a universal law "of nature," since his discussion of the four examples actually proceeds in terms of the formula of the law of nature (FLN) — a variant of FUL which he introduces at G 4:421. For our purposes, however, the differences between FUL and FLN are unimportant.

8. See Christine Korsgaard, "Kant's Formula of Universal Law," reprinted in her *Creating the Kingdom of Ends* (New York: Cambridge University Press, 1996), for a fuller discussion of these and other interpretations, including a defense of the second.

9. Unfortunately, Kant seems to be confused on this point, sometimes apparently holding the view just shown to be mistaken — that the familiar moral rules are themselves *a priori* as well. (See, e.g., G 4:389, 408, or 410–12.) In any event, the claim that *FUL* is *a priori* is less clearly mistaken, and Kant certainly believed it too (see, e.g., G 4:419–21), though whether it is correct depends on, among other things, whether the autonomy of reason is something that can be established *a priori*.

10. This has an interesting implication, which I will mention in passing. People often take the familiar moral rules (to keep your promises, to tell the truth, and so forth) as themselves being categorical imperatives, binding upon everyone. But in light of what we have just noted, we must reject this view. (We would need to reject it in any event, if we insisted on taking seriously Kant's claim that FUL and its alternative formulations represent the *only* categorical imperative.) If the derivation of particular moral rules makes essential use of contingent empirical facts, then those rules will themselves only be binding *given* the facts in question. This means that moral rules will not be binding upon *all* rational beings, *regardless* of what else is true. Thus the familiar moral rules are not categorical — since categorical imperatives must be binding upon all rational beings without condition (see G 4:416). What *is* true, of course, is that they *are* binding, nonetheless, for those rational beings for whom the relevant empirical facts do obtain, and in a world like ours that may well mean for all human beings whatsoever. In particular, then, while the familiar moral rules are not categorical, they are not conditional upon the particular desires and goals of the people involved. (It must be admitted, however, that Kant himself seems

confused on this point as well, suggesting at various places that the familiar moral rules are indeed categorical. See, e.g., G 4:389, 408, or 410–12.)

11. For one example of an argument to this effect, see Christine Korsgaard, "The Right to Lie: Kant on Dealing with Evil," in *Creating the Kingdom of Ends*.

12. Again, for the distinction between the two levels of moral theory see either "The Structure of Normative Ethics" or *Normative Ethics*.

13. I've argued elsewhere that, in general, deontological foundational theories need not support deontological normative theories (and, similarly, that consequentialist foundations needn't support consequentialist normative theories). See Part 2 of *Normative Ethics*.

14. Some deontologists are absolutists with regard to these constraints, holding the relevant types of acts to be forbidden no matter how much good would be done — or harm avoided — by performing them. Other deontologists are moderates about constraints, believing it permissible to infringe the constraint when enough good is at stake. For our purposes, however, the distinction won't be important.

15. Kant's own views on this subject are less clear. But it is striking that when discussing the aid example in terms of the formula of humanity Kant concludes that each person must "aspire, as much as he can, to further the ends of others" (G 4:430). This certainly looks like a denial of options. Perhaps, then, Kant would have agreed that FUL rejects options as well, since he believed that the formula of humanity is equivalent to FUL.

16. At least, not if we are taking the maxims to be *fully specified*. The consequentialist can readily admit, of course, that many other ("abbreviated" or "shorthand") maxims will also pass as well — when tested against the implicit background assumption that the act in question has good results overall.

17. Let me quickly mention another argument that is sometimes used to defend the claim that kantian foundations support deontology. It turns on the distinction between perfect and imperfect duties. A perfect duty, Kant says, "permits no exception to the advantage of inclination" (G 4:421 note) and is "unremitting" (G 4:424); in contrast, then, an imperfect duty presumably leaves one with some latitude as to how and when it is to be satisfied. Arguably this entails that one must never violate or otherwise infringe a perfect duty for the mere sake of fulfilling an imperfect one. If we then add the further assumption that the familiar duties such as the requirement not to lie, to keep one's promises, not to harm the innocent, and so forth, are perfect duties (because, supposedly, they all fall out of FUL at the

first step), while the duty to aid others is merely an imperfect duty (because it is generated only at the second step), we seem to have the desired deontological conclusion that one must promote the good, but not when this requires telling lies, harming the innocent, and so on. There are, however, a great many problems with this argument, not the least of which is the point, previously noted, that nothing in the account of FUL itself warrants investing the question of the stage at which a duty is generated by FUL with anything like this kind of significance. (For further discussion of the attempt to use the perfect/imperfect distinction as an argument for deontology, see Cummiskey, *Kantian Consequentialism*, chapter 6.)

18. Though I will note the obvious point that if one does accept more than one of these formulas as expressing a genuine categorical imperative, while denying their equivalence, one must deny Kant's claim, also previously noted, that there is exactly one categorical imperative. (Of course, it could still be the case that one of these categorical imperatives was the most basic, and the others could be derived from it.)

19. Though, again, see Cummiskey, *Kantian Consequentialism*, for a defense of the claim that it is actually consequentialism rather than deontology that is supported by the formula of humanity.

What Is Kantian Ethics?

ALLEN W. WOOD

Kant is the most influential moral theorist of modern times. Many philosophers, of whom I am one, think that of all figures in the history of ethics, Kant did the best job of identifying what lies at the heart of moral values and principles, providing a philosophical defense of our core moral convictions, and constructing a moral theory on the basis of them. At the same time, nobody today actually subscribes to every aspect of Kant's thought about morality, especially to Kant's moral opinions on certain subjects. To enlightened people in our day, some of Kant's views on lying, or suicide, or the death penalty, or the duty to obey political authority, or human sexuality — taken literally — are unacceptable. Even some of what Kant took to be fundamental tenets of his ethical thought, such as his theory of noumenal free will, seem dubiously metaphysical to most level-headed people.

Some take these stumbling blocks to indicate the theory's basic spirit. I think that is wrong, but we Kantians have to concede this much to them, that it is a bit anachronistic for us to insist on talking about 'acting from duty' and 'categorical imperatives', perhaps even about 'autonomy', 'ends in themselves', and the 'realm of ends'. We do so because we want to link ourselves to the spirit of the Enlightenment, of which Kant is the most influential representative. And we are entirely right to want to link ourselves to *that* spirit. At the same time, we have to admit that the eighteenth-century Enlightenment is far from where we are now, partly because of the very success of the Enlightenment in changing people's minds, but largely because of the many victories of countermovements to the progressive Enlightenment tradition, many of them in the second half of the twentieth century.

As a result, even in our fierce anachronism, we Kantians relate positively to Kant's writings only because we are silently transposing their content, hearing them in a different key, so to speak, from that in which they were originally written. But that metaphor is still too timid. For it is necessarily the entire style of our moral convictions that has changed. Kant can be to us only as Haydn or Mozart or Boccherini is to Shostakovich or

Bartók or Ellington. For this reason we owe it not only to the critics but to ourselves to do more than Kantians usually do by way of saying what exactly we think Kant got right, and how it should be expressed now.

I have been talking about "us Kantians" in the plural, but I can't go on pretending that I am speaking for anyone but myself. However, I do hope that many of those favorably disposed to Kantian ethics will share the views I put forward. No doubt others will think my interpretation of Kant is wrong, or (what can be, but is not necessarily, the same thing) they will disagree with what I identify as the rational kernel of Kantian ethics and rush to the defense of what I have decided to discard as its inessential husk. But the resulting controversies can only help clarify both our actual ethical thinking and our view of how Kant's ethical thought is to be appropriated.

I. "Moralism"

Kant theorized about morality over two hundred years ago, and he wrote for a very different audience. Even now many people associate morality very closely with religious beliefs and commitments, but in Kant's time this connection was still closer, and in many quarters it was considered improper even to question it, or to attempt to discuss morality at all apart from religion. Because morality was often conceived as obedience to God's will, it was wholly natural for a philosopher to treat moral principles as a species of law or imperative, even if the philosopher is not thinking of the divine will as the author of such commands. It was a decisive step away from the spirit of moral authoritarianism when Kant considered our own rational will to be the author of morality's commands. Another important point is that in the eighteenth century moral duty was treated almost universally with what we can only regard as a kind of innocent earnestness, whose rhetorical expression we can receive only with condescending irony or cynical skepticism.[1] Kant writes about the authority of moral commands with a kind of assurance that no one could today.[2]

A large part of the common resistance to Kantian moral theory is simply a reaction to the rhetoric of stern "moralism" in which Kant presents his theory. Let's face it: we all know people who are "too moral by half" in their own lives — and also too intrusively interested in the morality of others. They are always ready with cloying platitudes, which they are ready to illustrate with tediously familiar little stories that grossly oversimplify the problems real people face in a complicated world, and at the same time they exhibit unrelentingly a viciously narrowminded, "moralistic" view of the world.[3] Such people are offensive enough in our private dealings with them, but when they turn their zeal toward public political ends, as they have in our country during the last generation, then the results are loathsome to contemplate. Many thinking people reject Kant's moral philosophy because they react to the rhetoric of his writings in the same way they do to the offensive spirit of such private or public moralists. The instincts of such people are healthy, but when they direct their rage at Kant, they seriously misunderstand him.

Once we get past his eighteenth-century rhetoric, I do not think Kant's *ethical theory* really is "moralistic" at all in this negative sense. Morality is a complex social and psychological phenomenon, but one of its chief elements — especially when it is preached by moralists — is a peremptory claim by certain cultural forces (often highly traditional and very regressive ones) to authority over the lives of individuals. Above all what makes it hard to take "moralizing" seriously is our understandable skepticism about the thought that letting "morality" (in this sense) have its way with me could be compatible with the attitude I should take toward my life. For as a mature adult human being, I rightly regard that life as mine to direct according to my own lights. I cannot permit myself to be ordered about submissively by pompous moralizers enforcing outworn codes of conduct or by religious fanatics claiming to represent God's authority over me.

It is one of Kant's chief merits that he articulated just those reasons for resisting "moralism" — but he did so in the name of "morality" itself. For Kant's basic idea is that our primary commitment should be to directing our own lives according to our own best rational judgment, and he accordingly reconceived the principle of morality itself as a principle of *rational autonomy*. Our resistance to Kant is often a result of the understandable difficulty we have in taking seriously the revolutionary concept of morality he is proposing. We hear only his moralizing talk, and interpret his theory of morality as though it were just another shabby subterfuge some moralist is using to manipulate us. In this light, I think it would help us to understand Kant better if instead we heard his moralistic rhetoric partly as a desperate attempt to persuade the conservative audience of his day (including the morally conservative part of himself) that his fundamental idea of rational autonomy is compatible with traditional moral standards and values. In other words, Kant has good reason to fear that "moralists" (in the sense we rightly find objectionable) will regard his theory as dangerously libertine. We should perceive his moral sternness as an attempt (perhaps not wholly successful) to disarm such fears. One of the things about Kantian ethics that should most appeal to us, therefore, is that it helps us explain and justify our resistance to the very rhetoric in Kant's own writings that we often find most offensive. We rightly resist any morality based on tradition or custom (perhaps sanctified by religious humbug) as an affront to our worth as self-directing adult human beings, who have the capacity to think for ourselves and the right to regard our own free thinking as the final arbiter of whether morality (or anything else) deserves our allegiance.

Of course "moralism" is out of fashion for bad reasons as well as good ones. People also reject it on the basis of various shabby rationalizations and self-serving illusions. Kant was aware of many of them in their eighteenth-century forms. Many people succumb to the sentimental notion that in directing our lives our "natural feelings" can always be trusted. Or they hold the shallow belief that there really are no reasons except selfish reasons, or the vicious philosophy that things go best for all if we forget about other people and just "look out for number one." Or they say that whether this is "best" or not, it's the way things are and one has to be a "realist" about life. Or perhaps they subscribe to the absurd Romantic (and Nietzschean) idea that some people are "special" ("higher" or more "creative" — that is, that some people are like themselves as they imagine themselves to be), and special people do not need to respect other people's rights or concern themselves with their needs.

Since Kant's day, the self-deceptive appeal of these ideas to our selfish complacency has been fueled by misunderstandings of Darwin's theory of evolution and by the perceived failure of all sorts of attempts, whether religious or secular in inspiration, to make the world a better place. I confess that Kantian ethics also appeals to me because it *is* "moralistic," in the sense that it gives no quarter to any of these widespread and pernicious notions. Kant had a conception of human nature that was in many ways dark and cynical, but that only made him the more insistent that we must not give in to the temptation to treat what is done as the proper standard for what should be done. Kant's moralistic rhetoric, I submit, is not offensive (but is even appealing) if we perceive it as a reflection of his recognition that human affairs are very far from being what they should be, and an attack on the self-complacency with which too many people rationalize their shortsighted and selfish ways of life.

II. Moral Deliberation

As Kant's theory presents it, morality is fundamentally a way of thinking about what to do. It is a mode of deliberation that could be described as 'free' or 'ultimate'. It is *free* in that it is unrestricted regarding the kind of reason one offers for a course of action, and *ultimate* in being the last instance of decision about how we should live our lives. *Moral* deliberation is, first, not restricted to reasons arising from *instrumental* reasoning about particular ends we have contingently set. It may consider the best way to attain an end, but it is fundamentally about which ends should be ultimate and primary in our lives. Second, it is not restricted to considering self-interested ends, such as my own welfare, or the welfare of some particular group to which I belong or which I happen to care about. Moral deliberation provides grounds for being concerned about my own welfare and happiness, but it is not limited to *prudential* reasoning about how my — or anyone's, or everyone's — happiness is best to be promoted. Moral deliberation is concerned also with knowing why, and deciding under what conditions, anyone's happiness is a worthy object of pursuit.

Kant treats moral deliberation as a species (even a paradigm) of rational deliberation. The Kantian conception of moral deliberation thus goes against a familiar dogma that rational deliberation is solely about means and can never be about ends (whose adoption is not supposed to be subject to rational considerations at all). The basic error behind this dogma is the assumption that practical reasoning is always grounded on desire. It is one of Kant's chief insights that there are some desires we have only because we have *reasons* to have them, and these reasons are independent of any desire.

Some desires (such as hunger) we just find in ourselves. Others we have for reasons (even hunger is a *rational* desire to the extent that we recognize it as expressing our need for nutrition). Some rational desires are nonmoral and some are moral in content. Morality, in fact, is about the objects of all these desires and the reasons grounding them. Moral deliberation creates rational desires by making these reasons evident to us. It focuses on a certain type of ultimate value and ultimate rational concern about how we should act. This value, as Kantian theory conceives it, is the *worth* of the rational beings who are moral agents, who have the value Kant describes by saying they have 'dignity' and by calling them 'ends in themselves'. Moral deliberation is usually concerned with someone's welfare or happiness, but not only with the agent's own welfare, or with the welfare of those agents she may happen to like or with whom she may sympathize. Moral deliberation regards the value of happiness or welfare as grounded on something deeper, namely on the objective worth of the beings themselves whose happiness is in question. Because other rational beings have the same worth that I do, moral deliberation therefore necessarily takes the welfare of others into account as well as my own.

This feature of moral deliberation has led some philosophers to think of morality as a kind of expanded or collective prudence, based ultimately on a single end, the common good or greatest happiness of all. John Rawls famously criticized this type of moral theory for overlooking (or under-estimating the importance of) "the distinction between persons."[4] The ar-gument associated with this last slogan is often taken to be the most basic and authentically Kantian reason for resisting the "greatest happiness" morality. But I think we badly misunderstand Rawls's Kantian objection to utilitarianism if we depict the disagreement between Kantian and utilitarian views as fundamentally one in which the utilitarians favor human commu-nity or the unity of human ends while the Kantians ignore these values or give them second place to the abstract rights of isolated individuals. This is a basic misunderstanding. Kant's own basic principle is that we must see ourselves as part of an ideal community, a "realm of ends" in which all human ends are united and mutually supporting.[5] The most basic object of value in Kantian ethics is therefore the rational being not as an isolated individual but as the object of a set of common laws *uniting rational beings into a community*.

The right way to put Rawls's Kantian criticism is rather to say that it charges utilitarianism with misunderstanding the true nature of that human community which is (for both Kantianism and utilitarianism) the primary value. Kant holds that people should be united by ends they freely and rationally pursue in common. The fundamental aim of moral theory is to determine the principles according to which to achieve that agreement, hence the *right kind* of community. The point of Rawls's criticism is that when utilitarianism conceives of the right end as simply the collective maximization of personal good, it thinks of human community as if it were best guided by a single prudential reasoner (in effect, a benevolent despot) who dictates actions to an aggregation of will-lessly obedient (or perhaps craftily manipulated) subjects. Respect for individual human beings, and for their role as independent judges, equal participants in the process of deciding for the community, must then be taken account of subsequently, as something that the utilitarian dictator integrates (of necessity, paternalisti-cally) into the collectively prudential calculations as one factor among many in what is most beneficial to them. For the Kantian, however, a community of rational beings must be conceived from the ground up as the rational agreement of a plurality of distinct and equal persons who freely choose to unite their ends on terms that respect each one's autonomy. The crucial thing, therefore, is not to determine the means to a single given collective end. It is something more basic than that: It is to determine the principles of association through which any rational system of collective ends is to be set.

This point has far-reaching implications for the way we should reason about collective goods. We cannot simply integrate "process values," associated with the way ends are set and actions chosen, into the ends people pursue, as if these were simply one kind of good to be weighed against others in determining the content of the ends and the most efficient means to them. It gets the fundamental role of these values wrong to ascribe "utility" to the fact that an action keeps a promise or an institutional arrangement respects the rights of those who participate in it, and then to treat these as "utilities" to be weighed against other "utilities" in determining the best "overall consequences" of actions or social arrangements.[6] To flatten out moral deliberation into a system of collective prudence, with all goods treated as products of action, is to ignore the fact that the value of individual agents and of certain kinds of community among them has the *first* claim on us in structuring the way we should deliberate both as individuals and as communities.

Both the ground and the nature of these objections to consequentialist theories are distorted when they are represented as a mindless devotion to rule-following under the traditional title of "deontology" — as though the Kantian position is that the rules themselves (although they represent nothing of value) have some overriding authority to which we should be prepared to sacrifice everything that is of value. Kant's theory is based rather on the overriding value of rational beings themselves, whose rational choice, on terms of mutual respect, is to be the final authority over what might have enough value to make it worth pursuing as an end of action.

III. Three Features of Morality

"Morality," as a kind of rational deliberation, has three crucial features from which Kant's theory proceeds. The *first* is that it considers on their merits *all* reasons for acting, whatever their character. Thus although Kant holds that every action is for the sake of some end that is to be brought about, he also recognizes that the most fundamental reasons are those that do not presuppose an end but ground the *setting* of the highest ends we should bring about. The Kantian way of putting this point is that the imperative of moral deliberation is "categorical" rather than "hypothetical." This leads to Kant's first formulation of the principle of morality, the *formula of universal law* (FUL) and its variant, the *formula of the law of nature* (FLN) (G 4:421).

The *second* feature, in one way still formal but in another way the most substantive value thesis on which Kantian ethics rests, is that it is concerned with the *reasons* we have for taking account of the standpoint of others, hence for caring about their welfare as well as our own, and choosing on principle to unite that standpoint with ours under common laws for common ends. This presupposes that as a rational agent I have good reasons for respecting other rational agents, and treating their existence and their welfare as having objective value in principle equal to my own. From these considerations arises Kant's second formula of the principle of morality, the *formula of humanity as an end in itself* (FH) (G 4:429)

The *third* feature of morality, easier to overlook but just as important as the other two, is that it motivates us by appealing to our conception of *who we are* and to incentives of *self-worth* associated with this conception. This leads to Kant's third (and most definitive) formula of the moral law, the *formula of autonomy* (FA), and its variant, the associated *formula of the realm of ends* (FRE) (G 4:431, 433).

It is essential to moral deliberation that the fundamental reason I have for following it is that in my own eyes *I* will have less worth if I do not. A being that always did the morally right thing, and always desired to do what it does, would nevertheless not be a moral agent at all if it did not think (or had no tendency to be moved by the thought) that it had greater self-worth for so acting and less self-worth if it had not so acted.[7] This is why Kant begins the *Groundwork* by appealing to the *esteem* we feel for the good will, and regards the moral law as adequately grounded only when it has been shown how obedience to it is associated with our *self-respect* (G 4:393–99, 431–38). It is also why Kant regards autonomy of the will and the dignity of self-legislation as the only possible grounds for a categorical obligation.

IV. Morality as Social Custom

One common criticism of moral theories (both Kantian and non-Kantian) is based on the thesis that morality is *not fundamentally* a kind of rational deliberation at all. Morality, it is said, has its origin not in individual ratiocination but in social customs and the shared attitudes they involve. A society has certain rules of conduct whose observance involves the subordination of individual preferences, and even individual well-being, to what is regarded as the good of the whole. Failure to comply with those rules subjects the offender to disapproval and contempt in the opinion of others. Some theories of the origin of morality locate the truly original expectations and opinions more precisely, in the threat of paternal disapproval of the child, or even in the mother's refusal of the breast to the infant, which subsequently become "internalized" or take the form of the "superego" or "ego-ideal" standing over against the real person and her interests. Others fasten on the variety and contingency of social customs, using this as an argument that we should not expect moral principles to be universal or grounded in anything we should dignify with the name of 'reason'. Some of these approaches to morality insist that moral philosophy, instead of adopting the intellectualistic and individualistic form of practical deliberation, should orient itself toward this more basic "ethical life" *(Sittlichkeit)*, or lived social practices, and the set of traits, feelings, and "thick" self-conceptions corresponding to them.[8]

It may come as a surprise to some who argue this way that Kant largely agrees with them as far as the historical origins and social roots of morality are concerned. Yet he holds that this does not support their objections to his kind of moral philosophy, but in fact discredits them. In his essay *Conjectural Beginning of Human History*, Kant locates the primal origin of morality in the act of *sexual* refusal through the concealment of desired genital organs. This device excites sexual *desire* by transforming its object into something imaginary, and simultaneously awakens *respect* for the person by closing off access to what is desired (MA 8:113). The effect is to bring into being a kind of social power over individual agents located within these agents themselves. By means of this power their behavior can be controlled through their sense of their own worth and the worth of others and through an experience of conflict between that kind of worth and their natural desires. Kant calls this new state of consciousness the sense of "decency" *(Sittsamkeit)* or "propriety" *(Anständigkeit)*. By conforming to accepted customs *(Sitten)*, or acting in a manner that is deemed fitting *(anstehend)*, people arouse the esteem of others, which they value as a condition of their sense of self-worth. Kant regards such behavior as closely tied both to people's competitive impulses (their "unsociable sociability") and to their propensity to deceive both others and themselves, by concealing what would lead others to think less of them and by pretending to supposed merits they do not possess.

Kant thereby recognizes that the psychological and historical origins of morality are something toward which thinking people are right to adopt a critical and even a highly ambivalent attitude. Kant thus recognizes some of the good reasons why reflective people are rightly skeptical of "morality" and "moralism." He acknowledges the continuing dominance of these patterns in social life when he treats "semblance" *(Schein)*, "illusion" *(Täuschung)*, and "deception" *(Betrug)* as characteristic of human sociability, and even as increasingly characteristic of it as it becomes more fully developed or "civilized" (VA 7:149–50).[9]

No doubt some of the most conspicuous examples of bad conduct involve the defiance of what is socially approved, whether the infringement of people's recognized rights or the disregard of their accepted claims to respect and concern. A view that roots morality in social practices and customary attitudes has no trouble giving an account of what is wrong with such conduct. It has a harder time, though, in accounting for what is objectionable in the evils that spring precisely from this *Sittlichkeit* itself, from the conformity to accepted customs and the display of traits recognized as "virtues" and from the harmonious relation to all those feelings and "thick" conceptions that express the life of an existing community. If the basic principles of existing communities really embodied a decent approximation of the way people should think about themselves and should treat one another, then such approaches to morality might get things at least approximately right. But as long as the truth remains closer to the reverse of this — as long as our societies remain scenes of massive oppression, injustice, and corruption — moral philosophy does better by encouraging us to alienate ourselves from the ethical life of our existing communities and instead to take as fundamental a purely rational deliberative standpoint. It is therefore one of the chief *advantages* of Kantian ethics that it is abstractly rationalistic and self-alienating in precisely this way.

Kantian ethics is "individualistic" in the sense that it takes the capacity for rational deliberation in individuals to be the ground of the moral life, or even to be the ground of all value whatever. It is also individualistic in its assertion of the importance of the rights of human individuals and in its rejection of notions of collective moral responsibility or guilt. But it is not individualistic at all in several other important respects in which it is too often thought to be. First, as we have just seen, Kantian ethics recognizes that the psychological origins of morality are social. Kant agrees with Rousseau in regarding moral evil (what Kant calls the 'radical propensity to evil in human nature') as a product of our social condition (R 6:27, 95–96). Second, and just for this reason, Kant also holds that the struggle against evil cannot be effective unless it is social. He does not think that individuals struggling on their own against their evil propensity will make much progress toward good (R 6:96–102). Third, the final end of morality is social rather than individual: it is a realm of ends, in which the ends of all rational beings would be systematically united and mutually supporting (G 4:433–35).

For Kant the clearest model of a realm of ends in ordinary human life is friendship, in which (he says) friends unite their ends into a collective end in which their individual happinesses are swallowed up (MS 6:469–72, VE 27:422–23, 675–77). Genuine friendship also involves a commitment to the ideal of perfect friendship, in which human ends are united in this way. Because it involves this commitment, friendship, for Kant, makes us worthy of happiness (whether or not it actually makes us happy); and we have an ethical duty to enter into relations of friendship with others (MS 6:471). These fundamentally anti-individualistic strains in Kant's ethics have often been neglected by his sympathizers and his critics alike.

V. Morality as a Doctrine of Duties

Kant's aim in the *Metaphysics of Morals* was to present a "doctrine of duties" — a system of moral obligations that results from applying this principle to human nature (G 4:388, MS 6:216–17). No doubt we find it harder than Kant or his audience did to think about our lives as something to be structured by our "duties" — as though we should carry around a little handbook of moral duties for our edification and consult it hourly to decide what we should be doing. But down to this day it is also sadly fashionable in moral philosophy, both Kantian and non-Kantian, to think that moral theory must consist in some kind of rational decision procedure (such as some version of the principle of utility or Kant's FUL or FLN), through which we could reckon up what we ought to do in every situation that presents itself to us. An ethical theory then becomes a kind of meat grinder into which we feed empirical facts, turn the crank, and out comes the series of acts we ought to perform, one after the next, like neat little sausages on a string. The position known as "Kantian constructivism," which emphasizes the FUL (or FLN) and regards moral goodness or rightness properties constructed through the application of a "CI-procedure," is a sad example of this repellent picture, in which an abstract, hidebound, and often counterintuitive process of formulating maxims and testing them for universalizability is supposed to take over our lives, tell us at every juncture what to do, and leave us no room to direct our conduct in the wide variety of ways that intelligent people actually do direct it.[10]

Kant's famous four examples in the *Groundwork* (G 4:421–25) are often misunderstood as his chief contribution to the theory of ordinary moral deliberation. But there is no reason to regard them as intended in any such way. They occur in the course of Kant's development of a system of formulations of the moral law, and they are intended to illustrate the first and most abstract formulation (FUL or FLN), so that the reader may see how that formulation, and the reasoning involved in it, might relate to some relatively familiar cases of moral duties and temptations to violate them. It is absurdly hasty to jump to the conclusion that a philosopher would think that illustrations suitable to that purpose are also a universal model for all moral reasoning.

Kant gave a very different account when he actually came to work out his system of duties in the Doctrine of Virtue. There he redescribed our ethical duties as *ends* (MS 6:382–86, 394–95). He saw the moral life not as a matter of applying a decision procedure, but of devoting ourselves to certain ends, working out our own personal priorities among them (with a good deal of latitude, or *Spielraum*, about this) and making specific judgments about how best to pursue them under particular circumstances. He also conceived of these ends, regarded as objects of morality, not as general categories of good to be maximized (as utilitarians want to maximize the sum or average of pleasure over pain) but rather as particular ends set under contingent conditions — for instance, as the development of a certain talent or capacity in ourselves or the promotion of the happiness of a certain individual or group (MS 6:386–88). This is why Kantian ethics regards both the choice of the specific ends and the order of priorities among ends as necessarily involving latitude — as fundamentally a matter of individual choice (MS 6:388–94).

Following Kant's theory, the choices between ends and maxims are constrained only by the enforceable rights of other people and by specific relationships in which we stand to specific individuals (through relationships of family or friendship or through professional obligations) (MS 6:468–69). In his personal moral opinions, Kant is infamous for his defense of certain inflexible moral rules (against lying and suicide, for example). But his theory clearly allows for exceptions to moral rules — treating *exceptivae* as one of the twelve fundamental categories of moral thinking (KpV 5:66). The "casuistical questions" discussed in the *Metaphysics of Morals* are mostly questions about when we should or may make exceptions to common moral rules (conspicuously among them, rules about lying and suicide). On many of the issues raised in these questions Kant does not come to any firm or general conclusion, regarding the proper reflection on these questions as "not so much a doctrine about how to *find* something as rather a practice in how to *seek* truth" (MS 6:411). The spirit of Kant's theory is open-textured and flexible regarding the scope and demandingness of moral duties.[11]

VI. The Supreme Principle of Morality

Kant's aim in the *Groundwork* was to "seek out and establish the supreme principle of morality" (G 4:392). It may seem anachronistic to think of our moral ends as grounded in a single "fundamental principle of morality." We may think of moral values as an unordered plurality, and insist that different people might subscribe to different moral principles, which would seem to be incompatible with regarding all moral deliberation as falling under a single fundamental principle. But in recognizing a fundamental principle of morality, Kantian ethics really has no such implications. For Kant's theory itself directs us to pursue an indeterminate plurality of ends, and to apply the fundamental moral principle through a plurality of moral laws, principles, and precepts. Ideally, all could be arrived at by applying the supreme principle to empirical facts about human nature and the human condition, many of them only imperfectly binding, and nearly all of them admitting of exceptions. Such a derivation, however, is far removed from everyday life, although as an ideal it can sometimes play an important role in our deeper critical reflection on what principles we should follow and what ends we ought to pursue.

The point of looking for a supreme principle can be seen when we reflect on the fact that morality arises out of social custom or propriety when people begin to *think for themselves* (MA 8:144–46). Thinking for oneself is a prerogative, even a duty, of rational adulthood; Kant thinks of it as a critical historical development not only in the life of an individual but, even more significantly, in the collective historical life of human civilization. Kant's name for this historical crisis is 'enlightenment' (WA 8:35). He characterizes the thinking of enlightenment by providing three rules, or "maxims," for its successful practice: (1) think for yourself; (2) think from the standpoint of everyone else, and (3) think consistently (KpV 5:294–95; VA 7:200, 228–29, VL 9:57). To "reason" is to think for oneself, to draw the ultimate source of one's acts and judgments from oneself rather than taking them from the opinions of others or even from one's own feelings and desires, regarded uncritically as something simply given. The first maxim of rational thinking also explains how we are to understand Kant's insistence that the principle of morality is *a priori*, a thesis that often proves a stumbling block to the acceptance of Kantian ethics because of empiricist confusions and prejudices. All cognition for Kant is the result of our faculties' operating on what is given to us in sensible intuition. A proposition is known *a priori* for Kant if its content is determined not by what is given to us from outside but through the exercise of our own faculties (KrV A1/B1). To say that the fundamental principle of morality is *a priori* is therefore to say that its source lies in my own critical reflection on the reasons I have for acting, rather than in commands coming from outside me, or on desires I happen to find in myself prior to any rational reflection, rather than produce in myself through considering the reasons why their objects are valuable and worth pursuing. The claim that there is an *a priori* practical principle means that as reasonable beings we are always capable of reflecting critically on what is given, and accepting or rejecting it for reasons we are capable of recognizing and validating through our own thinking.

Thinking for oneself is genuine thinking only if it subjects itself to the authority of reasons, which means grounds that are equally valid for all thinkers. For finite and fallible beings such as ourselves, such grounds can be found and critically certified only if one tests one's thoughts by adopting the standpoint of others — ideally, of all others, since genuine reasons must be equally valid for all. In the second maxim of thinking, Kant is asserting that we can do this only through coming to understand the viewpoint of others by communicating with them, and in a manner in which all are free to express their viewpoints freely. It is for this reason that he declares freedom of communication to be a necessary condition for the very existence of reason itself (KrV A738/B766). The universal validity of reason also depends on uniting the thinking of all standpoints into a set of principles that can claim to be grounded for all of them. This is what Kant means by the third maxim, that of thinking "consistently" — which he declares to be the most difficult of the three maxims to apply successfully (KpV 5:295).

This free, unconditional, unified, and critical thinking from a universal standpoint is a never-ending process. Anything concrete that we identify as a "principle" for such thinking enjoys this status only provisionally; our thinking should continue to test and correct it, or at any rate to refine, reinterpret, and rearticulate it in response to new circumstances or to viewpoints we still have not adequately considered. Philosophical formulations of such a principle are really placeholders for something that philosophers and reflective individuals will forever seek after, collectively as well as individually.

VII. Formulations of the Moral Principle

In the *Groundwork* Kant formulates the moral law in three different ways. They constitute a developing progression, and correspond closely (as I have already indicated) to the three features of moral deliberation distinguished above. Kant begins with the form of the law, as a categorical imperative, which leads to FUL and FLN: the requirement that every maxim be consonant with the form of universal law (or law of nature). Then he takes up the matter of the law, or the end that could motivate rational obedience to a categorical imperative, which is found in FH, based on the dignity of humanity or rational nature as an existing end in itself. Putting together the concept of universal law with that of the dignity of rational will, Kant then derives the final and most comprehensive formula, the idea of every rational will as universally legislative (FA), and the moral law as grounded on autonomy. Morality is conceived as a system of laws that, if universally followed, would constitute the community of rational beings as a "realm of ends," a mutually supporting purposive system in which the ends of all rational beings form a harmonious community (FRE).

The fact that Kant *develops* the moral law in this systematic way entails that the later formulas of the law are in general both more adequate and more definitive expressions of the principle than the first formula — the well-known FUL or FLN and its much-discussed universalizability tests for maxims. Thus when Kant derives his system of ethical duties in the *Metaphysics of Morals*, it is the worth of humanity as an end in itself, not the testing of maxims for universalizability, to which he appeals.[12] When Kant presents a "universal formula" of the moral law in the *Groundwork*, the *Critique of Practical Reason*, and the *Metaphysics of Morals*, the formula he uses is that of autonomy (FA), or the adoption of maxims that not only might be willed as universal laws, but *include in themselves the volition* that they can actually hold as part of a system of universal laws.[13] In the final section of the *Groundwork* Kant provides a deduction of the moral law through its equivalence with the freedom of the rational will that must be presupposed in all our actions, making use once again of FA.[14] Kant never undertakes any unconditional validation of FUL or FLN, apart from its development into and subsumption under the principle of autonomy (FA).[15]

The most important idea in Kantian ethics is that the authority of moral deliberation is based on the autonomy of the agent's rational will. This idea rests fundamentally on the assertion of an objective value: the equal dignity of all rational beings as ends in themselves. The best picture of what moral deliberation seeks is that of the realm of ends, or a rational community in which all the freely set ends of human beings ultimately converge. The most useful formulation of the fundamental principle for generating moral rules is the principle that the dignity of every rational being is entitled to equal and unlimited respect. By contrast, for Kantian theory the practice of testing maxims for universalizability has a relatively limited role to play in moral deliberation.

The overemphasis on FUL, both by Kant's critics and by his sympathizers, has had a mischievous effect on the interpretation, and therefore the reception, of Kantian ethics. On the one hand, it has misled many of Kant's sympathizers into thinking that what is distinctive and valuable about his ethical theory consists in some distinctive "decision procedure" rather than in its substantive conception of rational nature and autonomy as the real grounds of ethical value. Kant's own quite limited use of the universalizability tests (in his complex exposition of the moral principle in the *Groundwork*) is then ignored, and the tests are treated as if they were some sort of universal moral decision procedure or algorithm (a sort of Kantian response to the equally bogus act-utilitarian project of precisely calculating and comparing all the felicific tendencies of all the practical options open to us in any situation). On the other hand, it has misled Kant's critics into thinking that when they find defects in Kant's first formula when it is regarded as a universal and self-sufficient moral decision procedure, they have discovered a good reason simply to dismiss Kantian ethics as a whole without further ado.

If the main issue about Kantian ethics were whether the universalizability test for maxims is a satisfactory universal algorithm for all moral deliberation, then the right assessment of Kant's ethical theory would be that it is pretty worthless. There are several reasons why the universalizability tests are not up to playing any such role. First, since the tests are suited only to testing individual maxims, one by one, for permissibility, they can never yield anything like a positive moral rule or duty. The test never enables you to conclude that suicide or making false promises is wrong, but only that it is wrong to perform these actions on the specific maxims tested in the *Groundwork*; for all the universalizability tests might ever show, there might be other, wholly universalizable maxims on which acts of suicide or lying promises could be made. Second, the universalizability tests are notoriously subject to false negatives — entirely innocent maxims that nevertheless fail the tests. Take the maxim that whenever I arrive at a doorway at the same time as another, I will always yield right of way to the other and will never go through first. There is nothing wrong with that maxim, but it could never be adopted by all agents as a universal law. The problem here is simply that there are many maxims that cannot themselves be made (or willed as) universal laws (or laws of nature) but also do not violate universal moral laws (on any plausible conception of what these might be). Third, the universalizability tests are also threatened with false positives — maxims that pass the tests but are impermissible on any reasonable moral view. The most basic reason for this problem is that any action is intentional (or follows 'maxims') on many different descriptions and at many levels of generality or specificity. The universalizability tests by themselves provide no criterion for determining how, or at what level of specificity, the maxim is to be formulated, or (therefore) which intentional features of the action are relevant to its moral evaluation. As Hegel correctly put it, the universalizability test would be fine if we already had determinate moral laws, but the test itself can never generate any such principles.[16]

None of these problems is fatal to Kantian ethics when FUL, FLN, and the associated universalizability tests are used in the limited way they are actually employed by Kant in the Second Section of the *Groundwork*. There he says explicitly that when we find ourselves tempted by a maxim that violates the moral law, we are aware of "willing the opposite of our maxim to hold as a universal law" (G 4:425). In other words, Kant intends us to presuppose determinate moral laws and categories of duty deriving from the autonomous will. The aim of the tests, as Kant tells us, is to illustrate his first (preliminary) formulation of the moral principle. Through his illustrations, we recognize the contradiction in our will that would result if we tried to integrate these specific unlawful maxims into what we will as universal laws. In these examples, Kant is *not* attempting to use FUL (or FLN) as an algorithm for generating all moral principles or making all moral decisions. The examples are only a device for enabling us to see how certain maxims that we already recognize as contrary to duty can be exhibited as unlawful in the light of the (first and most abstract) formula of the law that he has just derived.

The same four examples are considered again a bit later in light of the formula of humanity as end in itself (FH). This later treatment is in every case a more transparent and cogent way of motivating the general principle of duty involved in the examples. Kant grounds the prohibition of suicide, for instance, on respect for humanity in our own person, and the duty against deceiving others on respect for the other and the requirement that we adopt only ends that others can rationally share. Whether or not these considerations ground the particular duties cited (I think they equally ground large categories of exceptions to the prohibition on suicide, for example), they also involve an appeal to substantive values on which determinate positive duties could be based — something that cannot be said about the universalizability tests.

Why don't readers of the *Groundwork* see this, and direct more attention to Kant's more authentic derivations of duties? The reason, I think, is that it is all too evident that arguments from the formula of humanity do not provide even the appearance of an ethical sausage machine — a universal algorithm for grinding out what any agent whatever should do under any conceivable set of circumstances. Although it may sometimes be self-evident what the dignity of humanity requires of us, sometimes it is not. Sometimes this is a matter of dispute, and clearly there is no simple, general way of resolving such disputes by anything like a mathematical calculation or universal decision procedure. Hence readers who are looking for the universal moral algorithm (in spite of Kant's lack of an intention ever to provide one) are not tempted to think they have found it in FH, but they can integrate a certain interpretation of FUL (and FLN) into their delusions about what moral philosophy is supposed to be. This misguided expectation, however, only sets up Kant's theory for quick dismissal when it is soon recognized that these formulas fail to satisfy the unreasonable demands being made on them.

If we rest our theory of duties on FH, as Kant actually does in the *Metaphysics of Morals*, then we have to admit that the fundamental principle of morality yields no universal decision procedure for all cases. Moral deliberation generates moral rules applicable in particular cases only in a loose fashion, leaving (as Kant himself says) considerable "play-room" for individual discretion and judgment (MS 6:390). It will also depend heavily on what Kant called "practical anthropology," that is, on our fallible, constantly changing, and always deeply problematic knowledge of what human beings and the human predicament are like (both in general and under specific social and historical conditions).

A major source of error here is a common misconception about what moral theory is for, and especially about the function of the fundamental principle in such a theory. The function of a fundamental principle can never be directly to settle difficult moral issues; it can serve only to provide the right general framework in which moral rules and controversial issues should be raised and discussed. Even then, any formulation of it must be regarded as provisional — an object of constant critical reflection and continual reinterpretation and rearticulation. The rethinking of traditional misinterpretations of Kant's own formulations of the moral law and their relation to one another is intended here as only the beginning of such a process, which of course should go beyond getting Kant right and begin to say how even his concepts of 'universal law', 'rational nature', and 'autonomy' might be reinterpreted or revised.[17]

VIII. Supernatural Freedom

I will conclude by taking up a vexed topic I barely touched on at the beginning, which becomes a major theme in the Third Section of the *Groundwork*: Kant's thesis that morality depends on transcendental or noumenal freedom. I think it was an important insight on Kant's part to see free agency as a special kind of causality, namely a causality that acts under normative principles, hence a capacity to choose between alternatives according to one's judgment about which alternative is permitted or required by a norm. I also think he was correct to argue, on the basis of an acute analysis of what rational normativity involves, that if we are free in this sense, then we are bound by the moral law whose content he developed through FUL, FLN, FH, FA, and FRE. But a great many of us today regard all our rational capacities, including those required to give ourselves moral laws that are categorically binding, as belonging to what we must ascribe to ourselves as beings of nature. We are animals who have evolved through a process of natural selection, and all our rational capacities must in principle be wholly explainable through causal laws of nature. To the extent that we believe this, we do not need to resolve the metaphysical problem of freedom as Kant did, by transporting ourselves into an unknowable noumenal world. If our position is as I have described it, then morality should be grounded on freedom, as Kant thought, but on the sort of freedom we recognize ourselves as having as part of our equipment as the rather remarkable but contingently evolved natural animals that we are, and not on the sort of unknowable supernatural freedom Kant thought we must postulate if we are to think of ourselves as free at all.

Of course I do not mean to deny that the metaphysical problem of free will is a genuine problem. I especially want to make it clear that I am not representing myself as having some final solution to it. We still need to investigate empirically the nature and biological underpinnings of our rational capacities. It will be no trivial task to reconcile our scientific theories about ourselves with the freedom and reason we necessarily presuppose in ourselves even in the act of undertaking such investigations. I am not convinced that we have yet reached that theoretical goal, and I think that there are philosophical as well as empirical obstacles still standing in the way of our human self-understanding. Like Kant, I am dissatisfied with the shallower compatibilist solutions to the free will problem that have been offered to it (and are still offered today).[18]

If, in order to account for our capacities as rational beings and agents, the best we could ever do were to postulate that we are supernaturally free in a noumenal world, then that is what we would be stuck with. Kant would be sadly right about the free will problem. But I doubt that Kant's extravagant metaphysics is the best we will ever be able to do with this problem. The basic point, however, is that Kantian ethics is no more hostage to the free will problem than any other ethical theory would be that regards us as reasonable and self-governing beings. Any defensible ethical theory has to deal with us as beings who ask ethical questions about what we should do, can answer them according to reasons, and can act in accordance with the answers they come up with. That's what we have to start with in formulating any ethical theory, whatever psychology, biology, or metaphysics we think lies behind it.

Any ethical theory that tried to deny that we are free, or to reduce our natural capacities to empiricist mechanisms of sentiment and desire, would get us obviously wrong in ways in which Kantian ethical theory gets us right. Kant's own doctrines perhaps play into the hands of such theories, by representing our practical freedom and capacity for rational self-government as something metaphysically controversial — something that requires a mind-boggling leap of faith into the supersensible. Kant did this because he actually found it appealing to associate our human dignity with the thought that we are supernatural beings, or have a divine spark and destiny that transcends anything our empirical science can ever hope to grasp. It seemed fitting to him that those who are committed to morality would think of themselves as belonging to a supernatural realm (a *corpus mysticum* or Kingdom of Grace), while those who think of themselves only as natural beings are condemned to be enslaved by their lower desires, failing to live up to their rational capacities; we should expect such earthbound materialists to treat themselves and other rational beings with contempt (like the mere things they think we all are).

After two centuries, however, neither the philosophy nor the sociology of this picture any longer carries any conviction for an enlightened person. The picture itself is a holdover from the very religious prejudices Kant so admirably opposed in his own time.

If we are capable of rationally recognizing that people are free and equal self-governing beings and ends in themselves, then we do not have to bow down to anything supernatural in order to sustain our commitment to treating them as their dignity requires.

All thinking people reject the antiscientific attitudes of religious funda-
mentalists who reject the theory of evolution on the ground, as they sometimes put it, that "if we think of ourselves merely as animals, then we will
act like mere animals." It is one measure of philosophical progress since the
eighteenth century that then such thoughts were shared by a great many of
the most enlightened people (including Kant), whereas now they are characteristic only of people who are conspicuously unenlightened. The thing a
Kantian should now say is that of course we are animals — namely, animals
that have somehow evolved capacities to direct their lives according to
principles of reason and to recognize the objective value of their own
rational nature as an end in itself. The regrettable thing is only that we
animals with rational capacities too often fail to exercise them.

Kantian ethics is about having a rational conception of ourselves which
commits us to autonomy, human equality, and cosmopolitan community. It
is an ethical theory that is still as gripping in its inspiration and as radical in
its implications as it was when it emerged from the Enlightenment tradition
a little over two centuries ago. That is why Kant still is, and still should be,
the most influential ethical theorist in the philosophical tradition to which
our civilization belongs.

NOTES

1. A lack of innocent earnestness in one's attitude toward morality was,
of course, not unknown in Kant's time either; nor was it unknown even to
Kant himself, when he wrote that people "put on a show of affection,
respect for one another, modesty and impartiality, but without deceiving
anyone, because it is generally understood that they are not sincere" (VA
7:151). But Kant appears to regard this universal deception as inevitable,
and he even approves of it to the extent that he thinks people may actually
make themselves better through the attempt to live up to their false profes-
sions of moral goodness. In our time, even the pretense of moral earnestness
is not so universal, and people's reactions to it are much more varied, and
often openly skeptical.

2. We can no longer even take for granted, as Hume did, that those who
profess doubt about all moral distinctions and obligations must be insin-
cerely disputatious, and that no one will take these doubts seriously. Hume,
Enquiry concerning the Principles of Morals, in *Hume: Enquiries*, ed. P.
Nidditch (Oxford: Clarendon Press, 1975), sec. I, pp. 169–70.

3. If you don't know what I mean here, then just start reading William
Bennett, ed., *The Book of Virtues* (New York: Simon and Schuster, 1993),

and you should find out soon enough. Even the term 'moralist' — in the eighteenth century a perfectly acceptable word for someone who thinks about morality or ethics — now embarrasses us; but since a term for the same thing is still indispensable, people have had to invent the term 'ethicist' — arguably the ugliest neologism of recent times that can't be blamed either on the computer or on French literary theory.

4. John Rawls, *A Theory of Justice* (Cambridge, Mass.: Harvard University Press, 1971), p. 27.

5. Before making this criticism of classical utilitarianism, Rawls had already laid down as the "main idea" of his theory the concept of an "original agreement" through which free and equal persons might enter into a community; *A Theory of Justice*, p. 11.

6. For one attempt to do this see Amartya Sen, "Consequential Evaluation and Practical Reason," *Journal of Philosophy* 97 (September 2000): 477–502.

7. But we will mangle this point too if we are still stuck on the false thought that desire has to be the starting point for deliberation. For then we will express it by saying that the moral motive is a *desire* for self-approval. This is, of course, a desire we all have. But it is a commonly observed fact of human life that it can usually be satisfied most easily not by doing the right thing but by deceiving oneself into thinking one has done it, or by adjusting one's perception of moral demands so that they are satisfied by what one wanted to do anyway. Hence a moral theory that starts out this way, if it is consistent, can only be morally bankrupt, and that to a spectacular degree. The point is not whether we do or do not approve of ourselves, but rather whether we act in such a way as to be worthy of our own approval. So the issue for genuine moral self-concern is not how to satisfy the desire for self-approval, but how to satisfy the conditions under which we ought to approve of ourselves.

8. It is beyond the scope of this essay to say how far I think Hegel subscribes to that view, and how large a gulf separates him from some present-day "communitarians," who sometimes take his name in vain when advocating their popular but pernicious views.

9. Kant even argues that we must tolerate (or even welcome) the semblance of genuine moral virtue most people assume, because it, and the desire for honor that motivates it, are among the most readily available and least dispensable means we have for winning others, and even ourselves, over to genuine morality (VA 7:151–53). I will leave unexplored the question how far we ought to follow him in this dubious direction, although I do

want to point out that this line of thinking should move some of his critics, if they are consistent, to qualify their negative opinion of him.

10. The term "CI-procedure" and the notion that Kantian ethics involves a "constructive" (hence antirealist) metaethics have grown popular through the influence of Rawls's essay "Kantian Constructivism in Moral Theory: The Dewey Lectures 1980," *Journal of Philosophy* 77 (September 1980): 515–75. See also his interpretation of Kant in Rawls, *Lectures on the History of Moral Philosophy*, ed. Barbara Herman (Cambridge, Mass.: Harvard University Press, 2000), pp. 143–328. There is much in Rawls's presentation of Kant, especially in these lectures, that is true, illuminating, and important. But regarding the theme of "constructivism," I find Rawls's presentation of Kantianism in section 40 of *A Theory of Justice*, pp. 251–257, much more accurate and sympathetic. Further, I think Kantian ethics is both distorted and harmed by the attempt to associate it with metaethical antirealism and by the way the idea of a "CI-procedure" perpetuates overemphasis on the formula of universal law. Kant does not directly address issues in twentieth-century metaethics; any interpretation on these issues has to depend on the way one construes hints in Kant's texts or the overall shape of Kantian theory based on the interpreter's own philosophical predilections. My own predilections are in more a realist than an antirealist direction, and I think Kant's theory is read more sympathetically if it is read more realistically. But I also think that even textually the hints on the realist side are stronger than those on the antirealist side, so at least it should not automatically be taken for granted that Kantianism is not a metaethically realist view, as has been suggested recently by Philip Stratton-Lake, "Kant and Contemporary Ethics," *Kantian Studies* 2 (1998): 1–14. Far more harmful than the "constructivist" interpretation, however, has been its perpetuation of the traditional association of Kantian ethics with the universalizability test, and the common assumption that testing maxims for universalizability is Kant's chief (or even his only) significant contribution to ethical reasoning. For those who want to read Kant sympathetically, it is worth noting that Rawls himself clearly admits the "CI-procedure" is incapable of providing the content that (on this interpretation) it is supposed to provide. (See *Lectures on the History of Moral Philosophy*, p. 163.) Reading Kant in Rawls's way, therefore, seems best designed to yield an interpretation of Kant's ethical theory as an unsuccessful rough draft of the theory Rawls was later to provide. It is not, then, on the whole, a very sympathetic interpretation of Kant. To his credit, however, Rawls rejects the idea of the "CI-procedure" as providing something like an algorithm

for moral decision making: "It is a serious misconception to think of the CI-procedure as an algorithm intended to yield, more or less mechanically, a correct judgment. There is no such algorithm, and Kant knows this. It is equally a misconception to think of this procedure as a set of debating rules that can trap liars and cheats, scoundrels and cynics, into exposing their hand. There are no such rules" (*Lectures on the History of Moral Philosophy*, p. 166).

11. Kant famously denies that there can be any "conflicts of duty" (MS 6:224). But what he is denying in this very brief discussion of a very complex topic is only that there could be no case in which one obligation could "cancel" another. It is not clear that Kant ever truly raised the issue whether there are "moral dilemmas" (in the form in which that issue has been discussed recently by moral philosophers). He does allow that different obligating reasons *(rationes obligandi)* can conflict, requiring us to choose the stronger over the weaker.

12. In only one of the sixteen ethical duties enumerated in the Doctrine of Virtue is there an appeal to anything like universalizability. This is the duty of beneficence, which involves universalizability in the unique case of the one maxim that everyone necessarily adopts (namely, of willing one's own well-being and hence, on the basis of Kant's empirical thesis that the vital ends of all human beings are tightly dependent on the voluntary assistance of others, necessarily willing that others promote it too) (MS 6:452). Eleven of the fifteen remaining duties are based explicitly on appeals to the worth of humanity, and the other four are based on it by implication, because they are classified as falling under duties with that explicit basis. For documentation of these claims, see *Kant's Ethical Thought* (New York: Cambridge University Press, 1999), pp.139–41.

13. See ibid., pp. 182–90.

14. See ibid., pp. 171–82.

15. Kant's famous use of the formula of the universal law of nature in discussing the four examples at G 4:421–25 depends on and presupposes a system of duties, projected (but not supplied) in the *Groundwork*, and depending on the formulas of humanity as end in itself and of autonomy, which are still not available to him in this discussion. The fact that the universalizability tests for maxims have the intended background accounts, I believe, for the shortcomings critics have often noted in the formula of the law of nature (and to which Kant's defenders have misguidedly and unsuccessfully tried to reply) when this formula is interpreted (as I think, misinterpreted) as a universal and self-sufficient moral decision procedure.

16. Hegel, *Elements of the Philosophy of Right*, § 135A.

17. I view Rawls's conception of principles chosen in an initial situation and Habermas' and Apel's conceptions of an ethics of domination-free communication as recent positive examples of the sort of thing I have in mind here.

18. Nor am I convinced that there is anything but snake oil and pseudo-science in most of the flashy attempts to explain our moral and social capacities on the basis of such a reduction.

Glossary

Abbruch tun: infringe
ableiten: derive
Absicht: intention, aim
absondern: separate; abstract*
Achtung: respect
Affekt: affect
All: (the) all
allgemein: universal; general
Allgemeingültigkeit: universal
      validity
Allheit: totality
anerkennen: recognize
angenehm: agreeable
Anlage: predisposition
Anlockung: enticement
Anmaßung: presumption
Anschauung: intuition
Ansehen: authority
an sich: in itself
Anspruch: claim
Antrieb: impulse
Arbeit: labor
Art: way, kind, species
auferlegen: impose
Aufgabe: problem
aufheben: abolish
auflösen: resolve, solve; analyze
Aufmunterung: encouragement
aufsuchen: search

ausfindig machen: bring to light
ausmachen: constitute; settle

Bedeutung: significance, signification
Bedingung: condition
Bedürfnis: need
befördern: further, promote
Befugnis: warrant, authorization
begabt: endowed
Begehrungsvermögen: faculty of
      desire
begreifen: comprehend
Begriff: concept
beharrlich: persisting
beilegen: apply (to), attribute (to)
Belieben: discretion
Bemühung: toil, effort
Berharrlichkeit: persistence
berichtigen': correct
Beschaffenheit: constitution;
      property
Beschäftigung: enterprise, concern,
      business
besonder: particular
besorgen: take care
Besorgnis: concern
beständig: permanent, constant
bestimmen: determine

*When the word is so translated, a footnote will inform the reader.

Bestimmung: determination, vocation (in ethical contexts)
betrachten: consider
Betrachtung: inquiry; consideration
Beurteilung: judgment
bewahren: confirm
Bewegungsgrund: motive
Bewegursache: motivation
beweisen: prove
Bewußtsein: consciousness
Beziehung: reference; relation
Bild: image
billig: equitable, fair
billigen: approve
Boden: terrain
Böse: evil
Bösewicht: scoundrel

darlegen: establish
Darstellung: exhibition, presentation, display
dartun: establish
Dauer: duration
Deutlichkeit: distinctness, clarity
Ding: thing

echt: genuine
Ehre: honor
ehrlich: honest, honorable
Eigendünkel: self-conceit
Eigenschaft: quality
eigentlich: real, authentic
Eigenliebe: self-love
einbilden: imagine
Einbildungskraft: imagination
Einfalt: simplicity
Einfluß: influence
einräumen: concede
Einrichtung: adaptation

Einschränkung: limitation
einsehen: have (gain) insight into
einstimmen: harmonize
Empfänglichkeit: receptivity
Empfindung: sensation, feeling*
entlehnen: get
Erfahrung: experience
erfordern: require
Erhabenheit: sublimity
Erhaltung: preservation
erheben: elevate
erkennen: cognize, know*
Erkenntnis: cognition
Erklärung: explanation; definition; declaration
erlaubt: permissible
Erläuterung: elucidation, illustration
Erscheinung: appearance
erteilen: impart

fähig: susceptible; capable
Fähigkeit: capacity
festsetzen: establish
Freiheit: freedom, liberty
Freundschaft: friendship
Frist: term

Gabe: gift
Gebiet: domain
Gebot: command
Gebrauch: use, employment
Gebrechlichkeit: fragility
gefallen: like, please
gefällig: pleasing
Gefühl: feeling
Gegengewicht: counterweight
Gegenstand: object
Geist: spirit, mind
Geldnot: pecuniary distress
gemäß: in accord

gemein: common
Gemeinschaft: community
    (communio);
    interaction
    (commercio)
Gemüt: mind, heart*
genugtun: satisfy
Genuss: enjoyment
Geschäft: business, concern,
    enterprise
gescheit: clever
Geschicklichkeit: skill
Gesetz: law
Gesetzgeber: legislator
Gesetzgebung: legislation, giving law
Gesetzmässigkeit: lawfulness
Gesichtspunkt: point of view
Gesinnung: disposition
Gewalt: control
Gewerbe: trade
Glaube: belief, faith
Glied: member
Glück: (good) fortune; luck
glücklich: happy, fortunate
Glückseligkeit: happiness
Grad: degree
Grenze: bound(ary)
Grund: ground
gründlich: well-grounded
Grundsatz: principle
Gültigkeit: validity
Gunst: favor

Handlung: act(ion)
Hang: propensity
heilig: holy
herrlich: splendid
hervorbringen: produce, bring forth
hinreichend: sufficient
Hirngespinst: figment of the mind

Hochschätzung: esteem

Idee: idea
Imperativ: imperative
Inbegriff: sum total

Kennen: acquaintance
kennen: be acquainted with, know
Kenner: connoisseur
Kenntnis: acquaintance
klar: clear
Klugheit: prudence
Kraft: power, force (physical
    contexts)
Kritik: critique, criticism
Kunst: art

Laster: vice
Laune: mood
lauten: be stated
lauter: pure*
Lehrbegriff: doctrine
Lehre: doctrine
Leidenschaft: passion
liebenswürdig: amiable
Lob: praise
Lüge: lie
Lust: pleasure

Macht: might, power
Materie: matter
meinen: hold or express opinion(s)
Mensch: human being
menschlich: human (adj.)
Menschlichkeit: humanity
Mittel: means
Moral: morals
Moralität: morality
Muster: model
Mut: courage

Nachteil: disadvantage
Naturgesetz: natural law
Neigung: inclination
Not: distress
Nötigung: necessitation
Notwendigkeit: necessity
Nützlichkeit: utility

Oberhaupt: supreme head
oberst: supreme
Object: object

Person: person
Pflicht: duty
pflichtmäßig: in conformity with
    duty
Preis: price
Prinzip: principle
Prüfung: examination

Quelle: source

Ratgebung: advice
Ratschlag: counsel
Raum: space
Recht: right (n.)
Rechtschaffenheit: uprightness
Redlichkeit: honesty
Regel: rule
Reich: realm
rein: pure
Ruhe: tranquillity

Sache: thing
Satz: proposition
Schande: disgrace
schätzen: estimate; esteem
Schätzung: estimation
Schein: illusion; semblance
scheinen: seem

schicklich: suitable
Schlauigkeit: cunning
Schranke: limit(ation)
schwärmen: enthuse
Schwärmerei: enthusiasm
Seele: soul
Selbstbeherrschung: self-control
Selbstbestimmung: self-
    determination
Selbstliebe: self-love
Selbstmord: suicide
Selbstverleugnung: self-renunciation
Sinn: sense, meaning
Sinnenwelt: world of sense
sinnlich: sensible, sensuous
Sinnlichkeit: sensibility
Sitten: morals, morality
Sittlichkeit: morality
Sollen: 'ought'
Standpunkt: standpoint
Stoff: material

Tat: deed
Tätigkeit: activity
Tauglichkeit: suitability
Teilnahme: sympathy; sympathetic
    participation
Treue: fidelity
Triebfeder: incentive
Tugend: virtue
Tun und Lassen: deeds and
    omissions

Übel: ill
Übereinstimmung: agreement
Überlegung: reflection
Übermut: arrogance
übersteigen: surpass
Übertretung: transgression
Überzeugung: conviction

Umfang: range
unbegreiflich: incomprehensible
Unlauterkeit: impurity
unnachlaßlich: unremitting
Unschuld: innocence
unterordnen: subject
Untersuchung: investigation
Unvermögen: incapacity
Urbild: archetype
Urheber: author
Ursache: cause
Urteilskraft: power of judgment
Urwesen: original being

verabscheuen: abhor
verachten: despise
Verachtung: contempt
Veränderung: alteration
Verbindlichkeit: obligation
Verbindung: combination
                   (conjunctio)
verdienstlich: meritorious
Vereinigung: unification
Vergnügen: gratification
Verhalten: conduct
Verhältnis: relation
Verkehr: traffic; commercial traffic
Verknüpfung: connection (nexus)
Verlegenheit: embarrassment
Vermögen: faculty
vernuenfteln: ratiocinate
Vernunft: reason
verschaffen: obtain
Versprechen: promise
Verstand: understanding
Verstandeswelt: world of the
                   understanding
Versuchung: temptation
verwerflich: reprehensible
Vollendung: completion

vollkommen: perfect (v.)
Vollkommenheit: perfection
vollständig: complete
Vorgeben: pretense
Vorschrift: precept
Vorsorge: provision
vorstellen: represent
Vorstellung: representation
                   (repraesentatio)
Vorteil: advantage

wählen: choose
Wahn: delusion
Wahrnehmung: perception
Weg: route
Weltweisheit: philosophy
Wert: worth, value
Wesen: being, entity (ens); essence
                   (essentia)
Widerspruch: contradiction
Widerstreit: conflict
Wille: will
Willkür: (power of) choice
willkürlich: voluntary; arbitrary
wirklich: actual, real
Wirkung: effect
Wissen: knowledge
Wissenschaft: science
Witz: wit
Wohl: well-being
Wohlergehen: welfare
Wohlgefallen: satisfaction
wohltätig: beneficent
Wohltun: beneficence
Wohlwollen: benevolence
Wollen: volition
wollen: will
Würde: dignity

Zergliederung: analysis

zufällig: contingent
Zufriedenheit: contentment
Zusammenhang: connection; nexus
Zusammensetzung: composition;
            synthesis

zusammenstimmen: harmonize
Zustand: condition, state
Zwang: coercion
Zweck: end
Zweckmässigkeit: purposiveness

Index

Popular moral philosophy, 8, 22–29
Postulate, 46
Power, 9
Pragmatic, 33
Praise, moral, 14
Precept, 35
Predispositions of human nature, 47
Preserving one's life, 13–14
Price, 43, 52–53
Principle of morality, 28; a priori, 5–
  6; formulas of, 8; supreme, 8,
  169; synthetic, 62. *See also* Law,
  moral; FUL; FLN; FH; FA; FRE
Principle(s), 15–16, 17, 26; a priori,
  22–24; formal and material, 45.
  See also Law; Maxim
Promising, 18–19, 36, 29, 48, 126,
  129–132
Property, 48
Propriety, 165
Prudence, 18, 31–33, 60; counsels
  of, 33–35
Psychology, 6
Pufendorf, S., 38, 86
Purposiveness, natural, 10–11

Quantity, categories of, 54

Rational nature, 24, 26, 43, 46. *See
  also* Humanity, predisposition to
Rawls, J., 90–91, 162, 178, 179–
  180, 181
Realm (*Reich*), 51–52
Realm of ends, 51–52; 53, 56–57,
  78, 167, 176; member of, 51, 53,
  56; supreme head of, 52
Realm of nature, 54
Reason: instrumental, 31–32; practical, 28, 29–37, 77, 113–117; prudential, 32–35; pure practical, 7–

8, 45; theoretical and practical,
  113–116
Refusal, sexual, 165
Reich, K., x, 26
Respect, 16–17, 57, 165
Rights, human, 48

Schiller, F., 92,107
Schönecker, D., xv, 26, 107, 110
Science, pure and empirical parts of,
  3–5
Scripture, holy, 15, 23, 25, 48. *See
  also* Gospel
Self-contempt, 43
Self-control, 10
Self-legislation, 49–50
Self-love, 22–23,38, 39
Sen, A., 178
Seneca, 3, 52
Servility, 47
Sexual desire, 165
Shaftesbury, third earl of, 100–102,
  108–109
Sidgwick, H., ix, 111
Skill, imperatives of, 32
Socrates, 19, 85
South Sea Islanders, 39
Stoics, 3, 59, 89, 108
Stratton-Lake, P., 179
Strict duty, 42, 43, 57
Suicide, 13–14, 38–39, 47
Sulzer, J. G., 27–28, 38–39
Superego, 165
Sympathy, 14, 40, 102–103

Talents: duty to develop, 39–40, 48;
  of the mind, 9
Taste, 44, 62
Teleology, 54. *See also* Purposiveness, natural

Rethinking the Western Tradition

Also available in the series: